Tropes for the Past

96

Internationale Forschungen zur
Allgemeinen und
Vergleichenden Literaturwissenschaft

In Verbindung mit

Norbert Bachleitner (Universität Wien), Dietrich Briesemeister (Friedrich Schiller-Universität Jena), Francis Claudon (Université Paris XII), Joachim Knape (Universität Tübingen), Klaus Ley (Johannes Gutenberg-Universität Mainz), John A. McCarthy (Vanderbilt University), Alfred Noe (Universität Wien), Manfred Pfister (Freie Universität Berlin), Sven H. Rossel (Universität Wien)

herausgegeben von

Alberto Martino
(Universität Wien)

Redaktion: Ernst Grabovszki

Anschrift der Redaktion:
Institut für Vergleichende Literaturwissenschaft, Berggasse 11/5, A-1090 Wien

Tropes for the Past

Hayden White and the History / Literature Debate

Edited by
Kuisma Korhonen

Amsterdam - New York, NY 2006

Cover image:
Saint Sebastian with wounded chest
Day, F. Holland (Fred Holland), 1864-1933, photographer
Library of Congress, Prints & Photographs Division [LC-USZC4-8158]

Cover design: Pier Post

Le papier sur lequel le présent ouvrage est imprimé remplit les prescriptions
de "ISO 9706:1994, Information et documentation - Papier pour documents
- Prescriptions pour la permanence".

The paper on which this book is printed meets the requirements of " ISO
9706:1994, Information and documentation - Paper for documents - Requirements
for permanence".

Die Reihe „Internationale Forschungen zur Allgemeinen und Vergleichenden
Literaturwissenschaft" wird ab dem Jahr 2005 gemeinsam von Editions Rodopi,
Amsterdam – New York und dem Weidler Buchverlag, Berlin herausgegeben.
Die Veröffentlichungen in deutscher Sprache erscheinen im Weidler Buchverlag,
alle anderen bei Editions Rodopi.

From 2005 onward, the series „Internationale Forschungen zur Allgemeinen
und Vergleichenden Literaturwissenschaft" will appear as a joint publication by
Editions Rodopi, Amsterdam – New York and Weidler Buchverlag, Berlin. The
German editions will be published by Weidler Buchverlag, all other publications
by Editions Rodopi.

ISBN: 90-420-1718-X
©Editions Rodopi B.V., Amsterdam - New York, NY 2006
Printed in The Netherlands

CONTENTS

IV Literature as History

Acknowledgements

The idea for this book was born in the conference *Literature and its Others* that was held at the University of Turku, Finland, 8-10 May 2003. Therefore I would first like to thank the organizers of the conference: Finnish Graduate School for Literary Studies, and the Graduate School of Cultural Interaction and Integration and the Baltic Sea Region. Also the departments of English and Comparative Literature from the University of Helsinki, and the departments of Cultural History, Comparative Literature, and General History from the University of Turku helped us to create the conference. It was also sponsored by the Academy of Finland, University of Turku, and Turku University Foundation. Especially I want to thank the members of the Organizing Committee of the conference: Liisa Saariluoma, Mikko Laaksonen, Johanna Perheentupa, Bo Pettersson, Merja Polvinen, and Tomi Kaarto. Their tireless efforts made the conference and also this book possible.

We had two outstanding key-note speakers, Professor Hayden White and Professor Karlheinz Stierle , who both kindly offered their lectures to this volume. Their generous comments in the conference were highly valuable for the articles in this book.

Most of the articles are based on papers that were held at the conference. I want to express my gratitude to all those speakers who edited and sometimes rewrote their papers completely to make this book an integral, freestanding volume: Herman Paul, Stanley Corkin, Phyllis Frus, Andrew Burrell, Fiona McIntosh-Varjabédian, Claire Norton, Olabode Ibironke, and Lara Okihiro. Many of the papers that were held in the conference were not included in this volume; however, they all helped us to form an overall image of the history/literature debate, and in many cases their influence can be seen in the "Introduction" that I wrote to this volume.

I would also like to thank those authors that joined us later to complete the volume with their own contributions: Kalle Pihlainen, Matti Hyvärinen, and Markku Lehtimäki.

Especially I want to thank Liza Muszynski, who read carefully all the articles, checked their use of English, and made numerous valuable stylistic comments and suggestions. Great thanks also to Jenni Laitinen, who helped me in preparing this volume for the publisher, and to all the wonderful staff and colleagues at the Helsinki Collegium for Advanced Studies, where I have finished this volume.

Finally, I want to thank my wife and children – Kristina, Teo, Joona, and Mitja – for all their love and support.

In Helsinki, June 16th 2005,

Kuisma Korhonen

GENERAL INTRODUCTION

Kuisma Korhonen

The History/Literature Debate

In the beginning, there was no history or literature: there were just tales, mythic narratives of the legendary past. It was a storyteller's duty to praise the ancestors, both real and divine, so that the contact between the past and the present was not broken.

Then came writing. Historical time is, by definition, the time of writing, the time of written time and written documents. Writing freezes the moment of enunciation, turns it into a trace, a document. As traces from the past, written documents are both continuous and discontinuous with the past – often they are actual remains of what once was, but since they have been cut away from their original context, we must constantly interpret and reinterpret them as signs that refer to that virtual and constantly changing construction that we call "history."

With the advent of the calendar, it became possible to date events; by the use of written documents, it became possible to place events into that calendar time. Moreover, it became possible, to some extent, to distinguish between the events that one could verify from those that one could not – between the events that really took place from those that were either invented or were remembered only through some unverifiable oral tradition. Written stories about these events were, then, recognized as belonging to two different categories: those of "history" and those of "poetry." It is important to note, however, that the mental image of the past was – and still is – formed by both kinds of stories. How people see their place in the continuity of succeeding generations is determined not only by history but also by poetry and fiction.

In Ancient Greece and Rome, history and poetry were both treated as rhetorical arts: they both were written for some (political) purpose and composed according to the rhetorical techniques of *divisio*, *narratio*, etc.[1] Their main difference lay, as Aristotle famously put it, in their topics: history dealt with real events, whereas poetry dealt with possible events – that is, real, mythical, or invented events. Already then, however, history and literature were also seen as rivals. It is well known that, for Aristotle, poetry was more philosophical than historiography. Because poetry treated *possible* events – events that were plausible in their story context – poetry revealed the typical and thus the essential in human fate. Historiography, on the other hand, was tied to real events and thus to the accidental – events that were often more surprising than plausible – so it lacked the inner logic that made poetry so philosophically instructive.

---

[1] On the proximity of history and poetry in Rome, see, for example, Antoine Foucher, *Historia proxima poetis. L'influence de la poésie épique sur le style des historiens latins de Salluste à Ammien Marcellin* (Bruxelles: Latomus, 2000).

In the 18th-century, literature and historiography both still belonged to *belles lettres* and the rhetorical tradition.[2] The main challenge for a historian was to create as persuasive an authorial *ethos* as possible. This meant that *plausibility* (rather than documentation) was, just as it was in the classicist poetics of the 17th century, the main criteria for the historian's discourse (see Fiona McIntosh in chapter 8 of this book). In the early 19th century, however, new (more or less) scientifically motivated historians began to stress the importance of documentation and thus downplay the role of fictive and rhetorical elements in historical writing. At the same time, writers and literary scholars began to see *literature* as an autonomous field of writing that was either an alternative or a rival for historians' claims to truth. Romantics, and later symbolists, saw literature as a substitute for religious truth, as revelation of those existential basic principles that normally were hidden behind the banalities of bourgeois existence. Realistic and naturalistic trends, on the other hand, defined literature as research , research that analyzed the same reality as historians analyzed, but using methods that were capable of finding more elaborate truths than historians uncovered – the hidden experiences and structures of everyday life (see Hayden White in chapter 1 of this book).

New positivist historiography took on a seemingly more modest project than were those of literature or philosophy: it did not aim to reveal transcendental truths or private experiences, but aimed only to show the past "how it actually was" (*wie es eigentlich gewesen ist*), to quote Leopold Ranke's famous slogan. This "modesty" was, of course, twofold: it hinted that literature's and philosophy's claims to truth were illusory – not *eigentlich* – whether it was a question of such grandiose visions as the Hegelian "end of history," or of such "microhistories" as the intimate experiences described in 19th-century realistic novels. Moreover, in declaring that it was not itself rhetorical – that it did not try to manipulate its readers – historiography made its own discourse look as though being value-free and thus projecting an objective image of the world to readers. It followed, by definition, that the past that "actually was" consisted mainly of those things that were documented and that historians chose to describe in their writings: major wars, acts of diplomacy, deeds of great men, etc. Other realms of human experience – dreams, fears, and visions of marginalized people, for example – did not belong to "how it actually was."

During the 20th century, some authors like Collingwood saw historiography as storytelling rather than as science, but the majority of academic historians usually continued on emphasizing the empirical and thus scientific nature of their profession. The so-called French *Annalists* even proclaimed that historiography should be purged of all narrative elements – a program that they did not always follow in practice. At the same time, schools of literary scholarship, such as Russian formalism and the Anglo-American New Criticism, too, wanted to treat literature as separate from social, political, and historical questions. They did admit that some well-written historical studies like Michelet's *Histoire de France* could become recognized as literature, but only when they had ceased to be useful as historical sources. Both history and literary scholarship thus learned to live in mutual peace – each respected the other's sovereignty and did not make any open territorial claims.[3]

---

[2] See, for example, Everett Zimmerman, *The Boundaries of Fiction. History and the Eighteenth-Century Novel* (Ithaca: Cornell UP, 1996).

[3] About the relationship between history and literature in general, a good reader-type introduction is Tamsin Spargo (ed.) *Reading the Past. Literature and History* (Houndmills & New York: Palgrave, 2000). See also

This peace – or cold war – was then, in the beginning of the seventies, shattered by Hayden White and his followers.

Hayden White: Tropes of the Past

Hayden White's work, especially his *Metahistory*, published in 1973, had a huge influence in many different fields: in new philosophy of history, in literary studies, in cultural studies, in the so-called "narrative turn" in social sciences, etc.[4] For many professional historians, however, White was a traitor who smuggled literary theory into historiography, thereby undermining the scientific nature of historical research and turning it into mere literature.[5] However, also many literary scholars, often with a more or less formalist background, have been disturbed by what they have taken as a blurring of the distinction between fact and fiction.[6] Why has White's project been so dangerous, to both "history" and "literature"?

In *Metahistory*, White examined the narrative deep structure of historiography in 19th-century Europe, the "golden age of historiography." One of his main sources of inspiration was, nevertheless, rooted in literary criticism. Using Northrop Frye's vision of the literary universe, White went back to the common roots of literature and historiography: the archetypal forms of epic thinking.[7] Following Frye, White distinguished four kinds of narrative styles in historiography that, while all striving towards some kind of "realistic" representation of the past, used different strategies to achieve their "explanatory effect." Therefore he was able to describe Michelet's historical narratives by the notion of Romance, Ranke's by that of Comedy, Tocqueville's by that of Tragedy, and Burckhardt's by way of Satire.

White then related four different historiographical styles to four principal modes of historical consciousness on the basis of tropological theory that was mainly derived from Giambattista Vico, the great 18th-century precursor of the "linguistic turn." From Vico, White inherited the vision of four "metatropes" that prefigured all human thinking: Metaphor, Metonymy, Synecdoche, and Irony. Thus, not only historiographical discourse was predetermined by literary styles, but historical consciousness in general was predetermined by certain linguistic structures.

Leonard Schulze and Walter Wetzels (eds.), *Literature and History* (Lanham: University Press of America, 1983).

[4] Hayden White, *Metahistory: The Historical Imagination in Nineteenth-century Europe.* (Baltimore: Johns Hopkins, 1973). Henceforward cited as M. For the reception of Hayden White in different disciplines, see Richard Vann, "The Reception of Hayden White," *History and Theory*, 37, 2, May 1998 (the whole number is dedicated to White). The critical bibliography on White is extensive. Some useful introductions can be found from Keith Jenkins, *On "What is History"? From Carr and Elton to Rorty and White* (London and New York: Routledge, 1995), and "On Hayden White," *Why History? Ethics and Postomodernity* (London and New York: Routledge, 1999), pp. 89-158. See also Wulf Kansteiner, "Hayden White's Critique of the Writing of History." *History and Theory*, vol. 32, no. 3, 1993, pp. 273-295; and Nancy Partner, "Hayden White (and the Content and the Form and Everyone Else) at the AHA." *History and Theory*, vol. 36, no. 4, December 1997, pp. 102-110.

[5] See, for example, Arnaldo Momigliano, "La retorica della storia e la storia della retorica," *Sui fondamenti della storia antica* (Turin: Einaudi, 1984); and Gertrude Himmelfarb, "Telling It As You Like It. Post-Modernist History and the Flight From Fact." *Times Literary Supplement*, October 16, 1992, pp. 12-15.

[6] See, for example, Gérard Genette, *Fiction et diction* (Paris: Seuil, 1991), and Dorrit Cohn, *The Distinction of Fiction* (Baltimore: Johns Hopkins UP, 1999).

[7] Northrop Frye, *Anatomy of Criticism. Four Essays* (Princeton, NJ: Princeton UP, 1957).

In the nineteenth century philosophy of history (Hegel, Marx, Nietzsche, Croce), then, White saw the same kind of development as in historiography itself, from one trope to another. Modern history has, in his view, become more and more identified with the Ironic mode. In the end of his preface to *Metahistory*, White acknowledges that his own book, too, was cast in an Ironic mode, but wanted to turn the Ironic consciousness against Irony itself, hoping "for the reconstitution of history as a form of intellectual activity which is at once poetic, scientific, and philosophical in its concerns – as it was during history's golden age in the nineteenth century." (M, xii) As Herman Paul shows (see chapter 2), we may interpret White's "turning of the Ironic consciousness against Irony itself" as an attempt to turn *epistemological* irony against *ideological* irony that, often under the disguise of "objectivity" or "scientism," refrains from ideological choices.

In his following books, *Tropics of Discourse, Content of the Form* and *Figural Realism*,[8] White has developed his views further. Although he has often been accused of claiming that "everything is fiction," he has actually always made a firm distinction between historical and fictional *events*:

> Historians are concerned with events which can be assigned to specific time-space locations, events which are (or were) in principle observable or perceivable, whereas imaginative writers – poets, novelists, playwrights – are concerned with both these kinds of events and imagined, hypothetical, or invented ones. (TD, 121

In other words, there is, on the most elementary level, a clear difference between factual and fictional events, a difference that White rarely bothers to mention, taking it usually for granted. White also holds that one can achieve fairly reliable knowledge about past events, persons, and processes by using various approximate methods of research. However, the mere collection of facts, which can be compared to the work of a detective or a journalist, is for him not yet historical discourse, properly speaking, but rather formation of an *archive* that can be accessed and analyzed not only by historians but by other disciplines as well. For White, *historical discourse* is, by definition, interpretation of this archive of past events by means of narration. And it is here, by way of narration, that the techniques of literature and historiography overlap each other.

Because White has been interested in how the discourse of the historian and that of the imaginative writer "overlap, resemble, or correspond with each other," he has moved from the most elementary referential level to the deeper structures of meaning as they can be revealed by the use of different archetypal narrative forms and rhetorical figures. At the level of these deep structures, as he famously claims, history and fiction are "almost indistinguishable" as literary artifacts (TD, 121). Both are interested in communicating a certain vision of reality, although writers of fiction may refer to this vision by the use of such figurative devices as the construction of the "fictional world" (events that one cannot necessarily verify or falsify) whereas historians refer to this reality by their constructions of the "real world" (events that one can verify or falsify). However, in one sense both are fiction: the archetypal vision that they imply by their different textual devices and references cannot be verified or falsified – it is, in a way, fiction, something that is added to the world as it is.

---

[8]   Hayden White, *Tropics of Discourse. Essays in Cultural Criticism*, (London, Johns Hopkins UP, 1978; henceforth cited as *TD*); *The Content of the Form* (Baltimore: Johns Hopkins UP, 1987); *Figural Realism: Studies in the Mimesis Effect* (Baltimore, Johns Hopkins, 1999).

For White, the world in itself is not inherently tragic, comic, or romantic – it simply is – but when people try to make sense of their past they rely on certain modes of emplotment that refer to such archetypal visions of the world (whether implied by fictional or historical discourse) that can be called tragic, comic, romantic, etc. Or, in the deeper "tropological" level, the use of one trope instead of some other already implies some vision of the world, although we cannot say that reality *in itself* is metaphorical, metonymic, synecdochean, or ironic.

For White, then, life in itself is merely a sequence of events without any narrative structure of its own. Narratives are made afterwards. However, many critics have pointed out that the human Life-World (*Lebenswelt*) is always already intentional and is formed by those narratives that live in our culture. Or, as Karlheinz Stierle puts it, we are all entangled in the web of stories (see chapter 5). A world without narratives is, as Matti Hyvärinen shows, referring to Paul Auster's novels (see chapter 6), a world of horrors – narratives of everyday life are perhaps never as structured and finished as those of history or fiction, but narrativity, the never-ending attempt to construct some kind of narrative identity for oneself, is an essential part of human existence.[9] One may claim that White's notion of life as a sequence of events in time and space is, in fact, surprisingly close to positivist one; prior to narrative structures, "world" in itself is seen merely as a physical world without human will, plans, or intentions.

Many critics have also opposed the view that historians are free to impose whatever emplotment they want upon the events. As Mary Fulbrook notes, history is today essentially a collective enterprise. There is an ongoing struggle between different stories, and individual historians cannot impose storylines as they wish – different emplotments are continuously tested in an ongoing discussion about the right interpretation of events.[10] Moreover, many historians have felt that White reduces a struggle with an endlessly changing historical reality to that of merely a few styles and tropes that predetermine all historical discourse.

However, according to Frank Ankersmit, White's main intention in his theory was not to shut history into some structuralist "prisonhouse of language" (Jacobson) but, on the contrary, to help us to free ourselves from those figures that, at least if we do not recognize them, predetermine our discourse.[11] For White, the great classics of 18th- and 19th-century historical writing (Gibbon, Tocqueville, Michelet, Burckhardt) were admirable just because they were aware of their own rhetorical choices and could therefore develop new ways of dealing with the past.

There is no doubt that the professionalization of historiography by Ranke and his followers did create more reliable research methods. Today, we can distinguish more easily between reliable and non-reliable sources than ever before. However, and according to Ankersmit, this has been White's main point throughout his career: the emphasis on sources and archives meant that historians eventually became blind to the very language and literary techniques they were using. They lost their sensitivity to the "content of the form" that the great classics of the 19th century still had, and the result was an image of the past that was seemingly accurate but, in practice, seriously limited by unimaginative and conventional

---

9   A now-classic study on the essential role of narratives in the formation of identity is Charles Taylor, *Sources of the Self. The Making of the Modern Identity* (Cambridge: Cambridge UP, 1989).

10   Mary Fulbrook, *Historical Theory* (London: Routledge, 2002).

11   Frank Ankersmit, *Historical Representation* (Stanford: Stanford UP, 2001), pp. 249-261.

use of language. The subversive otherness of the past was hidden by the automatized linguistic structures. At the same time, modernist literature was developing new ways of revealing formerly unknown realms of human experience, developing more revealing and, in
some ways, also more realistic images of our relation to the past than more professionalized
historiography ever could.

While *Metahistory* concentrated on 19th-century historiography, in his later works White
has become more interested in "the modernist event" and its effects upon literary and historical discourse.[12] In the same way that 19th-century historiography was tied to literary
realism and its narrative structures, so too can modern historiography, and especially its
distrust of narratives, can be seen in relation to the demolition of traditional narrative forms
in modernist fiction. The interests of White have expanded from literature and history to
film, and on to psychoanalysis, music, and even on to chaos and cosmology, but his main
hope is still the same: to develop a way of dealing with the past that would be "at once poetic, scientific, and philosophical in its concerns."

In his new article "Historical Discourse and Literary Writing" (in chapter 1 of this
book), White turns the old accusation – that through his vision history is reduced to fiction
– upside down. This time he stresses the *non-fictional* character of *both* history and modern
literature. For the great modernist literary tradition, from Flaubert and Dickens to Joyce and
Eliot, literature has not been the creation of escapist illusions, but on the contrary can be
accounted for by patient research for new ways of speaking about the reality of the real. In
this research, literature has been, claims White, in fact more innovative and *less* fictional
than historiography: "It is literature's claim to manifest, express, or represent reality, to
summon up and interrogate the real world in all its complexity and opacity, that brings it
into conflict with writers of historical discourse."

Postmodernists vs. Pomophobics

In the last decades, the question on the relationship between literature and historiography
has become intertwined with the debate between "postmodernists" and "pomophobics" (to
use Beverley Southgate's term).[13] All the details of this debate cannot be easily summarized, but perhaps it can be roughly sketched, or caricaturized, as follows.

Referring often to White, the so-called "postmodern" camp has stressed the close resemblance between literature and historiography, drawing attention to different literary and
rhetorical techniques used in historical narratives, as well as to some textual strategies of
(modernist) literary fiction that could be used as models for new, postmodern ways of dealing with the past.[14] "Pomophobics" – in historiography mainly the so-called "empiricists,"
but also some literary scholars who believe, in the spirit of good old New Criticism, in the
autonomy of literature – have put an emphasis on their difference, stressing that the distinc-

---

[12] See especially the essay "The Modernist Event," in White, *Figural Realism.*
[13] Beverley Southgate. *Postmodernism in history. Fear or freedom?* (London: Routledge, 2003). Southgate's
account is a wise and insightful attempt to reassure those "pomophobics" that see postmodernism as a threat to
the sense of history in general. By tracing the historical roots of postmodernism within the skepticism in An-
tiquity and Renaissance, Southgate places the recent debates in a wider context.
[14] On postmodernist philosophy of history, see, for example, Keith Jenkins, *Re-thinking history* (London:
Routledge, 1991); Jenkins (ed.) *The Postmodern History Reader* (London: Routledge, 1997); and Alun Mun-
slow, *Deconstructing history* (London: Routledge, 1997).

tion between non-fiction and fiction, between the real and the imaginary, must not be blurred. "Empiricists" have feared that if historiography is compared to literary fiction, the scientific nature of their profession will then be undermined.[15] At the same time, after "cultural studies" have threatened to take over the English departments, some literary scholars have apparently feared that if everything is read as fiction, then the specificity of literary discourse will be ignored and new generations will be superseded by those not knowing how to read literature proper.

This all takes place at the same time when, so we are often told, both literature and history *as we know them* are decaying, perhaps even dying – perhaps they both have come to the end of their historical project.[16] "Pomophobics" sometimes see the possible death of literature and history as nothing less than the end of Western Civilization and the beginning of a new barbarism, where nothing matters and everything is permitted. The paranoid title of Keith Windschuttle's book is telling: *The Killing of History: How Literary Critics and Social Theorists are Murdering our Past.*[17]

"Postmodernists" claim, on the contrary, that the death of literature and history *as we know them* is a good thing – that in the new postmodern era the old modernist power structures, based on the centralized production of knowledge and aesthetic values, will be deconstructed, which allows new forms of cultural creation and new ways of thinking to emerge. For example, in his deliberately provocative book *Why history? Ethics and postmodernity*, Keith Jenkins argues that we should forget history *as we know it* – as an academic discipline that has been, at least traditionally, tied to the values of modernity, scientism, and bourgeois society.[18] The old ways of doing historiography do not apply any longer to our postmodern condition, claims Jenkins, and the very word "history" seems to be so infected by the values of modernity that we could perhaps do better without it. Why are we so tied to our past in the first place? Should we not think rather in terms of presence or future? Jenkins suggests that we should form our relation to the temporality of human existence starting from a new basis that would no longer be automatically governed by the assumptions of the modernist agenda.

The picture I have just presented is, of course, oversimplified and does not do justice to all different arguments made. However, one is tempted to ask if the intensity of the literature / historiography debate has revealed the hidden agony of two modes of discourse that know that time has passed them by? That new unseen forms of writing and thinking are really coming to replace them? Or is there some sense, still, in using concepts like "history" and "literature" – and maintaining some distinction between them?

---

[15]   See, for example, G. R. Elton, *Return to Essentials* (Cambridge: Cambridge UP, 1991); and Richard Evans, *In Defence of History* (London: Granta, 1997).

[16]   For the end of literature and its reasons, see, for example, J. Hillis Miller, *On Literature* (London: Routledge, 2002), pp. 1-12. On the threats towards our notion of history, see Alexander Stille, *The Future of the Past. How the Information Age Threatens to Destroy our Cultural Heritage* (London: Picador, 2002).

[17]   Keith Windschuttle*, The Killing of History: How Literary Critics and Social Theorists are Murdering our Past* (New York: The Free Press, 1996). Windschuttle attacks those narrativists who see that historians have the freedom to choose whatever narrative pattern which they desire for their histories. As he stresses, "one of the most common experiences of historians is that the evidence they find forces them, often reluctantly, to change the position they originally intended to take." Ibid., p. 231.

[18]   Keith Jenkins. *Why History? Ethics and Postmodernity* (London: Routledge, 1999).

History as Quasi-fiction, Fiction as Quasi-history

One of the key-terms in the history vs. literature debate has obviously been 'fiction.' However, the word 'fiction' has been used in so many different contexts and meanings that it is practically impossible to give any single definition for the word.[19] As Karlheinz Stierle reminds us (see chapter 5), the Latin word *fictio* referred originally not so much to lies or poetic inventions, but to molding and shaping pre-existing material (*fingere* = to model a figure out of the shapeless clay). And it is worth noting that still in the 18th century the opposite of 'fact' or 'truth' was not 'fiction,' but rather 'fancy' or 'error.' We may thus claim that all knowledge involves a certain amount of *fictio* in the original sense of the word – a certain amount of molding and shaping pre-existing material. In this sense of the word, the word 'fiction' refers to a system of poetic techniques that are used in all literature and, arguably, in all historiography, too.

However, already in Roman times *fictio* could refer also to lies and poetic inventions – to things and events that did not exist in our real physical world. In this sense, 'fiction' is used as an ontological term that refers to the physical non-existence of the referent. Anything that cannot be reduced to some physical basis can therefore be called fiction: theoretical or scientific hypotheses are fictions since they have not yet been proven, money is fiction since it exists only as a shared illusion of its value, values like 'democracy' and 'freedom' are fictions because they do not have a physical existence. Or, from a Buddhist perspective, all material reality is fiction since it, as everything else in this world, is only illusory.

This ontological use of 'fiction' must, then, be separated from its use as an epistemological term: in judicial language, for example, 'fiction' is used as synonymous with 'lie' or 'conjecture' as opposed to 'truth.'

With literature, however, we use the term 'fiction' mostly as a generic term, as referring to novels and short stories, whether they are based on real events or on pure imagination. In this modern, literary use of the term, 'fiction' is distinguished from 'lie' – the author of fiction cannot lie because by defining the text as fiction he or she has stated that the work is not meant to be read as referring directly to our real world. Literary fiction is thus based on a pact between the author and the reader where some visible signs, some "signposts of fiction," inform the reader that he or she is not supposed to take different statements of the text at their face value.[20] All is stated "as if," as a form of make-believe, where all statements are only pseudo-communication that refer to some larger communicative figurations. As Kalle Pihlainen argues (see chapter 4 of this book), the way this kind of fictional writing refers to the world is in some ways different from historical writing. Whereas assertions in traditional fiction writing become significant mainly in the internal context of the text itself and achieve their "truth-effect" by referring to those private experiences that all readers can share, assertions in historical writing refer to clearly defined singular events outside the textual sphere itself and can thus present, by the aid of documentation and other generally accepted textual advices, referents that readers are not usually familiar with.

---

[19]   One may claim, for example, that part of the misunderstandings concerning Hayden White's work has resulted from his sometimes unstable use of the words "fiction" and "fictive."

[20]   For "signposts of fiction," see Cohn, *The Distinction of Fiction*.

However, there are numerous borderline cases that make this division problematic, for example the so-called "non-fiction novels" that seem to combine many generic characteristics with novels (intra- and intertextual references, inner focalizations, etc.), while still claiming for some kind of non-fictional status (see Markku Lehtimäki in chapter 10 in this book). Also in essayistic tradition fictional and non-fictional references are often intertwined: there is no doubt that Virginia Woolf addressed, in her famous essay *A Room of One's Own*, real historical problems of her own age, but she addressed them by creating a fictional (or composite) town of "Oxbridge" and an arguably fictionalized first-person narrator. We must be careful, then, in not defining 'fiction' and 'literary' simply as synonymous.

We must also remember that the use of imagination in fiction does not mean creation *ex nihil*. All fiction selects and combines elements from the real world, and the reader fills in all the gaps that exist in all literary texts according to his or her own experiences in real life. In the end, all literary fiction becomes meaningful only when we read it in relation to our own experiences in the world. They form the background of all fiction, and there is no fiction that cannot be interpreted as an allegory of this world.[21]

In the third volume of his monumental *Time and Narrative*, Paul Ricoeur sees both history and fiction as crucial for our relation to the question of time, and thus he sees narrative poetics as a necessary supplement for phenomenological analysis of temporality.[22] For Ricoeur, in addressing the "pastness of the past," history and fiction are necessarily intertwined: history is quasi-fiction, fiction is quasi-history. The fictionalization of history, the use of imagination in order to provide ourselves with a figure of the past, begins already in the reinscription of the time of narrative within the time of the universe, and becomes more visible still when we move towards "seeing" the past and re-enacting its events in our mind. According to Ricouer, narrative imagination is crucial for historical understanding: for example, without some kind of "fictionalization" we cannot understand the challenge and meaning of those choices that the characters of history had to face. Moreover, fiction's capacity for creating both an illusion of presence but also a critical distance to its objects is needed especially in cases when the event is too close, too sublime, or too horrible to be told in accordance with traditional methods.[23]

On the other hand, Ricoeur sees historization of fiction, where fictive narratives are based on an "as if past" effect, as the basis for all literary narratives. Fiction receives its attitude of detachment from a temporal "quasi-past" that treats the events as if they belonged to the past:

> If it is true that one of the functions of fiction bound up with history is to free, retrospectively, certain possibilities that were not actualized in the historical past, it is owing to its quasi-historical character that fiction itself is able, after the fact, to perform its liberating function. The quasi-past of fiction in this way becomes the detector of possibilities buried in the actual past. What "might have been" – the possible in Aristotle's terms –

---

21 See, for example, Wolfgang Iser, "The Significance of Fictionalizing." Anthropoetics III, no. 2 (Fall 1997 / Winter 1998).

22 Paul Ricouer, *Time and Narrative, volume 3* [Temps et récit, vol. 3, 1985]. Translated by Kathleen Blamey and David Pellauer (Chicago: The University of Chicago Press, 1988). Henceforward cited as TN.

23 "Individuation by means of the horrible, to which we are particularly attentive, would be blind feeling, regardless of how elevated or how profound it might be, without the quasi-intuitiveness of fiction. Fiction gives eyes to the horrified narrator. Eyes to see and to weep," (TN III, 188).

includes both the potentialities of the "real" past and the "unreal" possibilities of pure fiction. (TN III, 191-192)

Lately, the considerable success of different kinds of "virtual histories," pseudo-historical accounts of possibilities that were never actualized, shows that the importance of this fictionalizing moment in historical research has now been recognized more widely than before.[24]

Virtual Histories

In a way, all writing is historical – it preserves a certain moment of writing, as if a text could preserve the very voice and soul of the author for centuries so that by reading old texts we could raise the dead from their graves.

From historical novels to lyrical memories, from imaginary histories of Space Wars and other fantasy worlds to non-fictive essays, literature and, increasingly, other forms of artistic expression such as films (see Frus and Corkin in the chapter 3 of this book) have thematized our relation to the past. Literary and artistic representations of history may not have enjoyed the same kind of official status as academic historiography has, but no one can deny that they have had a crucial impact on those mental images that we have formed from our past. Often these images may have contradicted the results of scholarly research in one way or another, but without them our reception of all historical narratives, both factual and fictive, would arguably have been far less vivid and less urgent.[25] History of literature, film, and other artistic expressions is, then, not only a story about the development of different styles, schools and individual talents, but it also contributes to the history of imaginary relations to the past and therefore helps us to understand how such textual constructions as "Middle Ages," "Renaissance," or "Wild West" were born and how they undergo changes from one time to another.

However, artistic imagination also has a more serious role in our attempts to encounter the past in its otherness. Not all pasts have been documented – there are, as Oladobe Ibironke underlines (see chapter 11), whole civilizations that do not possess the same kind of written documents and monumental traces as Western civilization possesses. According to Jacques Rancière, one of the reasons that made Michelet a great historian (and a great writer) was his introduction of *silent witness* into historical discourse – a choice that also showed the limits of documented histories.[26] As the representations of the Holocaust or Hiroshima (see Lara Okihiro's essay at the end of this book), or the important role of poetical and essayistic historiography in Africa or the Caribbean show,[27] artistic imagination is an essential supplement to historical discourse when the intention is to give voice to those

---

[24] See, for example, Niam Fergusson (ed.), *Virtual History. Alternatives and Counterfactuals* (London: Picador, 1997).

[25] About the role of historical consciousness in literature, especially in historical novel, see, for example, David Courart, *History and Contemporary Novel* (Carbondale: Southern Illinois UP, 1989); Herbert Lindenberger, *The History in Literature: On Value, Genre, Institution* (New York: Columbia UP, 1990); and Dominick LaCapra, *History, Politics, and the Novel* (Ithaca: Cornell UP, 1989).

[26] Jacques Rancière, *The Names of History* [Les Noms de l'histoire, 1992] (Minneapolis: University of Minneapolis Press, 1994), pp. 54-59.

[27] See, for example, Ado Quayson, *Strategic Transformations in Nigerian Writing. Orality and History in the Work of Rev. Samuel Johnson, Amos Tutuola, Wole Soyinka, and Ben Okri* (Bloomington: Indiana UP, 1997).

who are marginalized from the centralized production of knowledge, or to those who are silenced forever.

Naturally, one should be wary of the nostalgic and sentimentalist approach to the past that is familiar to us from the ever-growing flow of historical entertainment where, little by little, the American Civil War has been replaced by *Gone with the Wind*, and the history of medieval Europe by the history of Middle Earth. And certainly, as Kalle Pihlainen notes, some fictive techniques are less suitable for historical representation than others. However, this should not prevent us from seeing what modern literary writing could offer to historiography. Literature is not only nostalgic entertainment, but serious research on world-making, language, and their multifaceted relationship.

In all scholarly discourse, the reader should be informed not only about the results of the research, but also about the methods used – methods of research and writing. Consistent academic historiography usually does (or at least it should) lay its basic *research* methods open for all to see, so that the reader can estimate the validity of the study by him- or herself: what has been the underlying question or hypothesis of the study? What theoretical basic assumptions have directed the research? How reliable the sources used are? How the material has been analyzed? To what other studies have the results been compared? And finally, how reliable are the conclusions? However, one may claim that traditional academic historiography has not been as eager to estimate its own means of *representation* and how they may have directed the research process itself. Here historiography could, perhaps, learn something from the metatextual techniques of postmodern fiction.

Moreover, some recent works show that it is totally possible to write texts that are both historically sound, in terms of traditional empirical historiography, and aesthetically innovative, in terms of literary discourse. Different forms of hypertextuality may open new ways of relating our lives to the past – after all, the traditional linear form is not necessarily the best one when describing the highly complicated web of different causal connections and individual viewpoints that mold historical events.[28] And, while we still may recognize the distinction between "historical" and "aesthetic" levels of discourse, it is also possible to recognize that both levels imply some philosophical, ethical, and even political levels that reach far beyond the distinction between literature and historiography.

* * * * *

---

[28] For example, Sven Lindqvist's admirable work *A History of Bombing* [Nu dog du – Bombernas århundrade, 1999], translated by Linda Rugg (London: Granta, 2001). As a historical study, it charts the history of Western aerial bombings from their roots in 19th-century colonialism and racist imagination through Dresden, Hiroshima and Vietnam to the possible lines of development in the future. It is based on careful research, it is heavily annotated, and its bibliography is one of the most thorough that one can find from any book on the subject. However, *A History of Bombing* is also very self-consciously a literary text, constructed as a kind of hypertextual network of textual fragments. Fragments are arranged so that they form two different logics, and consequently two different ways to proceed: thematical and chronological. Close to Kafka's *Castle* or Robbe-Grillet's *Last year in Marienbaden*, to mention only two of such literary adaptations of the mythical figure of the labyrinth, *A History of Bombing* creates a forceful and intense ethical experience, urging the reader to search his or her own way beyond the politics of mass destruction.

The past comes to us through traces that it has left behind, and through those mental processes that form worlds and stories out from those traces. We are, at the same time, one with our past – our identity being formed by the very narratives that we make out of it – and strangers to it, incapable of fully grasping either our own or our ancestor's past mentalities and intentions. What did they think? (What did we think?) How did they perceive their world? (How did we perceive the world?) Why did they choose as they did? (Why did we choose as we did?) In order to encounter the past, in order to deal with our own temporality and finitude, we need both history and literature – and we also need texts that question their distinction and thus force us to rethink the very nature of our relationship to the past.

I Hayden White and Textuality of History

Introduction to Part I

Hayden White and Textuality of History

The key note for this book comes from Hayden White, whose role in launching the contemporary history/literature debate has been crucial. In his new, previously unpublished essay "Historical Discourse and Literary Writing," White not only reiterates and clarifies his basic views on the close relationship between literature and historiography, but develops further his analysis on the truth-value of figurative language and its consequences for modernist literary writing. White examines these issues through consideration of the work of Primo Levi, a writer who, by general consensus, has attained to canonical status as an objective, even-handed, and dispassionate witness to life in Auschwitz. However, as White shows in his detailed textual analysis, it is exactly the careful use of figurative expressions that creates Levi's "realistic" and "plain" style. What makes Levi so valuable to our understanding of the Holocaust is, then, not only his being an eyewitness, but the very "literary" character of his writing.

In the following chapter, Herman Paul analyzes White's major work Metahistory *in the light of his early career, and takes a close look into irony, that is one of the most central literary tropes in White's vision of historiography. Although White openly admits the ironic character of his own work, he seeks to provide certain grounds for a rejection of irony by "a turning of the Ironic consciousness against Irony itself." Paul argues that this ironic battle against irony can be understood as an attempt to reconcile two separate tendencies in White's earlier work: the wish for a historiography that would contribute to the shaping of a "humanistic" future, and the critique of ideology as "false consciousness."*

The two following chapters deal with Figural Realism, *the most recent book of Hayden White, and its notion of "the modernist event." Phyllis Frus and Stanley Corkin advance Hayden White's theories by applying them to visual narratives, particularly to contemporary films that define historical consciousness in the late 20th and early 21st centuries. Frus and Corkin shift the analytic precepts from the form of texts to a method for apprehending the historicity of these texts, and they pay particular attention to forms such as docudrama and fictional films that are specifically historical, as in Oliver Stone's controversial film* JFK.

As we have seen, White suggests that the most appropriate forms to describe "the modernist event" could be found from modernist literary fiction. In the fourth chapter, Kalle Pihlainen challenges this view. He argues that historical narrative is ultimately committed to engaging the reader in a process that needs to be returned to the world, whereas a literary narrative may well remain content with leaving its reader somehow privately edified. Thus, while historical narratives are clearly linguistic figurations, just as White argues, Pihlainen holds that this should not be regarded as their determining feature when one searches for alternative representational strategies of the modernist event. Rather than constantly referring to the formal similarities between historiography and literary fiction, one should, he argues, focus on the strengths entailed by the commitment to referentiality.

CHAPTER 1

Hayden White

Historical Discourse and Literary Writing

Before the nineteenth century, the relation between historical writing and literary writing was not problematical. Since Aristotle, it had been thought that, although both history and imaginative writing were rhetorical arts, they dealt with different things: historical writing was about the real world while "poetry" was about the possible. During the nineteenth century, however, the concept of history was reformulated, historical consciousness was for the first time theorized, and the modern scientific method of historical inquiry was inaugurated. History was no longer simply the past or accounts of the past, but now became identified as a process, a dimension of human existence, and a force to be controlled or succumbed to. During the same time, what had formerly been called discourse and *belles lettres* underwent reconceptualization. Now literary writing – as practiced by Balzac and Flaubert, Dickens and Scott, Manzoni, etc., was detached from of summoning up the unconscious or latent dimensions of human reality. Now, literature became history's other in a double sense: it pretended to have discovered a dimension of reality that historians would never recognize and it developed techniques of writing that undermined the authority of history's favored realistic or plain style of writing.

It is often thought that history's principal enemy is the lie, but actually it has two enemies considered to be more deadly to its mission to tell the truth and nothing but the truth about the past: rhetoric and fiction. Rhetoric because, according to the doxa philosohica, it seeks to seduce where it cannot convince by evidence and argument; and fiction because, according to the same doxa, it presents imaginary things as if they were real and substitutes illusion for truth.

History is one of the "others" of literature inasmuch as literature is understood to be identifiable with fiction. Because history wishes to make true statements about the real world, not an imaginary or illusory world. Secondly, history is literature's other inasmuch as literature is understood to be identifiable with figuration, figurative language, and metaphor, rather than with literal speech, unambiguous assertion, and free or poetic (rather than bound) utterance.

It has to be said, however, that, in general, literature – in the modern period – has regarded history not so much as its other as, rather, its complement in the work of identifying and mapping a shared object of interest, a real world which presents itself to reflection under so many different aspects that all of the resources of language – rhetorical, poetical, and symbolic – must be utilized to do it justice. So history's antipathy to literature is misplaced. It has been a long time since the primary business of literary writing has been conceived to be the spinning of stories about imaginary worlds for the entertainment of people seeking relief from reality. The great modernists (from Flaubert, Baudelaire, Dickens and Shelley down through Proust, Joyce, Woolf, Pound, Eliot, Stein, and so on) were as interested in representing a real instead of a fictional world quite as much as any modern historian. But unlike their historian counterparts they realized that language itself is a part of the real world and must be included among the elements of that world rather than treated as a transparent instrument for representing it. With this realization, modernism created a new conception of realistic representation itself and beyond that a new notion of reading which permits a creative re-reading even of the formerly transparent historical *document*.

For an older historiography, the historical document was to be read for what it yielded in the way of factual information regarding the world about which it spoke or of which it was a trace. The paradigm of the historical document was the eye-witness account of a set of events which, when correlated with other accounts and other kinds of documents bearing upon these events, permitted a characterization of "what happened" in some finite domain of past occurrences.

The operation involved in this process of determining what happened in some part of the past presupposes that the object of study remains *virtually* perceivable by way of the documentary record (which attests to both its existence and its nature or substance). The aim was to extract a number of facts from the reading of the documentary record which could be measured or correlated with facts extracted from other records. This meant reading through or around whatever a given testimony might contain in the way of figurative speech, logical contradiction, or allegorization. None of these would be admitted as testimony in a court of law and consequently were not permitted to remain, as it were, untranslated into literal equivalents in the reading of a historical document.

But here we are interested in how or in what ways a modernist notion of verbal representation can expand understanding of the world of which it speaks. One way is to ask how it is that figurative language can be said to *refer* to extra-textual phenomena and what kind of information about the world such language provides us with. That is to say, what is the status or truth-value of figurative statements about the real world, and what kind of information does an anaysis of figurative language in the historical document yield to us?

I want to examine some of these issues by means of a consideration of the work of Primo Levi, a writer who has attained to canonical status as an objective, even-handed, and dispassionate witness to life in Auschwitz concentration camp. Levi, more than any other writer of the Holocaust, I would say, has shown not only that this event is representable in writing but is *realistically* representable as well. But what makes Levi's prose so compelling as a kind of model of objectivity and realism in the representation an event, the Holocaust, which is often held to be "unrepresentable"?

Levi's objectivity and precision of utterance are often attributed to the fact (promoted by him in interviews and personal statements) that he was not really a writer but only a "simple" chemist who brought the same kind of "weighing and measuring" procedures to his depiction of life in the Lager that he had utilized in the research labs of the paint company for which he worked. The suggestion is that whereas many other Holocaust writers depend upon rhetoric and aestheticization to render the horror of their experiences in the camps, Levi has purged his language of rhetoric, developed an anti-rhetorical "plain" style, and is all the more effective for eschewing any openly artistic tricks or techniques.

In my view, however, it can be easily demonstrated that Levi's text is full of rhetorical figures and tropes and is never more rhetorical than when he is or purports to be simply "describing" a place, situation, or individual he knows.

I want to indicate what I mean by these remarks by analyzing – so far as time will allow – a passage in *Se questo è un uomo* ("If this is a man" translated into English as "Survival in Auschwitz" and into French as "Si c'est un homme").[1] I choose this passage because it is a point in Levi's text in which his theme – indicated in the title of the English translation of his book, *Survival in Auschwitz* – is condensed into brief characterizations of four types of "the survivor" met with in the Lager. I will suggest that if we read these descriptions literally, for whatever information they give us about life in the camps, we will miss what is most important in them as evidence. The use of figurative language and tropes is what give them a concreteness and vividness – indeed, a humanity – that no conventionally "objective" description of these individuals could ever produce.

The passage I will analyze extends over seven pages of the 1989 Einaudi edition of *Se questo è un uomo*, a little over one-half of the chapter "I Sommersi e I Salvati," which comes at the exact middle point of the text. A proper "close reading" of this text would comment on every trope and turn of its elaboration – only thus could we do a proper job of bringing to the surface its latent content, what a psychoanalytical criticism would call the "unconscious of the text." And this latent content of the text, the level on which the motivation of the figures of speech marking its surface features is to be grasped, this latent content is as significant as historical evidence as any of the factual information we can derive from a literal reading of it. Indeed, I would argue that this latent content is more important than *the information about life* in the camps and what it took to survive therein, contained in the text, because it tells us not only "what happened" in the camps but also "what it felt like."

I will not here attempt such an extensive excavation of the *whole* of this text for want of time, but will concentrate on what kind of historical knowledge can be extracted from Levi's text by a "literary" reading of it – a reading, I would argue, without which the deep content of the work (what Hjelmslev would have called "the substance of its content") will remain unregistered or simply unseen. I will concentrate on the last of the four descriptions of the "survivor type" which Levi gives us, not least because the person whom Levi is describing (under the pseudonym of "Henri") turned up some fifty years later, identified himself, and responded to what he took to have been something less than a fully adequate account of who he was and how he saw life in he Lager.

The person in question turns out to have been a young Russian Jewish man named Paul Steinberg, resident of Paris in 1943, where he was picked up by the police and shipped off to Auschwitz, at the age of sixteen or seventeen. Here is what Levi tells us about him:

> Henri, however, is eminently civilized and sane, and possesses a complete and organic theory on the ways to survive in Lager. He is only twenty-two, he is extremely intelligent, speaks French, German, English and Russian, has an excellent scientific and classical culture. (English edition, p. 98; Italian, p. 89) [Note: here is factual error number one: Henri was not twenty-two but seventeen in 1944; he had not even graduated from high school, and knew more about the street life of Paris than he did about science much less about classical culture, which he had gotten from reading in his father's polyglot library.]

"His brother died in Buna last winter," Levi continues, "and since then Henri has cut off every tie of affection; he has closed himself up, as if in armour, and fights to live without

---

[1] Primo Levi, *Se questo è un uomo* [1947] (Torino: Einaudi, 1989), English translation by Stuart Woolf, *Survival in Auschwitz* (New York: Touchstone, 1996).

distraction [...]" [Note: factual error number two, this was not his brother, but a friend.]
"There is no better strategist than Henri in seducing [circuire] (coltivare, dice lui) the English POWs. In his hands they become real geese with golden eggs ... Henri was once seen
in the act of eating a real [autentico] hard-boiled egg." (English ed., p. 99, Italian ed., 89)

[The figures in this passage make up a skein of essentially ironic symbolizations: the
cold, carapaced isolate, the seducer of the geese that laid the golden eggs; the consumer of
an "authentic" egg. . . These figures build up a set of oppositions between the shifters: hard-
soft, cold-warm, seducer-victim, not to mention that between authentic and fake – Henri is
being "fictionalized," to be sure, but fictionalized as a real type, what Gayatri Spivak calls
an "authentic fake"?]

These figures are distilled in the paragraph which follows into a synecdoche of the piti-
less seducer who himself uses pity [la pietà] as "suo strumento di penetrazione." (Italian
ed.., p. 89, English, 99.) Then follows a physical description of Henri's visage, but by way
of an allusion to a famous painting:

> Henri ha il corpo e il viso delicati e sottilmente perversi del San Sebastiano del Sodoma: I suoi occhi sono neri
> e profondi, non ha ancora barba, si muove con languida naturale eleganza (quantunque all 'occorrenza sappia
> correre e saltare come un gatto, e la capacità del suo stomaco sia appena inferiore a quella di Elias). (Eng., p.
> 99, It., p. 89.)

Henri, we are told, exploits these, his "natural gifts" with "la fredda competenza di chi
manovra uno strumento scientifico: i risultati sono sorprendenti." [It., p. 89 It; 99 Eng]

[This passage is important for me, because a couple of years after I started studying
Levi's style, Paul Steinberg's book came onto the market, accompanied by a photograph of
the author, at the age of sixteen or seventeen, or the age just before his arrest and deporta-
tion to Auschwitz. I had already looked up Sodoma's famous portrait of San Sebastiano,
and of course, empiricist that I am, I could not resist comparing the two, in order to determine how accurate was the characterization, first of Sodoma's San Sebastian ("his eyes are
deep and profound, he has no beard yet, he moves with a natural languid elegance, etc.")
and then of Henri, whose visage was recorded in that photograph on the cover of his Lager
memoir, *Chroniques d'ailleurs* ("Speak you also" – from Celan – in English)].

But surely here a literalist empiricism is misplaced. Henri's physiognomy is being likened to that of Sodoma's San Sebastian, to be sure, but it is less on the level of the signifier
than on that of the signified that the resemblance is being asserted. It is to the San Sebastiano of "Il Sodoma," the well-known "patron saint" of homosexuals, that Henri is being
likened and with which his essence or substance is being identified, in a complex interplay
of attraction and revulsion that brings to the surface an erotic dimension to the act of observation ("penetration"?).

The motif of penetration is picked up and condensed into a truly gruesome image in the
paragraph following: Here Henri is likened to a kind of wasp, the ichneumon which kills its
prey (the "hairy caterpillar") by drilling into its body and depositing its eggs therein, leaving the larvae to feed off the body of the host and ultimately killing it. Henri is quoted as
confirming the aptness of this simile by referring to his stints in the infirmary, where he can
avoid the selections of the gas chambers, as his "svernare" (hibernation).

So this is why it is "gradevole discorrere con Henri," why it is "utile e gradevole," but
also frustrating since, when Henri seems to be warming up and becoming friendly, even

affectionate, he can turn quite suddenly once more into the cold and armoured "enemy of all, inhumanly cunning and incomprehensible, like the serpent in Genesis." (It., p. 90, Eng., p. 100)

Indeed, Levi closes his portrait of Henri with a bitter personal remark:

> From all my talks with Henri, even the most cordial, I have always left with a slight taste of defeat; of also having been, somehow inadvertently, not a man to him, but an instrument in his hands.

> I know that Henri is living today. I would give much to know his life as a free man, but I do not want to see him again. (Eng., p. 100, It., p. 90)

Now, if we had read this passage for information, factual information about life in the camps, what would we have learned? We know that some of the factual information about Henri is mistaken. But what about the figuration of Henri, the characterization of him in a series of metaphors and similes that effectively assimilates him to a conventional symbol of evil, "il Serpente del Genesi"? This operation, I suggest, is compelling and convincing as a description of a kind of human being that we have all encountered. And it is compelling and convincing because of the specific combination of specific images that add up to a symbol of a certain type of humanity.

But so what? What does this example of figurative description passing for objective description tell us about the relation between literature and its other, "history"?

The debate over the status of historical knowledge, knowledge of the past, or knowledge of the complex relations between the past and the present, has been pretty much resolved by the recognition that historical research is something less than a rigorous science and something more than common sense. It is recognized that inquiry into such questions as causality in history, the intentions of historical agents, and responsibility for the unforeseeable consequence of large scale social actions in the past require a combination of practical procedures, rather more like those used by judges and detectives than of scientists in a laboratory or of anthropologists in the field. The epistemological problems of historical inquiry stem from the fact that the events and persons with which historians deal are no longer present to perception, the evidence available for inspection is incomplete and contingently assembled, and eyewitness accounts of events can be checked only against other accounts, not against the events themselves. All of this means that, as a component of what Reinhart Koselleck calls a community's "space of experience," its "archive" of practical knowledge, historical knowledge is pretty weak. We have long since given up "learning from history" (cf. Gumbrecht) because the knowledge with which history provides us is so situation-specific as to be irrelevant to later times and places. This does not mean that historical knowledge is of no use at all; on the contrary, it has a vital function in the construction of community identity.

But problems arise precisely in any effort to use historical knowledge for purposes of identity construction – as the European Union is rapidly discovering as it tries to construct a European identity as a necessary step in the construction of a European subject and citizen. And these problems arise because historical knowledge always comes to the present in a processed form, not as raw data or information stored in an archive or data bank. It is only as represented knowledge, as written, filmed, videotaped, photographed, dramatized, and narrativized, that historical knowledge enters into the public domain. This is not to say that, simply as archived information, historical data are not already processed – named, identified, and classified and assigned a provisional relevance to the community's interests. But as archived, data are only minimally identified as being historicizable, of potential use as historical knowledge, and really belong in this preliminary state to the history of the archive rather than to that communal history which the archive wishes to serve. And, as the philosopher Paul Ricoeur has said, "C'est à ce niveau [de la representation] que se concentrent les difficultés les plus tenaces concernant la representation du passé en histoire." For it is here (but not only here; also at every stage of the research process), in the process of composing the historian's text that the problem of the relation between the factual and the fictive in historical discourse arises.

It is not a matter of style understood as the relatively benign process of using standard educated language to describe complex social processes or translating arcane terms (such as metic) into modern equivalents (foreigner). It is rather a matter of endowing sets of events with, first, chronological and, then, narratological order and, beyond that, transforming persons and groups into figures in a scene that has more in common with the theatre than with real life.

The discussion over the nature of historical representation has an importance far exceeding the rather banal problem of telling the truth about the past as best one can on the basis of the study of the documents. No one denies that historians – of whatever stripe – want to tell the truth about the events and persons of the past; the question is: can they ever do so, given the constraints on both unambiguous referentiality, on the one side, and the fictionalizing effects of narrativization, on the other?

For my part, I have no doubt that discourse and especially historical discourse refers to objects and events in a real world – but would add that since these objects and events are no longer perceivable, they have to be constructed as possible objects of a possible perception rather than treated as real objects of real perceptions. I will come back to this when I discuss the strategy of description by which objects in the past are worked up for subsequent treatment as specifically historical kinds of objects. For the moment, however, I want to stress that, in my view, one cannot historicize without narrativizing, because it is only by narrativization that a series of events can be transformed into a sequence, divided into periods, and represented as a process in which the substances of things can be said to change while their identities remain the same. (Cf. Collingwood). Insofar as historical discourse is willy-nilly condemned to narativization it is by this circumstance alone committed to ideologizing practices, by which I mean the endowment of past events with meanings and values relevant to the promotion of political and social programs in the present for which historians write. For narrativization has to do with the problematic of action, whether action is considered to be possible or impossible, a good thing or a bad thing, a burden or a gift of the gods, of fate, or of history. This is a view long held by the Left, as Lukacs, for example.

Braudel was wrong to think that, by its form alone, narrative always implicitly supports the Right and conservatism. Narrative, even when written from a "conservative" or "traditionalist" pespective, as in Dante, or Balzac, always asks: how is action possible? It may answer this question by a negative result: alas, action is not possible; or a positive one: yes, it is possible. But by raising the question, narrative itself is positive: it answers the question: is it possible to ask whether action is possible?

So, historical narratives refer to a real world (that no longer exists but of which we have traces) and presents that world as having narratological coherence. And the question is:

does the manner in which they refer and techniques used in narrativization render their accounts more fictional than realistic, more imaginary than rational, more artistic than scientific in nature?

So let us look once more at the passage from Primo Levi's work that I analyzed previously. This work is not so much a history as a privileged piece of historical evidence, an eye-witness account of events that happened in a particular time and place. But if it does not quite qualify as a history, it certainly qualifies as a model of the kind of account that historians, working from a variety of sources, might wish to have been able to produce as an account of life in the camps. For Levi's book tells us, not only what happened in Auschwitz between his arrival in October 1944 and June 1945; it tells us – more importantly – what it felt like to have been the victim of the kind of humiliation which the camps had turned into an art. In any event, the passage from Levi's text which I analyzed is presented as a bit of "factual" discourse. It is certainly not presented as fiction. Indeed, as Levi says at the end of the Preface to his book, "Mi pare superfluo aggiungere che nessuno dei fatti è inventato."

One could linger over this assertion. Does it say, "None of the facts has been invented"? or does it say "None of the facts has been invented"? If we take it as saying the former, then the statement is superfluous, since we would already assume that none of the facts has been invented. If we take it as saying the latter, that the facts have not been invented, it leaves aside the question of what else, other than the facts, the work might contain. None of the facts have been invented, OK, but what other than the facts are to be found in this work? Of course, the irony of the statement is already signaled in the remark: "Mi pare superfluo, . . ." which says: "It appears to me superfluous" to add, etc. If it is superfluous, why add it? Yet it is added: "none of the facts has been invented." The statement "None of the facts has been invented" is superfluous; it need not be added; yet it is added. Why? Is this an example of hyperbole (I add what need not be added) or litotes ("It seems superfluous to add…").

I hope that this will not be taken as mere pedantry: It seems superfluous to me to add that none of this is pedantry. I am just trying to read some passages in Primo Levi's Se questo è un uomo carefully and with full attention to what it says, rather than project my interpretation onto it in the form of a paraphrase about what I think it means to say. What I think it means to say is that "It appears [to the author] superfluous to add that none of the facts has been invented" but that this addition appears superflous because facts are facts and cannot be invented or made up and still remain facts but that whatever else is in the text, besides the facts, may have been invented or not. So, I think that this sentence, placed at the end of the preface, leaves considerable room for invention. But what is invented cannot be easily distinguished from what is not invented. It is a matter of trope and figuration.

Figuration is a necessary device for characterizing persons for roles in narratives and troping is necessary for making the kinds of connections between events that endow them with plot-meaning. Art may resemble life but life does not resemble art, even when it is intended to do so. The kinds of plots that endow sets of events with meaning exist only in art, not in life. Are there tragic lives or tragic events? I do not think so, however much we may wish to believe that it is so. The term "tragic" describes or refers to a structure of meaning, not a factual situation. Lives may be described as tragic, but it is the description that makes or makes them appear to be tragic, not the lives that justify the description.

Here is how figuration works. In Chapter 6 of *Se questo è un uomo*, Levi sketches portraits of four kinds of prisoner who possessed the kinds of talents necessary for survival in Auschwitz. These are a prisoner named Schepschel who has survived in the camps for four years – "a poor wretch who retains only a humble and elementary desire to live, and who bravely carries on his small struggle not to give way." Then there an engineer, Alfred L., who shows among other things "how vain is the myth of equality among men." He had learned early on that "the step was short from being judged powerful to effectively being so" and always practiced what Levi, citing the Gospel of St. Matthew, calls the rule that "to him who has it shall be given." Alfred L. survived by eliminating all rivals for the few privileges vouchsafed to those enjoying "protection." Next, Elias Lindzin, #141565, a dwarf of enormous strength, "whose whole face looks like a battering ram, an instrument made for butting." Elias is an animal, possessed of "bestial vigour." He is a "madman, incomprehensible and para-human," an "atavism," "insane." Elias shows that "the only road to salvation leads to … insanity and deceitful bestiality" (*Survival*, pp. 93-98).

These are characterizations of real people, all treated as instances of a type, the "survivor type" but more specifically the type of person capable of surviving in the extraordinary world of Auschwitz.

How are we to assess these characterizations? Here are the wretch, the confidence man, and the dwarf strong as an elephant. Are these characterizations true and if so, what kind of truth do they convey? One could, to be sure, treat these characterizations as what the philosophers call "singular existential statements" meant to be confirmed or disconfirmed by observation or other kinds of evidence. But we cannot check these statements by observation and we have no other evidence that bears on these specific individuals. We can say that these characterizations of the survivor-type are "true to their kind," based on information we have from other survivors about the kind of person who survived places like Auschwitz. But these are figurations, the truth of which must be accorded to the extent to which they seem to be consistent with what we know, on the basis of a wide body of evidence, about "survival in Auschwitz."

Literature – in its modern sense – has many others, not least of which is fiction. This is not to say that fictional writing cannot be literary writing. It is only to say that not all fictional writing is literary and, moreover, there is a great deal of literary writing that is not fictional. I am not sure that "literary" is the term I want to use as the genus of which fictional writing and non-fictional writing might be called a species. It may well be that the term poetic or poetry would do, since all poetic writing, whether it is in verse or prose, is non-fictional, which would allow one to speak of historical and a great deal of other social science writing as artistic without consigning it to the category of fiction. But I will stick to "literary" to characterize artistic writing since the term poetic suggests a difference from prose that I want to elide. I will say, then, that literary writing can be poetic or prosaic but differs from pre-literary writing by its claim to being non-fictional.

In this antipathy to fiction, modern literature shares ground with poetry, which may be fictive and fictionalizing but need not be so and, indeed, insofar as it is mimetic, especially of language itself, is never so. It is literature's claim to manifest, express, or represent reality, to summon up and interrogate the real world in all its complexity and opacity, that brings it into conflict with writers of historical discourse. This conflict is usually conceived as a battle between fact and fiction or between rational argumentation and imaginative presentation. But it is a feature of (modernist) literary writing that it brings under question the fact-fiction distinction and, along with that, the distinction between the real and the imaginary.

Modernist writing dissolves the event, shatters plot, and ambiguates point of view, thereby revising the basis for treating narrative as adequate to the representation of series of events in a specifically historical mode of presentation. In compensation modernist writing authorizes the examination of experience in terms of surface-depth, the spread of event, and the instability of the subject. Above all, literary writing focuses on language itself as both medium of expression and a thing in the world.

CHAPTER 2

Herman Paul

An Ironic Battle against Irony: Epistemological and Ideological Irony in Hayden White's Philosophy of History, 1955-1973

Hayden White's *Metahistory*, published in 1973, is often regarded not only as the author's most important book, but also as his first important piece of work. *Metahistory* was, after all, the first book-length study in which White explored the notions that are now considered as his most original contributions to historical theory: the notions of emplotment, tropology, prefiguration, et cetera. Moreover, *Metahistory* is one of the few books that have put the notion of "style" on the agenda of intellectual historians. Besides, the book has given a strong impulse to historical theory in America and Western Europe. It has become rather common to date the birth of narrativism in historical theory to 1973. In all of these perspectives, *Metahistory* is regarded as the starting point of a development or as the beginning of a still ongoing debate among theoretically minded historians.[1]

But *Metahistory* had, of course, a history of its own. It can be read as the result of White's research in intellectual history and historical theory during the 1950s and 1960s. In other words, *Metahistory* may be studied not only as the *starting point* of certain developments, but also as the *outcome* of several lines of thought developed during the early years of White's career. Given the large amount of attention paid to White's later work – defined as his publications from 1973 onwards – it seems worthwhile to focus this essay on some aspects of his early work.

There are several ways in which *Metahistory* can be connected to the early stages of White's scholarly development. Interesting (and almost completely unknown) is the relation between the *Ideologieanalyse* or "analysis of ideologies" in White's 1955 PhD thesis and the "metahistorical analysis" in *Metahistory*. White's search for the worldviews underlying the conflict concerning the succession of Pope Honorius II, in the early twelfth century, resembles in many respects his search for the ultimate beliefs of nineteenth-century historians and philosophers of history. In both cases, White tried to explain a cultural practice (church politics, historical writing) by referring to the way in which the main practitioners "prefigured" the world by means of a *Weltanschauung*.[2] Another suggestion could be to study White's opinions on nineteenth-century liberalism, on German historicism and on Hegel's and Burckhardt's philosophies of history. A comparison between his 1966 Hegel-

---

[1] Some scholars, however, have suggested that White's 1966 essay, "The burden of history" (in Hayden White, *Tropics of discourse: Essays in cultural criticism* [Baltimore/London: Johns Hopkins University Press, 1978], 27-50), rather than *Metahistory*, should be regarded as the starting point of White's philosophy of history. David Harlan, for example, characterizes this essay as "the polestar that has guided virtually everything [White] has written since then." David Harlan, *The degradation of American history* (Chicago/London: University of Chicago Press, 1997), p. 106.

[2] Hayden V. White, "The conflict of papal leadership ideals from Gregory VII to St. Bernard of Clairvaux with special reference to the schism of 1130" (PhD thesis, University of Michigan, 1955).

article and the 1973 chapter dealing with this German philosopher might reveal how White's methods of historiographical analysis only gradually took the form of the tropological system outlined in the introduction to *Metahistory*.[3]

I would prefer, however, to focus on one of the central motifs in *Metahistory*: the hope that the trope of irony, so characteristic of the modern Western view of history, will one day be replaced by the trope of metaphor. It might be recalled that in *Metahistory*, the development of historical culture in nineteenth-century Europe is portrayed as a movement from a metaphorical understanding of reality by way of a metonymical and a synecdochical consciousness to an ironic understanding of the world. From White's perspective, the irony of this last phase is, in a sense, unavoidable for anybody living in a late-modern society ("It may not go unnoticed that this book is itself cast in an Ironic mode").[4] But at the same time, White was convinced that historians should fight this irony with its own weapons in order to create an opportunity to "return" to a metaphorical comprehension of reality. As White himself stated at the very beginning of his book:

> [The] Irony which informs [this book] is a conscious one, and it therefore represents a turning of the Ironic consciousness against Irony itself. If it succeeds in establishing that the skepticism and pessimism of so much of contemporary historical thinking have their origins in an Ironic frame of mind, and that this frame of mind in turn is merely one of a number of possible postures that one may assume before the historical record, it will have provided some of the grounds for a rejection of Irony itself.[5]

In this paper, I first would like to reconstruct what the concept of "irony" is understood to mean. I will attempt to clarify White's argument by distinguishing between *ideological* and *epistemological* irony. Secondly, I will seek to demonstrate that in the quotation just given – especially in the "turning of the Ironic consciousness against Irony itself" – White tried to reconcile two independent lines of thought from his earlier work. Finally, I will argue that this attempt at conciliation reflected White's preference for an understanding of history in terms of sublimity and human moral freedom. In doing so, I will attempt to give new support to Hans Kellner's and Peter Novick's characterization of Hayden White as an existentialistic philosopher of history.[6]

– I –

First of all, what exactly is the irony White wanted to use as a weapon against irony? In *Metahistory*, the concept of irony is used in several ways. Eward Gibbon, for example, is called an ironic writer, because *The Decline and Fall of the Roman Empire* demonstrated

---

[3]   Hayden White, "Hegel: historicism as tragic realism," *Colloquium* 5:2 (1966), 10-19. Most of these early publications are listed in Ewa Domańska, "Bibliografia prac Haydena White'a," in Hayden White, *Poetyka pisarstwa historycznego*, edited by Ewa Domańska and Marek Wilczyński (Kraków: Universitas, 2000), pp. 361-381. In my PhD thesis on Hayden White's philosophy of history (in preparation), I will include a more complete bibliography.

[4]   Hayden White, *Metahistory: The historical imagination in nineteenth-century Europe* (Baltimore/London: Johns Hopkins University Press, 1973), p. xii.

[5]   Ibid.

[6]   Hans Kellner, "A bedrock of order. Hayden White's linguistic humanism," in *Language and historical representation: Getting the story crooked* (Madison/London: University of Wisconsin Press, 1989), pp. 193-227, here 212; Peter Novick, *That noble dream: The "objectivity question" and the American historical profession* (Cambridge: Cambridge University Press, 1988), p. 601.

(among other things) that in Rome, none of the "fanatical" religions that had succeeded each other through the years had been able to lay an exclusive claim on the city. Elsewhere, Hegel is called ironic, because the German philosopher believed that the world of human affairs is always characterized by paradoxes and dilemmas. Friedrich Nietzsche is named an ironic thinker as well, because he judged historical representations not so much by standards of truth but rather from the standpoint of a human will to power.[7]

These three examples make sufficiently clear that the word "irony" – just as several other central notions in *Metahistory* – is not used in a very uniform manner. In his review of the book, John S. Nelson even concluded that there are four ways in which the nineteenth-century thinkers discussed in *Metahistory* are called "ironic," and that in this set of four, five different levels can be distinguished. That is to say, in the first place, that there are several *degrees* of irony – ranging between "critical" and "nihilistic" – and that irony, secondly, can refer to different *subjects* – varying from archival sources to the *raison d'être* of historical research.[8] Obviously, this observation is aimed at criticizing the carelessness in White's terminology. Although it is possible to disagree with Nelson about the relevance of this criticism, it is necessary to follow Nelson at least to some degree, in order to grasp what is at stake in White's "ironic battle against irony". At the very least, it is necessary to distinguish between what I will call *epistemological* and *ideological* irony.

The first variant can be found in White's own definition of irony. "The trope of irony," White wrote, "…provides a linguistic paradigm of a mode of thought which is radically self-critical with respect not only to a given characterization of the world of experience but also to the very effort to capture adequately the truth of things in language."[9] In *Metahistory*, this irony is associated with epistemological skepticism. It suspects the "realism" – the attempt to represent reality as accurately as possible – that metaphorical, metonymical and synecdochical worldviews pretend to offer. Its anti-realism originates in the awareness that human knowledge can never achieve a perfect representation of reality and that, for that very reason, "realism" is doomed to fail. Thus, epistemological irony is an attitude that questions the historian's ability to offer a representation of the past that meets the standards of truthfulness set by metaphorical, metonymical, and synecdochical worldviews.

But this epistemological irony was certainly not the target of White's criticisms and the stage he wanted to leave by means of a Vichian *ricorso*. For one of the central motifs in White's *Metahistory* is the idea that there are no epistemological grounds on which it is possible to discriminate among the various ways in which historians prefigure historical reality. Each of these prefigurations, in its own way, rather determines what counts as "reality" and "epistemology". If there are reasons to prefer one way of prefiguring reality over another, these reasons, according to White, can only be moral or aesthetic in nature. So, White's attitude towards historical knowledge perfectly met the definition of epistemological irony given above.[10]

---

[7]   White, *Metahistory*, pp. 55, 109, 371-372.

[8]   John S. Nelson, review essay on Hayden White, *Metahistory* in *History and Theory,* vol. 14 (1975): pp. 74-91, here 81.

[9]   White, *Metahistory*, p. 37.

[10]   White, *Metahistory*, xii, p. 433. In his essays from the 1970s and 1980s, White has repeated this argument so often, that Peter Novick could observe a tendency among the American public to see White as something like

The type of irony which *displeased* White, by contrast, is apparent from the final chapters of *Metahistory*, on Jacob Burckhardt's and Benedetto Croce's philosophies of history. Croce, who had been one of White's intellectual heroes during the early 1960s,[11] was criticized because of his conviction that historians ought not to intervene in contemporary political debates. Although Croce warmly supported a morally committed historiography, he believed that present-day reality is always different from the past and that for that reason, historians can never tell their contemporaries what is good or wrong to decide in the present. By such a partition between the sphere of historical thought and the sphere of political action, White argued, the historian is forced "…to assume the most extreme Irony with respect to everything in his own social and cultural present."[12] Accordingly, the Crocean historian cannot be a "committed intellectual." Much to White's annoyance, no border traffic between history, on the one hand, and politics, science, philosophy and religion, on the other, seemed to be possible:

> Later philosophers of history, laboring under the felt necessity to provide some historically justified condemnation of the totalitarian regimes of the twentieth century, naturally regarded this position as morally agnostic or as a tactical move to discredit the "scientific" historiography of the Marxist Left. And so it appears from my perspective.[13]

This is not the place to discuss the adequacy of White's interpretation of Croce.[14] I would rather conclude that the irony White attributed to Croce was an irony with respect to the possibility for historians to contribute to the solution of political problems. It was the relation between history and politics that was at stake here, the relation between making the past and making the future, between the writing of history and the making of history. It was a lack of political idealism – or even a lack of utopian thinking – that White considered responsible for Croce's understanding of the historian's task. To put it differently, it was Croce's *ideological irony*, or his irony with respect to ideology, that elicited White's criticism.

As far as this ideological irony was concerned, White felt more attracted by the historiography Karl Marx had in mind. For this kind of historical writing was anything but "contemplative." From Marx's perspective, historical writing, just as other branches of scholarship, had to contribute to a transformation of reality. In White's concise summary: "For Marx, *history properly comprehended* not only provided an image of man come [*sic*] into his kingdom on earth; it was also one of the instruments by which that kingdom was finally to be won."[15] For this reason, Marx had little affinity with an ironic prefiguration of the historical field. Central to his philosophy of history – at least in White's interpretation –

a "symbolic embodiment" of epistemological irony (or even as an embodiment of "nihilistic relativism"). Novick, *That noble dream*, p. 599.

[11] Hayden V. White, "Translator's introduction. On history and historicisms," in: Carlo Antoni, *From history to sociology. The transition in German historical thinking*, translated by Hayden White (Detroit: Wayne State University Press 1959), pp. xv-xxviii; id., "The abiding relevance of Croce's idea of history," *The Journal of Modern History* 35 (1963): pp. 109-124.

[12] White, *Metahistory*, p. 402.

[13] Ibid., p. 401.

[14] Cf. David D. Roberts, *Benedetto Croce and the uses of historicism* (Berkeley/Los Angeles/London: University of California Press 1987), esp. pp. 345-349.

[15] White, *Metahistory*, p. 285.

was the *ricorso* from irony to metaphor that White had searched for in vain in Croce's thought. Whatever might be said about Marx's ideals, it was beyond doubt that the German philosopher did not envision a separation between historiography and politics.[16] He rather preferred to write history "in the active (…) voice," that is to say, in a way informed by his (radical) political views.[17] These two examples make clear that a "return" to the stage of metaphor as advocated in *Metahistory* would imply a revival of strong political commitments among historians.

– II –

In order to demonstrate how White's aversion to ideological irony was related to his preference for epistemological irony, I would like to make a few comments on the background of both. First of all, "ideology" can be regarded as a central theme in White's early work.[18] During the 1950s, White used this concept to refer to some basic human beliefs about the nature of reality, including ontological beliefs (about the present state of the world) and moral convictions (about the ideal state of the world). An equivalent of worldview or *Weltanschauung*, ideology was defined as a set of values that serve as a guide to human behaviour.[19] From this perspective, every human being could be said to adhere to a certain ideology.

During this period, moreover, White tried to unravel what Max Weber once called "the inner logic of the worldviews." Based on his reading of Weber, Karl Mannheim and Arnold J. Toynbee, he drafted a model that had to explain why the dominance of a certain ideology in a society almost automatically evokes opposition and, in doing so, starts processes that will inevitably result in revolution.[20] In Giambattista Vico and Michel Foucault, White also found useful theories on the diachronic development of "the deep structures" in human thought.[21] White's conviction that nineteenth-century historical consciousness lost its metaphorical character, passed two other stages and ended up in irony, is completely in line with this fascination for "the inner logic of the worldviews."

There are some indications that during the 1960s, the concepts of "worldview" and "ideology" grew apart, since the latter began to be used in a more critical way. In a 1963 essay on Croce, for example, White reserved the concept of "ideology" for political movements like Socialism, Fascism, and National Socialism. Characteristic of all these ideologies, White argued, was that they promised to solve the social and political problems of the day by simplifying the complexity of the reality they wanted to change. Their ready-made answers revealed that they evaluated the world of human affairs only from one particular point of view, thereby doing injustice to the many-sidedness of reality. If historical research

---

[16] Ibid., p. 316.

[17] Ibid., p. 329.

[18] See esp. Willson H. Coates, Hayden V. White and J. Salwyn Schapiro, *The emergence of liberal humanism: An intellectual history of Western Europe* I (New York, etc.: McGraw-Hill 1966); Willson H. Coates and Hayden V. White, *The ordeal of liberal humanism: An intellectual history of Western Europe* II (New York, etc.: McGraw-Hill, 1970).

[19] White, "Conflict of papal leadership ideals," pp. 15-16.

[20] Ibid., pp. 17-21.

[21] Hayden White, "The tropics of history: The deep structure of the *New science*," in *Tropics of discourse*, pp. 197-217; id., "Foucault decoded: Notes from underground," ibid., pp. 230-260.

teaches anything, White argued, it is that reality is always more complex than ideologies want people to believe.[22] So (interestingly, from the perspective of White's anti-realism), his objection against ideologies came down to the argument that they are not "realistic" enough.[23]

At the same time, White criticized these ideologies for discouraging independent thought. They prevented human beings from what White regarded as the first and most important human activity, that is, to think independently and to act according to self-chosen moral standards. During the 1950s and 1960s, White often repeated that he wanted human beings to be rational and responsible persons who choose for themselves what kind of future they want to realize. Especially in a "many-sided" and "complex" world, White argued, human beings cannot rely on the moral decisions of other people, made in other circumstances, but rather have to decide for themselves what is right or wrong in a particular situation.[24] This, I believe, can be regarded as the first expression of what Hans Kellner and Peter Novick called the existentialist dimension in Hayden White's philosophy of history.[25] In White's later writings, this existentialism – with its strong emphases on both reality's complexity and on the human being's personal responsibility to make moral decisions – would become most visible in the concept of the "sublime."[26] With hindsight it is possible to say that White's understanding of the world as a sublime (that is, chaotic and meaningless) reality already underlay his criticism of political ideologies in the 1960s.[27]

At first, White presented this existentialism as a modern kind of "liberal humanism" (just as Jean-Paul Sartre had done in *L'existentialism est un humanisme*) and as a principally anti-ideological body of thought.[28] Although such an opposition between political ideologies and *Ideologiekritik* would remain an important element in White's work (as demonstrated especially by "The politics of historical interpretation"), the separation of "ideology" and "worldview" gradually disappeared. White started to insist [set forth] that historians, in criticizing ideologies, cannot themselves pretend to be free of "ideological" biases.[29] But in this sense, ideology once again is used as an equivalent of the rather broad term *Weltanschauung*. Ten years after the essay on Croce, the identification of ideology with strong political ideology had already fallen into [felt in] oblivion. In *Metahistory*, "ideology" was said to refer to "…a set of prescriptions for taking a position in the present

---

[22]   White, "The abiding relevance," esp. p. 115. Cf. id., "Translator's introduction," esp. p. xxiv.

[23]   One might argue that White's frequently repeated warnings not to believe in the possibility of a historical representation that is adequate once and for all presupposes, in fact, a rather high (not to say positivistic) standard of "adequacy." A similar argument can be found in Chris Lorenz, "Can histories be true? Narrativism, positivism, and the 'metaphorical turn,'" in *History and Theory*, 37, (1998): pp. 309-329.

[24]   Hayden V. White, "Religion, culture and Western civilization in Christopher Dawson's idea of history," *English Miscellany* 9 (1958): pp. 247-287, here p. 287.

[25]   Cf. note 6.

[26]   Hayden White, "The politics of historical interpretation. Discipline and de-sublimation" in *The content of the form. Narrative discourse and historical representation* (Baltimore/London: Johns Hopkins University Press 1987), pp. 58-82, esp. pp. 66-73.

[27]   Cf. White's own reflections in Ewa Domańska, "Hayden White" in *Encounters. Philosophy of history after postmodernism* (Charlottesville/London: University Press of Virginia 1998), pp. 13-38, here pp. 26-27.

[28]   White, "The abiding relevance," esp. pp. 110, 112.

[29]   See, e.g., id., "Interpretation in history," in White, *Tropics of discourse*, pp. 51-80, here p. 69.

world of social praxis and acting upon it (either to change the world or to maintain it in its current state)…"[30]

According to this definition, White's existentialist humanism can be regarded as an ideology as well. Already in 1970, White seemed to acknowledge this, when he wrote that "…every 'ethics of ambiguity' actually presupposes a customary code that prescribes the main areas of aspiration and valuation in the individual's existential universe."[31] Although White's message of ambiguity and freedom was not a full-blown political ideology like Socialism or Fascism, it completely answered the definition of ideology presented in *Metahistory*. From this perspective, White's wish to re-establish a non-ironic kind of historical writing can be understood as a longing for a historiography that recognizes the complexity of human reality and emphasizes the freedom in which people have to live their own lives.[32]

This notion of human freedom can explain not only why White rejected ideological irony, but also why he felt attracted by what I called epistemological irony. It seems fair to say that White avoided dealing with epistemology in the strict sense of the word (defined as philosophical reflection on questions such as how knowledge of a past reality is possible, or what is characteristic of historical knowledge, compared to other forms of knowledge). When White claimed that the historian's knowledge of the past is never exhaustive and always mediated by social and intellectual perspectives, he usually preferred to present some examples from nineteenth-century historical scholarship and to point out where these texts expose the influence of the historian's personal predisposition.[33] So, instead of entering an epistemological debate, White claimed that historiographical practice teaches that there are usually multiple viewpoints on any topic.[34]

On the few occasions, however, when White tried to make his point on a theoretical level, he blamed "positivism" and "scientism" – alternately defined as fact-focused approaches to historical scholarship and attempts to drive back the plurality of viewpoints in history – for having caused damage to "cultural values" in the West.[35] By having made a split between historical writing and "metahistorical" reflection, positivism or scientism had brought "history proper" into a sphere of academic seclusion, where it was unable to respond to the challenges of contemporary cultural life. So, White's first reason for opposing positivism was its lack of cultural commitment.[36]

Secondly, the inclination to resist variety in historical viewpoints – a quality White considered characteristic of "positivism" – was hard to reconcile with the great significance

---

[30] White, *Metahistory*, p. 22.
[31] Coates and White, *Ordeal of liberal humanism*, 290.
[32] Another interpetation is offered by Ewa Domańska, "Hayden White: beyond irony," in *History and Theory,* 37 (1998): pp. 173-181, esp. p. 181.
[33] Usually, White derived his examples from the work of nineteenth-century historians like Jules Michelet and Alexis de Tocqueville (cf. *Metahistory* and "Interpretation in history," esp. 69-71 and 74). Elsewhere I have suggested that White's understanding of what historical writing is was based more on these early nineteenth-century examples than on late twentieth-century historical scholarship. Herman Paul, "Tegen reductionisme in de geschiedfilosofie. Hypothesen over eenheid en verscheidenheid in de geschiedschrijving," *Groniek* 36 (2003): pp. 501-514, esp. Pp. 506-507.
[34] White, "Politics of historical interpretation," p. 82.
[35] Hayden White, "Collingwood and Toynbee. Transitions in English historical thought," in *English Miscellany* 8 (1957): 147-178, here 148. Cf. id., "Religion, culture," p. 249.
[36] Cf. White, "Interpretation in history," p. 52ff.

White attached to human freedom. For White, after all, the freedom to choose a future was directly connected with the right to choose a past. "In choosing our past, we choose a present; and vice versa. We use the one to *justify* the other."[37] It was in the name of human freedom that White protested against a philosophy of history that sought to drive out a plurality of viewpoints. It seems reasonable to conclude, therefore, that White's belief in human freedom was among the most important driving forces behind his epistemological irony.

– III –

I would like to finish this paper with a brief discussion of White's thesis that a healthy irony might enable historians to go beyond the ironic consciousness of contemporary historiography. Several commentators have struggled with the apparent contradiction in this argument. For how is it possible to eliminate irony, if one uses irony as one's weapon? It brings to mind a story from the Gospel of Matthew, in which the Pharisees suspect that Jesus can drive out devils only with help of Beelzebub, "the prince of the devils." In his answer, Jesus points out the contradictory character of this argumentation. "If Satan cast out Satan, he is divided against himself; how shall then his kingdom stand?"[38]

In order to solve this problem, several readers of White's work, including Hans Kellner and John Nelson, have proposed to distinguish between a number of levels in the ironic condition of twentieth-century historiography. According to them, the modern world is so thoroughly ironic, that any attempt to overcome this ironic "over-trope" – to use Kellner's terminology – will require an *Unzeitgemäßheit* transcending the measure of human beings. Within this ironic over-trope, Kellner argues, each of the "normal" tropes has its own place. So, within the ironic "over-trope," four different phases can be distinguished, ranging from metaphor to irony. In Kellner's reading, a triumph over the trope of irony, as hoped for by White, is only possible on this minor level.[39] The problem with this "solution," however, is that it finds little support in White's own writings. Moreover, it neglects White's conviction that the tropes refer to the *deepest* level of the historian's understanding of the world.[40]

I would suggest that the distinction between epistemological and ideological irony, made in the first section above, is a better means for understanding what is at stake. For this distinction makes clear that White's "ironic battle against irony" is not a *contradictio in terminis* at all. In White's "battle," two completely different types of ideology stand opposed to one another: epistemological and ideological irony. The intra-ideological fight is, in fact, an attempt to overthrow the monopoly of the latter by means of the former. If we realize, White argued, that ideological irony is only one of the ideological points of departure a human being can choose – an insight made possible by means of epistemological irony – then we are no longer bound to this ideological irony. Then we are free to choose a

---

[37]   Hayden White, "What is a historical system?," in: *Biology, history, and natural philosophy*, edited by Allen D. Breck and Wolfgang Yourgrau (New York/London: Plenum Press, 1972), pp. 233-242, here p. 242.

[38]   Matthew 12: 24, 26.

[39]   John S. Nelson, "Tropal history and the social sciences: Reflections on Struever's remarks," in *History and Theory* Beiheft 19 (1980): pp. 80-101, here p. 100; Kellner, "Bedrock of order," p. 216.

[40]   Cf. White, *Metahistory*, x, where the tropes are said to refer to "…a deep level of consciousness on which a historical thinker chooses conceptual strategies by which to explain or represent his data." In "Interpretation in history," p. 72, White spoke about "some more basic level of consciousness."

metaphorical (or a metonymical or a synecdochical) prefiguration. In other words, it is an understanding of pluralism that opens the door to a non-ironic comprehension of reality. "Relativism" can teach that there is more than "relativism."[41]

It is remarkable, however, that although White called for a non-ironic, metaphorical understanding of the world, he did not spell out what kind of historiography the "new," non-ironic historian will produce. Neither is it clear how this new mode of historical thought will be related to politics and ideology, or which type of utopian thinking this history should serve. In his later work, White only said that historians should be critical of prevailing ideologies and that they have to show the sublimity of the past instead of trusting the beautiful stories told by the powers-that-be.[42]

Yet there is an indication that White had a specific kind of solution in mind. For the paradox contained in this battle is not completely solved by the distinction between ideological and epistemological irony. It is by no means certain that ideological self-confidence and epistemological irony can be consistent with each other. For is it not typical of worldviews that they pretend to offer the only true perspective on the world? Each ideology pretends to proclaim the truth, to defend the right doctrines and to spread the best morality. Usually, worldviews acknowledge the existence of other, competing ideologies, but without accepting their perspectives as equally valid as their own. For if they would do so, they would deny their own *raison d'être*. Karl Marx, one of the great non-ironic thinkers portrayed in *Metahistory*, was quite explicit about this: outside orthodox Marxism, there is only "false consciousness." This suggests that metaphorical and metonymical prefigurations of the historical field are inclined to deny the truth-claims of other, competing worldviews and to resolve the tension between epistemological irony and aversion to ideological irony in favor of the latter.

As far as I can see, the only way of resisting ideological irony, while remaining loyal to a form of epistemological irony, would be to adhere to a non-dogmatic ideology, that is to say, to an ideology in which diversity, tolerance and recognition of others are regarded as important values. Such an ideology would avoid claiming that it has a monopoly on truth – since it believes that reality is too complex to be fully grasped by one worldview – while simultaneously aiming at overcoming the irony White wanted to eliminate. If this is indeed the only way to combine ideological self-confidence with epistemological irony, then it follows that such an "open-minded" ideology served as an implicit model for the metaphorical worldview White presented as an alternative to the trope of irony. So, instead of allowing historians to choose whatever moral perspectives they would like – including "dogmatic," non-ironical ideological positions – White wanted them to be converted to an ideology that emphasizes reality's complexity and the importance of a moral commitment.

The obvious conclusion, then, is that White's pursuit to overcome the ironic condition of modern historiography is an attempt to place the study of history in the service of his own (existentialistic) understanding of the world in terms of sublimity and human moral freedom. *Metahistory* should be regarded as a book that incites development of a morally

---

[41]   Cf. White, *Metahistory*, p. 434: "If it can be shown that Irony is only one of a *number* of possible perspectives on history, each of which has its own good reasons for existence on a poetic and moral level of awareness, the Ironic attitude will have begun to be deprived of its status as the *necessary* perspective from which to view the historical process." See also ibid., p. 316.

[42]   White, "Politics of historical interpretation," esp. pp. 81-82.

responsible view of the past, informed by an existentialist understanding of the nature of the world.

CHAPTER 3

Stanley Corkin and Phyllis Frus

History and Textuality: Film and the Modernist Event

In his long and distinguished career Hayden White has repeatedly reminded us of the provisionality of all historical texts, convincingly arguing that written history is necessarily rhetorical and never apprehensible as fact itself. While this broad assertion allows for specific analytical operations on written texts, what of "history" when it becomes a visual presentation? White's writings on visual narratives are not as extensive as those on more conventional academic presentations of the historical in written form, and yet they are evocative.

In his latest collection, *Figural Realism*, Professor White makes a plea for a substantial revision of the normative mode of historical writing, asking that the more open form of modernist prose supplant traditional realist narratives. His motivations become most clear and expand into a broader cultural critique when he takes on the topic of mass culture in relation to the historical event. In an essay in this collection that appeared first in *The Persistence of History: Cinema, Television, and the Modern Event* (edited by Vivian Sobchak), White claims that "the notion of the historical event has undergone radical transformation as a result of the occurrence in our century of events of a scope, scale, and depth unimaginable by earlier historians and the dismantling of the concept of the event as an object of a specifically scientific kind of knowledge."[1]

The two primary causes of the "unnarratability" of certain events of the 20th century, according to White, are not only the "nature, scope, and implications" of phenomena like two world wars, population growth with concomitant hunger and poverty, instances of genocide capped by the six million murdered in the Holocaust, and environmental devastation, but also the sheer quantity and technological fragmentation of the mass media's representations of these events, which have made explanation, even rendering them in story form, impossible.[2] White says that historians, having experienced nothing comparable to mass exterminations, torture, radiation deaths, have no capacity for empathy – presumably for either perpetrators or victims.[3] But is it the event or our apprehension of it that has changed? Is the scale of violence of 20th-century wars greater than that of, say, the death of 13,000 Civil War prisoners at Andersonville, Georgia, in 1864-65, or the unknowable number of deaths suffered and caused by the Crusaders? Surely events such as the Black Death that spread across Europe in the 14th century, killing enormous percentages of the population, the battles fought by Napoleon's army, or the lives and deaths of scores of millions of Africans transported in the Atlantic slave trade are as incomprehensible in their way as

---

[1]   Hayden White, *Figural Realism: Studies in the Mimesis Effect* (Baltimore: Johns Hopkins UP, 2000), p. 72.

[2]   White, *Figural Realism*, pp. 69, 72.

[3]   White cites historian Christopher Browning's analysis of the difficulties he had in writing *Ordinary Men*, an account of a Polish police battalion's apparently willing murder of Jews in Poland. White writes, "[T]hese events seem to resist the traditional historian's effort at the kind of empathy which would permit one to see them, as it were, from the inside, in this case, from the perpetrators' perspective" (*Figural Realism*, pp. 80-1).

those invariably listed as horrors of the 20th century – the AIDS pandemic, genocide in Rawanda and Bosnia, the worldwide traffic in women for the sex trade. The difference that White defines as a cause – the enormity of modern events – is actually bound up in a mixture of cause and effect: our *sense* of events has been fundamentally altered by the persistence of mediated images and words, a profusion that characterizes modernity.

This alteration is apparent when we learn of sudden, unexpected, "unnatural" events. White cites Michael Turits's analysis of the media's saturation coverage of two "techno-air disasters," one of them the 1986 *Challenger* explosion just after liftoff (which was not surpassed as a media event by the 2003 Columbia breakup on re-entry, no doubt because the latter was not covered live), as an example of the failure of either repetition of the images or "morphing technology" to make the event "visually intelligible." Rather, the endless replay "produced widespread cognitive disorientation," even despair, over the impossibility of producing an explanation of the air disasters.[4]

As White himself acknowledges, the dimension of the thing in itself is not enough to paralyze our ability first to comprehend and then to explain or narrate the event in a meaningful way. A significant cause is the mode of representation, the fact that, since at least the assassination of President Kennedy in 1963, we apprehend catastrophic events instantly, in visual form, and then endure their repetition over days or even weeks.[5] Indeed, by enlarging White's vision of rhetoric to encompass cultural rhetoric or mediation, we can see that the modern historical event is reduced to trivia by its persistent reproduction, resulting in images that are everywhere and unintelligible at once.

Coverage of 9-11 by the news media (or as Europeans write it, 11.9.01) offers a highly relevant case. As those images of the airliners slamming into the Twin Towers and the sequential collapse of both buildings were replayed, we in the United States could get no sense of the complexity of the event, its possible causes, nor even its significance. Indeed, all analysis was submerged in the recurring lament, "Why do they hate us?" Less than a year later, when the first documentaries of 9-11 were shown on TV and released on video and DVD, they were little more than edited TV and video footage, or very limited, partial views of the attacks. The first docudrama (we define this term below) and the first feature film, appearing 18 months after the events, tell the story of safely heroic figures, New York Mayor Rudy Giuliani (a cable docudrama) and eight firefighters who lost their lives, as eulogized by their chief, aided by a journalist (*The Guys,* a film based on a stage play). Though the events of September 11, 2001, could be complexly rendered by any number of historians from any number of perspectives, such narratives would necessarily be partial and, due to their complexity, ineffective as public discourse. The documentaries and other footage reproduced, not surprisingly, submerge comprehensible images in formulaic and nationalist narratives. They are more concerned with affective engagement than with intellectual insight. Indeed, the profusion of un-illuminating visual images contributes not only to viewers' sense of the enormity of the event but to our fatigue. Despite the fact that such images bombard us and shed far more heat than light, we as scholars and critics have the responsibility to engage such images and narratives and take the opportunity to discuss their

---

4 White, *Figural Realism*, p. 73.

5 David Lubin, in *Shooting Kennedy* (Berkeley: University of California Press, 2003), p. ix, says that within fifteen minutes of the shooting, . . . half the population of the United States learned of the event, and within the hour, nine out of ten Americans knew. . . ."

history and historicity, since all of us – not just our students – get so much of our history from popular visual narratives.

White's lament about our inability to make sense of disasters sounds to us suspiciously like the famous complaint made by novelist Philip Roth in 1960 that because of television's influence on our perception of events, Americans no longer shared a credible reality. The world was incomprehensible, Roth wrote, far beyond a mere novelist's imaginative powers to render a convincing account.[6] The absurdity of events in the last half of the 20th century soon became the inevitable explanation of the death of realism and the rise of postmodernist fabulism or metafiction on one hand, and documentary, even "zero-degree" narration on the other.[7]

But, we wonder, is it the incredibility of reality that baffles both Roth and White, or the excesses of its mediated forms and mode of transmission? For example, to take instances closer to our time, doubtless the New York draft riots of 1864 or the race riots in Tulsa in 1921 were just as confusing and horrific to the participants and onlookers as were the 1992 Los Angeles riots after the verdict in the Rodney King police brutality case. The primary difference may be the presence of television and video cameras in 1992, so that – even more so than in the case of Vietnam, the first televised war – viewers could watch the events unfold in real time from their living room.[8] (The New York draft riots were at least widely reported by the newspapers; the events in Tulsa were swept under the rug and not part of even historians' awareness until 80 years later.) A better explanation for the supposed incomprehensibility of events may be not simply the excessive mediation but the influence of these multiple images on us as readers and viewers – specifically, their reifying effect.

As many have pointed out in their discussions of the various phases of modernity, a defining element of 20th- and now 21st-century life has been the disposition to express complex systems – labor, economics, politics, and mass communication – in reified images that resist analysis. That is, images take the place of understanding, although if they were unpacked as constructions, they might reveal more complicated explanations of their genesis and meaning. In an early and prescient expression of how partial and omnipresent representations of a system come to stand for the world itself, Georg Lukacs wrote of the way in which modern industrial practices – what we have come to know as Fordist systems of production – oppress those who work in them and alienate labor from its producers. Similarly, much later in the 20th century, devices of mass communication have tended to perform the same structural process of estrangement, reifying horrible events as separate from human causation. (The most familiar analysis of this phenomenon is Raymond Williams' in *Marxism and Literature*.)[9] Indeed, we need look no further than the current war in Iraq and its buildup to see how "the message of the day," words and image, create a blindness that allows for patently illogical explanations to go unchallenged – in the US, at least. Our reifica-

[6]   Philip Roth, "Writing American Fiction," *Commentary*, March 1961:223-33.
[7]   Roland Barthes, *Writing Degree Zero*, trans. Annette Lavers and Colin Smith (New York: Hill & Wang, 1967).
[8]   Those who rescued Reginald Denny from near his truck, where he lay bleeding and unconscious, went to the scene after watching him on television and, furthermore, watching others walk by without stopping to help. See the video version of Anna Deavere Smith's play *Twilight Los Angeles* (PBS Home Video: 2001).
[9]   Raymond Williams, *Marxism and Literature* (Oxford: Oxford UP, 1977).

tion of technological effect allows Americans to will ourselves to believe that no civilians are the victims of our "smart" bombs, that we are defending "freedom" when we wage war against not just a dictator but a nation, and to believe that our freedom is further guaranteed by suspending any number of Constitutional guarantees.

We intend to disrupt this blithe nationalist rhetoric by effectively dislodging the practices that enable it. We begin by pointing out that the hardened notions of fact and fiction are both symptoms and devices of reification, and so we must move discussion over history-based films off the axes of fact or fiction, real or invented, history or imagination, historical or invented polarities. The next task is to demonstrate how films, like all narratives, can be read through their process of production, for the way they reveal their historical contingency, and we advocate training audiences – beginning with our students – to do this kind of reflexive reading. Finally, we show how generic conventions affect our apprehension of the historicity of texts.

One need only look at the reviews of historical films in the *Journal of American History* to see how common it is for historians to judge them primarily by their fidelity to the historical record. This is not to say that there is no distinction between fact and fiction, only that there is no inherent formal distinction – nothing at the level of text or signifier – between factual and fictional narratives. When critics and readers or viewers refer to a text's fictionality, they usually mean that the plot and characters are made up, not that they are made, that is, put together by a writer or filmmakers to give the illusion of a real world. But it is important to notice and analyze the constructed qualities of a movie or short story or novel in order to avoid mistaking the illusion of the real for the real itself. Because all so-called nonfictional narratives – journalism, biography, documentary film, and history – are invariably made or constructed, it is the preponderance of historical referents, not their plain or transparent style that distinguishes nonfictional texts. Nonfictional is a somewhat misleading term, however. The category of nonfiction obviously arose to name what is other than fiction, but because "fictional" has come to be associated with "literary," it is ambiguous. "Fictive" and "nonfictive" would be more apt, but because "fictional" is in such common use, we continue to use it to refer to the opposite of the historical – that is, for narratives with primarily fictive referents.

Whether in regard to printed texts or filmic ones, we believe critics and viewers should continue to distinguish between the two main categories of narratives, but that, following the Russian Formalists, we should differentiate them at the level of *story* – "what happens," i.e., the actions we derive from narration. The other level of any narrative is *plot* – "how we learn of what happens."[10] At the level at which we apprehend all texts, that is, plot, all narratives have the same status. Because historians and biographers set their subjects as historical actors on a stage, dramatize events as scenes, and so on, we cannot always distinguish between fictional and historical narration until we go outside the text to check the status of its primary referents. If we recognize some of the people, places, events, and proc-

---

[10]   Boris Eichenbaum, "The Theory of the 'Formal Method,'" *Russian Formalist Criticism*, ed. and trans. Lee T. Lemon and Marion J. Reis (Lincoln: University of Nebraska Press, 1965), p. 116. The Russian word for story or "story-stuff" is *fabula;* the Formalists' word for what we call plot is *sjuzet*. Film theorists also use the distinction between story and plot to analyze how film gets its effects, or as David Bordwell says, "to specify the objective devices and forms that elicit the spectator's activity." See Bordwell, *Narration in the Fiction Film* (Madison: University of Wisconsin Press, 1985), pp. 48-50. The quotation is from p. 48.

esses from other texts, it is a good bet that the story we derive from it is historical. If we recognize very few, and those are primarily locations or processes, or large events, such as a war or protest or presidential assassination, we are probably safe in assuming it is a fictive narrative or a fictional feature film, with the historical referents placed there to anchor the realistic text in a verisimilar, recognizable world. In general we assume that all texts are historical – that is, they are produced at certain places and in some ways all refer to their circumstances of origin. The task of critics and viewers is to expose that historicity.

Our example to illustrate these various interpretive strategies is Oliver Stone's fact-based film *JFK*. It is first of all an example of how assuming the inevitability of these binaries distorts critical response. This movie was widely lambasted by professional historians for offering an interpretation that the available facts could not support. These facts are primarily the conclusions of the Warren Report, which by the time *JFK* was made had become consensual truth despite the investigations of a substantial number of conspiracy theorists. Responding to such charges, Stone, though arguing firmly for the legitimacy of his vision, nevertheless repeatedly states, both in the film and in commentaries on it, that his interpretations are provisional. Stone's *JFK* offers an intriguing example of the status of history in the postmodern age, for it suggests that even when a filmmaker signals the construction of his attitude toward his subject, this self-consciousness has little impact on an audience that seeks to view a historically referential work as history itself.

Nevertheless, it is valid to ask how readers and viewers might differentiate fact from fiction when extra-textual assumptions, such as those around the assassination of President Kennedy, become so fraught. Thanks to popularization of theory by pundits and columnists, many educated readers believe that academics are saying history is relative, truth does not exist, there are no moral absolutes, and so on. No wonder readers are likely to believe in the assertions of "transparent" texts, including popular third-person history by the likes of Stephen Ambrose, Doris Kearns Goodwin, and Tom Brokaw, and realist films that go to great pains to give the illusion of truth. It seems plausible that audiences would assume that any version of history before them is the correct one, especially if it is the only one they read or watch. A likely means to counter this disposition to take the credibility of texts at face value is to demonstrate a different way of apprehending them. Rather than call for open forms of discourse, such as modernist antinarratives, texts that refer to their own process (as Art Spiegelman's *Maus* does, to White's and our admiration), we would point to the viewer's ability to interpret the way texts reveal their historical contingency and suggest that increasing that ability is vital. And so, rather than having somewhat more advanced versions of a "yes, he does"/ "no he doesn't" discussion, we would like to change the basis of the conversation about *JFK* from one of object to one of method, from one of expression to how viewers apprehend this version.

Stone's film, to refresh your memories, puts New Orleans district attorney Jim Garrison, played by Kevin Costner, at its center – it is based on Garrison's book *On the Trail of the Assassins* – to tell a highly embroidered tale about a government conspiracy to assassinate the President because Kennedy has let it be known that he will withdraw troops from Vietnam.[11] The film is highly stylized, constantly calling attention to its fictionality through a

---

[11]   A decade later the film's historical and analytical premises strike us as absurd, and noting this absurdity makes the furor the film caused seem overwrought. For example, it seems preposterous that JFK was taken so seriously as a threat by historians, who predicted young people would believe Stone's claim that the assassination

range of techniques, from Costner's overwrought acting, to the bizarre portrayal of Clay Shaw, to its ahistorical logic. Stone freely acknowledges that he signaled *JFK*'s dramatic form and intentions through a variety of conventional methods. In a conversation with Mark Carnes, editor of *Past Imperfect: History According to the Movies*, he says, "The film is looking at itself, conscious of itself. It moves from black and white to color; the angles are offbeat. Somebody says one thing in an external moment, but then the movie cuts to an internal moment and you see another expression wholly opposite [...]. "[12]

Stone acknowledges adopting this strategy in *Nixon*, another of his films that has been severely criticized for its mutilation of history.[13] It is telling that both films, though given major theatrical release, were labeled "docudrama," a term that originated to describe low-budget televised movies based on recent events which networks seized on and produced for the built-in audience who already knew part of the story from news and magazine features, often in the tabloids. Nora Ephron, screenwriter of the controversial film *Silkwood*, also dubbed a docudrama by *New York Times* critics and even by a *Times* editorial writer, concludes that the dominant definition of docudrama is "any film that the *New York Times* disagrees with."[14] Apparently Stone's movies were labeled docudramas to deflate them because of his deliberate subverting of the usual assumptions of fact-based films – that they will replicate the standard interpretations of events. These two films, instead, illustrate Stone's claim that he intends to "make you aware that you are watching a movie, that I'm playing with your mind, and that there is no objective reality."[15] Beyond his many signals that his is a made story and not a found one, one need only look at his sources to know that Stone has devised an interpretation that freely employs paranoid perspectives. Thus the mix of technique and perspective make this an occasion to discuss any one of a number of things – the relationship between history and film, between history and this film, the process by which a media event becomes the basis for mass hysteria, and so on. But what it seems not the occasion for is to lambaste Stone, since as a popular filmmaker engaging enormous resources to garner an audience for his film, he has done precisely what he was contracted to do. Yet, one need not look far or wide to find historians excoriating Stone and conspiracy aficionados lauding him.

Stone's narrative seems symptomatic in many ways of what Professor White terms the manipulation of images that in many instances makes it "impossible to tell any single authoritative story about what really happened."[16] But, unlike the critics who sought to marginalize *JFK* as an illegitimate blend of fact and fiction, we take this manipulation – when interpreted reflexively – as signs of its construction. And, like White, who points out that the absence of any authoritative version means that "one could tell any number of possible stories about it," we welcome alternative explanations for what really happened on November 22, 1963, of which Stone's film is just one.

---

was a coup d'etat, a betrayal by a few dissidents in the government. As White notes, critics objected to the form the farfetched conspiracy theory took in Stone's film; this is a credit to its power, for fewer viewers would have been threatened by Stone's fantasy if it had been ineffectually dramatized.

[12] Oliver Stone, "A Conversation Between Mark Carnes and Oliver Stone." *Past Imperfect: History According to the Movies.* Ed. Mark Carnes. (New York: Holt, 1996), p. 307.

[13] Stone, "Conversation," p. 306-7.

[14] Nora Ephron, "The Tie That Binds." *Nation*, 6 April 1992: p. 453.

[15] Stone, "Conversation," p. 307.

[16] White, *Figural Realism*, p. 73.

Clearly this method of reading an image or visual narrative historically owes much to Hayden White.[17] His work inspired both a "new formalism" and an attention to context; we emphasize the latter in reading novels, short stories, and films, but our understanding of context emphasizes materiality, while acknowledging, as Fredric Jameson has noted, that such materiality is provisional and available only in textual form.[18] This emphasis on reading for the referent separates our strategies from other contextualist methods of reading literary texts, for we believe that the New Historicists, those in cultural studies, and canon revisionists all have highlighted practices of signification at the expense of material occurrence. Keeping sight of the material history selectively referenced by Hollywood films and TV docudrama is even more problematic than reading narratives historically for a number of reasons, including the fact that cinema employs iconic signs that easily appear as reality itself, while the indexical signs of the written text more clearly refer to an approximation or interpretation of an event.[19] Further, such visual productions often follow a formula for narrative that, as David Bordwell and Kristin Thompson have pointed out, is both logically causal and character driven. They explain,

> The number of possible narratives is unlimited. Historically, however, fictional cinema has tended to be dominated by a single mode of narrative form. [...] This conception of narrative depends on the assumption that the actions will spring primarily from individual characters as causal agents. [...] Time is subordinated to the cause and effect chain in many ways. The plot will omit significant durations in order to show only events of causal importance. [...] Finally, most classical narrative films display a strong degree of closure at the end.[20]

History-based films are usually made the same way: to approximate the style of narration found in the classic realist novel. Such a narrative structure, through its form and its persistence, can so persuade viewers of the veracity of the story that they apprehend these visual fictions as though they were unmediated fact.

Furthermore, as products and objects of mass culture, such narratives typically engage in tales of the probable or that which is within the realm of the probable. The historicity of a production such as *JFK*, for example, enlarges on a strand of popular culture – the belief that Kennedy's death was a result of a mafia conspiracy – that, while not precisely main-

---

[17]   We have demonstrated historical readings of literary texts in various publications, including "An 'Ex-Centric' Approach to American Cultural Studies: The Interesting Case of Zora Neale Hurston as a Non-Canonical Writer" in *Prospects: An American Studies Annual* (1996); and a review-essay and two essays on Willa Cather. The review-essay is Frus and Corkin, "Cather Criticism and the Canon," *College English* 59.2 (Feb.1997): pp. 206-17. One essay is "The More Things Change: Canon Revision and the Case of Willa Cather" in *English as a Discipline; or Is There a Plot in This Play?*, a collection of papers from the 1993 Alabama Conference (ed. James Raymond (Tuscaloosa: U of Alabama P, 1996); the second is "Willa Cather's 'Pioneer' Novels and (Not New, Not Old) Historical Reading." *College Literature* 26.2 (Spring 1999): pp. 36-58. See also the placing of texts by journalists and novelists from Stephen Crane to Tom Wolfe in reflexive historical context in Frus, *The Politics and Poetics of Journalistic Narrative* (Cambridge and New York: Cambridge UP, 1994), and our edition of Stephen Crane in the New Riverside Editions, *The Red Badge of Courage, Maggie: A Girl of the Streets, and Other Selected Writings* (Boston: Houghton Mifflin, 2000).

[18]   Fredric Jameson, *The Political Unconscious* (Ithaca, NY: Cornell University Press, 1981), p. 82.

[19]   Andre Bazin argues that cinema, like the photograph, is the ultimate form of realism. In his formulation, a photograph or film frame is both iconic and indexical, in the sense of depending on the reality of the object it represents. An image not only resembles its referent but "share[s] a common being." Bazin, *What Is Cinema?* Vol. I (Berkeley: University of California Press, 1967), p. 15.

[20]   David Bordwell and Kristin Thompson, *Film as Art*, 6th ed. (New York: McGraw-Hill, 2002), pp. 76-78.

stream, has been publicly aired and that many people find intriguing. In treating more main-
stream historical material with nationalist significance, such as *The Alamo*, historical films
tend to dramatize all manner of national myth, such as assuring viewers that the battle at
San Antonio was a principled one for "freedom" although one of the issues that led to the
secession of Texas from Mexico was the fact that Texans refused to comply with the Mexi-
can government's banning of slavery. Seeing John Wayne as Davy Crockett repeatedly invoke "liberty and freedom" as the reasons the Anglos must vanquish Santa Ana reminds us
that the Texan George W. Bush has employed both the posture and rhetoric of the John
Wayne persona toward similar political ends – empire and uncritical nationalism – thus
revealing their cultural resonance.[21]

Another important strategy for avoiding being caught up in the mythmaking so prevalent in movies like *The Alamo* is to "read" through genre by noticing the conventions common to many other films, such as plot and character types, settings, even costumes. These
elements usually make history-based, realistic films transparent, because the conventions
are so familiar that we do not notice them. They make us comfortable, and we accept the
habitual framework of melodrama or documentary realism as the assertion of truth. But
genre conventions are important devices for our understanding of certain historical events
in specific ways. If we regard the overarching narrative of *JFK* as a detective film, for example, we can see how Jim Garrison is a conventional figure, one part Phillip Marlowe, one
part Sherlock Holmes (maybe Edward G. Robinson's Johnny Blake in *Bullets or Ballots*?).
Such a figure does not easily jibe with the historical James Garrison, who was an erratic and
colorful figure as a New Orleans district attorney and judge. He was not Kevin Costner
smoking a pipe. Indeed, in a *New Yorker* article of 1992, journalist Edward Jay Epstein describes Garrison's conspiracy obsession in terms that connect him to Sam Spade and thus to
his generic role in the film:

> Garrison, having broken out of this enchanted maze and penetrated deep into the other dimension, portrays
> himself as battling to wrest from the invisible elite the dark secrets that perpetuate its power. His weapon in
> this titanic struggle is the missing evidence that he, but not others in the naive realm, can see and interpret.[22]

When we lay bare the generic character Costner plays, that is, see his Garrison as a "type"
or stock figure common in other detective films, we are less likely to believe in him as a
historical character. We start to consider the unnatural casting decision and, similarly, regard the conventionalized screenplay as artificial, not close to history. Compare this to other
signs of the process of production that Stone himself emphasizes, such as the change from
black-and-white to color, the alternation between simulation of the motorcade and Zapruder
footage, the casting of Tommy Lee Jones and Edward Asner against type. These elements
of construction, rather than reminding the viewer that this is Stone's particular view, may
be reifying in themselves because they encourage aestheticization of the form; critics note
them in appreciation, rather than as means of apprehending Stone's process of production.
Therefore, we cannot praise reflexivity as a textual strategy in itself, since that method can

---

[21]   An example of a 2003 Western interpreted to expose its mythmaking is Stanley Corkin's review of *Open
Range*, *Journal of American History* 90 (December 2003): pp. 1128-9. Corkin calls this Kevin Costner vehicle
perhaps "the first compassionate conservative Western" (p. 1129).

[22]   Edward Jay Epstein, "Epitaph for Jim Garrison: Romancing the Assassination." *New Yorker* 30 Nov. 1992. 2
April 2003 <http://edwardjayepstein.com/archived/ garrison3.htm>.

be a kind of truth-claim. However, seeing Garrison as Sam Spade-like helps us to see the intertextual relationships among a range of historical narratives so that we are not bewitched by that which was not.

To see the significance of viewing history-based films with some skepticism we have only to consider how willingly some Americans have accepted contemporary versions of Manifest Destiny. Clearly such triumphal notions of US history have been enabled by uncritical readings of popular film genres – Westerns, war films, and so forth – which collapse these fictional texts into history itself. As Professor White urges his students to read with analytical precision, we ask our consumers of mass-produced images to engage such images in dialogue with other historical texts.

CHAPTER 4

Kalle Pihlainen

The Confines of the Form: Historical Writing and the Desire that It Be
what It Is Not

A difficulty for alternative literary approaches to historical writing can be seen to lie in the
parallel strategies utilized in interpretation and narration. In calling for the adoption of
"new" and unconventional methods by historians, Hayden White has often emphasized the
similarity and occasional conflation of these two means of organizing knowledge. Although
endeavoring to understand the past, he argues, historians resort to established representational means, choosing from among a limited choice of emplotments. This involves them in
a rhetorical or narrative structuring of their material which – in addition to leading to numerous problems with regard to the "truth" of their presentations – marks a move from the
sphere of the logical to that of the figural.[1]
    If we agree with White's view that understanding and interpretation largely follow quite
general and discursively determined tropes, the tendency for conventional historical narratives is quite understandable. The definition of the interpretive move specifically as a fictionalization or figuration in the sense of becoming metaphorical is, however, based on an
underlying analogy between historical narratives and literary writing. It is, in other words,
on the basis of drawing a formal equivalence between historical writing and literary fiction
that White can claim that "[t]he similarities between interpretation and narration argue for
the essentially figurative nature of the discourses in which they are typically represented in
speech or writing."[2] While this is clearly not far from the truth of the matter, my intention in
what follows is to question the comparison of historical narratives to fictional ones on the
basis of shared form and the coincident disregard of what seems to be their determining
feature, namely their commitment to reference and to representing the past truthfully. The
main thrust of my argument is to question the general emphasis on interpretation rather than
presentation. As will be seen, I defend a strategy of deferral of the interpretive moment in
the reading process to the reader to the extent that this is feasible. Thus, while historical
narratives are clearly linguistic figurations and in this aspect resemble literary works, I argue that this is not their determining feature when we search for alternative representational
strategies. Rather than constantly referring the investigation of the historical narrative to its
similarity with literary fiction, we should, then, focus on the strengths entailed by the commitment to referentiality.

---

[1]   As White himself describes the process: "the sequence of turns taken in interpretative discourse resembles
      more the path traversed in the search for a plot structure adequate to the configuration of a diachronic series of
      events into a paradigmatic structure of relationships than it does the progressive accommodation of a set of
      perceptions to the exigencies of a nomological-deductive demonstration." Hayden White, *Figural Realism:
      Studies in the Mimesis Effect* (Baltimore: Johns Hopkins UP, 1999), p. 127.
[2]   White, *Figural Realism*, p. 127.

– I –

Beyond formal similarities, the association of historical and literary texts reflects a general yearning within historical research for subjective access to the past. Setting aside the issue of its material nature, we can say that literary fiction, like consciousness, exists in the manifestation of its contents alone. There is no story to be had separable from the one presented since the contents have no life of their own. They are fully known to the point-of-view from which they are narrated. History, on the other hand, or the ideal of history, objectifies these contents and their relations, and thus remains – to stay with the metaphor of consciousness – always only a representation or reconstruction of subjective experience. Indeed, historical writing reveals its reification as two conflicting desires: it hopes to re-present the directly experienced nature of the past and simultaneously to produce the referentially unhindered encounter with the subjective experience of the reader had by the fictional narrative. Naturally, both of these ambitions cannot be realized at the same moment. At least not when they are formulated in this way.

The particular phenomenological yearning that White's theorizing posits in historical narrativization comes about largely as a result of the comparison between historiography and prose literature. This comparison, in turn, seems inspired by the common conception of literature as enabling a transfer of understanding between distinct and often incommensurable world-views. The attribution of a similar mediating function in historical narration to something like empathy or identification alone is not, however, justified since the recognition involved goes beyond an admission or understanding of shared similarities. Where empathy furnishes – to some extent – an ability to "see" and "experience" things from another's point of view, it fails to provide the kind of critical distance also required in seeing the other as different from one's self. To provide a means for re-conceptualization and change, literature also has to address *the reader* in his or her specificity. This point has recently been well summarized by Winfried Fluck:

> By engaging the reader's interiority, ranging from mental images to bodily sensations, in the transfer that transforms the words on the page into an aesthetic experience, fiction provides recognition of the reader's subjectivity. This individual empowerment goes beyond any identification with single characters or events in the text. It arises from the necessity of the individual reader to actualize a whole world along the lines of her own interiority.[3]

The main thrust of White's arguments concerning the need for historians to utilize modern and postmodern literary means centers on his wish that historical writing be similarly emotionally effective, that it permit an experiential identification by the reader. This transformative – and clearly political – power of fictional discourse is thus something that White would like to see historical narratives achieve, especially since their social efficacy has been greatly undermined by the recognition of their epistemological troubles. At the same time, it is clear that the formula of the realist nineteenth-century novel can no longer provide a means for such emotional involvement given the political difficulties linked with such overly determined and unifying forms. Rather, the poststructuralist call for the disruption of representative closure needs to be heeded, if not for political purposes, then simply

---

[3] Winfried Fluck, "Fiction and Justice," *New Literary History* 34:1 (2003): p. 25.

for the reason that readers have come to expect representations to allow for more ambiguity. White has made this clear in his *Figural Realism.*[4]

Although the evocation of culturally shared attitudes through recognizable images is surely something that even the most fictional texts carry out, the subjective appeal of literature does not come from these. Nor is it sufficient to attribute this appeal to general textual strategies that situate the reader in a familiar context. As narratologists have repeatedly pointed out, the literariness of the literary text is tied to its employment of the unfamiliar, its ability to stop readers from continuing along familiar tracks in their thinking. Or indeed, even, along a route clearly marked by the text. For literature to be referential would require that it give up this ethereal, otherworldly quality, its ability to conjure up subjective, textually underdetermined images from within the reader that would resonate with hopes and desires that are essentially private.

But is there anything that would prevent a historian from writing in this fashion?

In addition to the obvious but difficult issue of referentiality and its role, a more specific question that I raise here with regard to the use of contemporary literary forms as models for historical representation concerns the centrality of intertextuality in their creation. Obviously, because of their different referential commitments, historical narratives cannot utilize intertextual means in the same manner or to the same effect as they could if they eschewed their promise to be truthful representations of reality. Although I make very general use here of the term intertextuality in a way that cannot do justice to the different forms it takes, the claims I make are based on the assumption that intertextual references are those that open up the significance of the work, displacing meanings from the overt narrative in a way akin to that performed by various tropes. They serve, in other words, to undermine the literal meaning of the work, or at least to provide it with a richness or complexity that a straightforward realist account could not.

A related point, but one that White at least has been less explicit about, is that of the role of the reader's involvement. While it is true that readers perhaps expect more ambiguity in and less control over their interpretation, there is also a distinct change to be perceived in the way we view interpretation itself. Traditionally seen as an intellectual process involving an attentive encounter with the text, it seems – to me at least – that increasing emphasis is being placed on the way that interpretation is not so much guided by the text as provided with loose parameters for free-play and association on the basis of the reader's particular background and experiences. This is, of course, where the troubles with historical writing begin. The issue is not so much one of literary form or the presentational techniques utilized but rather of the commitments of the text. The historical narrative is ultimately committed to engaging the reader in a process that needs to be returned to the world, returned, to borrow a phrase from Herbert Marcuse, "from the illusion to the reality of the illusion,"[5] whereas a literary narrative may well remain content with leaving its reader somehow privately edified. This distinction is of course not clear-cut.

---

4 See, e.g., White, *Figural Realism*, p. 66 ff.
5 As Marcuse argues: "Unless the analysis takes the road of return from the symbolic to the literal, from the illusion to the reality of the illusion, it remains ideological, replacing one mystification by another." Herbert Marcuse, "Love Mystified: A Critique of Norman O. Brown," *Commentary* (February 1967): p. 73.

– II –

My general point of departure for what follows is in the idea that literary fiction effects its meaning-making through an overdetermination of semiotic significance; in other words, through giving priority to the overall meaning of the work as it is constituted in and by the form and general coherence of its various elements. While certainly an exaggeration, this claim is often accepted as a useful heuristic by White[6] and has been extensively defended by literary theorists of different persuasions. In Michael Riffaterre's formulation, for example, "the literary text is a sequence of embeddings with each significant word summarizing the syntagm situated elsewhere."[7]

As Gary Saul Morson has recently noted, however, literary theory tends to prioritize issues that are not necessarily central to most readers of literary narratives. Questions of significance of the narrative as a whole are peculiar to a way of reading that seeks to foreground literary narratives as dense and coherent works of art, conforming to the shared interpretive bias of literary critics.[8] This same interpretive bias could, conceivably, be extended to the reading of historical narratives despite the counter-intuitiveness of doing so. Even if historical narratives are accepted as being guided by their referential commitments to such an extent that their material cannot be structured around a single meaning, it might still be argued – as White clearly does – that the linguistic figuration of historical material could lead to overall interpretive schemes. There is, however, a difference to be noted: where historical narratives may and certainly most often do similarly incorporate material into their form, subsuming it to a greater meaning, the selected elements do not cohere primarily on the level of semiotic signification but with regard to emplotment. The significance of this difference seems to be generally overlooked in discussions of historical narrative. Where literary theory can be seen to fetishize meaning (the "message" of the text), narrative theories of history similarly raise historiography to the level of a literary artifact

---

[6]   Cf., e.g., Hayden White, *The Content of the Form. Narrative Discourse and Historical Representation* (Baltimore: Johns Hopkins UP, 1987), p. 202; Kalle Pihlainen, "The Moral of the Historical Story: Textual Differences in Fact and Fiction," *New Literary History* 33:1 (2002): passim.

[7]   Michael Riffaterre, "Syllepsis," *Critical Inquiry* 6:4 (1980): p. 627. For Riffaterre, the constants in the text become visible by means of "anomalies" or "ungrammaticalities," leading the reader to search for a more comprehensive interpretation – the text's significance – rather than being content with a mimetic meaning. By disrupting the construction of a literal interpretation such anomalies indeed force the reader to search for an alternative way of reading. As he elaborates elsewhere: "Undecidables are pointers showing us at what spots comprehension will be blossoming once the real meaning-units have been grasped, once the other way of looking at the crux has been hit upon, once the right viewing-angle has been discovered." Michael Riffaterre, "Interpretation and Undecidability," *New Literary History* XII:2 (1981): p. 239, my emphasis. While it is true that Riffaterre's views are based on a very single-minded approach to literary texts, it should be noted that the readings he produces are extremely persuasive. Admitting the problems involved in an interpretive theory that hinges on the reader having sufficient "linguistic competence" for reaching correct interpretations, I hope to show that the assumptions Riffaterre makes lead to useful insights and observations when related to historical writing.

[8]   Cf. Gary Saul Morson, "Narrativeness," *New Literary History* 34:1 (2003): p. 70 ff. As Morson writes: "When we understand a work as a whole, contemplate its design or structure, we see it as a pattern in which everything fits. It is, so to speak, visible at a glance. Process exists only within the narrated world, not in the artifact taken as a whole. A radical divide typically separates the characters from the author, critic, or rereader. The characters experience open time and process, but the critic has overcome it."

without noting that the literariness of these artifacts is of an altogether different kind. Historical narratives are structured around the ideal of understanding external processes whereas literary narratives focus on internal processes.

The desire to access experiences directly is difficult for historians to incorporate into their work. The obvious route to this kind of historical writing seems to lie in the sphere of autobiography. Yet even with the privileged access to material afforded in the writing of autobiography, the author is left with many unsolved epistemological problems. The narrativization of material and the theoretical complications to do with remembering and self-understanding deny this form of writing any special position with regard to "truth". The objections to epistemological "accuracy" raised by White and like-minded narrative theorists with regard to selection, framing, and emplotment are at least as serious in the case of autobiography as they are within other genres of referential discourse. The difficulties with autobiography serve to remind us, then, that there is an inherent problem in the linguistic presentation of reality that is not a result of a particular historiographical way of thinking. Realizing this, we may also note that linguistic form – or, to apply White's more recent terminology, linguistic figuration – is not a problem for fiction since fiction by definition does not abide by a similar commitment to represent reality. Rather, as we have learnt from much so-called post-1968 theory, literary writing is linguistic through and through.

To begin to draw out the implications of this "ontological" commitment of given genres to particular "recipes"[9] with regard to reality and reference, we must refuse the extreme view that historical texts are literary artifacts in the more straightforward way of literary fiction. The first consequence of this refusal is to begin to see historical narratives as paradoxical in their very conception. To tell a true story of people, processes and events without recourse to intentions, aspirations, causes, or indeed sufficient documentation generally, is an impossible goal. In fact, even with sufficient access, the imposition of story-form on so diverse a material effects a totalization that leaves out more than it can include. For this reason, the recent suggestion by Morson that historical narratives would do well to present alternatives that did not take place, while still continuing to narrate the factual (as opposed to counterfactual) histories constructed around them, seems an approach that could better convey an understanding of the reality of the past:

> Perhaps a better alternative, one much more consonant with the thinking of Tolstoy, Dostoevsky, and Bakhtin would be to imagine the what-ifs – several of them, most likely – and then follow the choice that was actually made; and at the next moment of choice, do the same, repeatedly. In that case, one would have a sense of history as constantly presenting alternatives and the history we know as one possibility among legions.[10]

Making the past more real in this way, by allowing readers to explore situations in their (if not full, then at least) expanded potential, would lead to a historical writing that might satisfy one aspect of the phenomenological yearning that I have attributed to the historical enterprise. Namely, the desire to relive the choices of an agent in the past.

In White's theorizing, of course, the general (and sometimes disappointingly vague) call for the adoption of different literary strategies is aimed at satisfying this very desire. There is, however, a problem with employing points of view that are interior to a character – to

---

9   Cf. Thomas Pavel, "Literary Genres as Norms and Good Habits," *New Literary History* 34:2 (2003): p. 210.
10   Morson, "Narrativeness," p. 69.

take an example that is familiar from much biographical writing – in historical narration since, in most cases, the author has no access to these. Admittedly, seeing such narrative strategies as unsuitable may simply result from a narrow conception of historical narration and its scientific aspirations. Indeed, microhistorical approaches have also gone a long way in successfully stretching these boundaries.[11] With the commitment to factuality, historical narratives – at least when taken as ideal constructions – are, however, clearly limited in their opportunities for figuration.

A further difficulty historical narratives face with regard to systematic determinations of meaning is to be found in their general lack of focalization. The "who sees?" of historical narratives is – once again, due to their commitment to reality – less clearly determined when compared with literary fiction. Following from the need for transparency in their processes of truth-creation, historical narratives by nature refrain from imposing closure with regard to perspectives for re-emplotting the material presented. Similarly the "speakers" who may be introduced to the story are not limited to those presented by the text, whereas it would be quite uncalled for to bring a character from Margaret Atwood's *The Blind Assassin*, for example, to a reading of Alice Munro's "Meneseteung"; despite their close thematic and historical overlap this would provide no textual resonance or interpretive insight since the significatory systems and textually determined worlds of the two are so overtly self-contained and mutually excluding.[12] This, again, suggests a distinction between narratives where the imposition of form is a consequence of meaning-making (history) and where the same imposition is an integral part of the process itself (fiction). Between, in other words, linguistic figurations that incorporate content and those which construct it in the telling.[13]

– III –

Intertextual references as well as references to general knowledge or historical events, for example, appear to aim at opening fictional narratives outward, of placing them in context for the reader. The nature of this seeming outward-directedness is, however, quite distinct from the referentiality of historical narratives. Instead of informing the reader of alternative but actual ways of thinking or events, these references serve to situate the text in and through a world of meanings and interpretations that are already enfigured; their meaning in the narrative is solely a linguistic one, either opening the text "outward" to prefigured associations and interpretations that are familiar to the reader in his or her present or appealing to knowledge that the reader brings to the reading to deepen and actualize the narrative's exercise in meaning-production. While this kind of meaning-production is essential to what Riffaterre has called the "truth-creation" taking place in fictional narration, it effects a displacement and broadening of meanings that permits these texts to have significance for the reader without having a point of reference outside the reader's personal experiences of the

---

[11] For a good discussion of this see Mark Salber Phillips, "Histories, Micro- and Literary: Problems of Genre and Distance," *New Literary History* 34:2 (2003): p. 222 ff.

[12] In this kind of reading "historical," "geographical," or even thematic overlaps and parallels between non-referential texts are thus clearly secondary to textual considerations and intertextual relations.

[13] To perhaps exaggerate a little, historical events can be said to receive their telos in the imposition of the form, whereas properly literary narratives conform to this telos even prior to the creation or selection of the events.

world.[14] Given this difference in ways of meaning production, it seems more apt to say that fictional texts are directed "inward," to the unfolding and deepening of the narrative itself as well as to the subjective processes of the reader's world reflected in his or her self-experience.

To simplify, we might say that the strategy of meaning-making utilized by complex fictional texts is effected through referring the reader to material with which he or she is already familiar, and, by playing with the range of associations afforded by the text as a whole, gradually narrowing the range of interpretations that can be made of the text's overall significance. A simple example of fictional truth-creation is given by Riffaterre to illustrate this process. In *Fictional Truth*, he presents us with a typical truth-creating move from Proust: "No one yet was to be seen in front of the church except for the lady in black one sees leaving hurriedly at any given time in provincial towns."[15] In historical narratives the dynamic is quite similar *but directed outward*: the reader is presented with new material that is taken as true at face-value and the evidence presented provides a link with the real world even if it is unfamiliar to the reader.[16] With the ability to use its referential agreement for the purposes of introducing new material, the historical narrative is able to abandon fictional means of truth-creation completely.

The displacement of meaning encountered in a historical narrative is thus quite different from the use of intertextual references in literature. The text transfers its argument or meaning (its "message" or interpretation) to evidence that is textually manifested as "real" through various documentary conventions. The pact between the reader and the author reserves certain literary devices as referring to extra-textual evidence. The most obvious of such devices is quotation. Dialogue that is presented directly in the text is marked as opening up on the extra-textual through a system of notations demonstrating its origin. Yet this is something that also happens in fiction where speech is attributed to particular characters. The difference here, then, is obviously not textual despite the divergence between the means for indicating origin since we might quite easily accept a different convention in referential narration for attributing a comment to a character in a given context:

> This time, I had no misgivings regarding what I said as I could hear a familiar voice in my head, repeating: "The similarities between interpretation and narration argue for the essentially figurative nature of the discourses in which they are typically represented in speech or writing."

While this is of course a fictional moment on the level of the *narratio*, or rather, an emplotment that greatly simplifies the (temporal, spatial and perhaps ideational) relations between the characters present, it in no way makes the ideas expressed less real or detracts from their referential quality. Were we to write historical accounts with recourse to more involved literary conventions, the distinction between factual and fictional narration would still remain in place simply on the basis of the agreement regarding their genre and intentions.

Instead of emphasizing the potential for displacement of meaning offered by reality (the tending of the historical narrative to the extra-textual), focus has, however, been on a more

---

[14] Cf. Michael Riffaterre, *Fictional Truth* (Baltimore: Johns Hopkins UP, 1990), passim.
[15] Riffaterre, *Fictional Truth*, p. 8.
[16] The associations the reader makes from the presentations of this new material are similarly outward-directed. They appeal to ideas and actions concerning the concrete situations the reader encounters in the world.

literary (intra-textual) displacement and slippage from one possible interpretive moment and context to another in the manner of much contemporary literature. Yet why is this so if the purpose is to provide historical writing with alternatives?

In addition to being generically committed to reference and truth, historical narratives mark their referentiality by presenting the reader with sources. Differing from much fictional truth-creation, these presentations are generally quite straightforward. The convention of abiding by documentable evidence relieves the historian of the need for involved narrative means for making things "ring true." In other words, historical narratives present references and evidence with an eye on the validation of the truth of the account they offer. Yet, although this is the position from which criticisms of more traditional historical writing come, this is not the whole story. The way in which references are presented in historical narratives differs radically from the strategies of fictional truth-creation. Historical narratives present references that they assume to be unfamiliar to the reader, appealing to the reader that he or she situate this new material in the context of the familiar, perhaps producing a new understanding of the whole. To make this process even more truth-like, historical narratives that are conscious of the complications involved in narrativization often engage in a form of "thick description" that allows readers to "see for themselves" the materials that are used and the voices that are ultimately (most often) subsumed to the interpretation itself. Despite the opportunity for personal evaluation that this affords, the reader has, of course, only the generic agreement as insurance that the evidence is real. Clearly then, truth-creation in historical narratives is not a textual feature but is based on a shared understanding between the author and reader concerning the legitimacy of interpretations and the epistemological standing of acceptable evidence.[17]

Despite White's long-standing emphasis on "the content of the form," it seems to me that he would make a similar distinction between inward- and outward-directed forms of discourse.[18] Yet he takes the extra-referentiality of the discourse for granted (quite naturally given his general argument) and leaves its full implications unexplored. The extra-referential attitude or commitment of historical narratives is, however, something that requires further mention since it is this particularity that has surprisingly been neglected in discussions of their possibilities. Although effective historical narratives may, like their fictional counterparts, well begin from the observation of an individual or situation as a

---

[17] Although it does not provide a very interesting or conclusive means for distinguishing between genres, the manner in which historical narratives present their sources and evidence in the form of footnotes, for example, provides – to quote Dorrit Cohn – an additional "textual zone intermediating between the narrative text itself and its extratextual documentary base." Dorrit Cohn, "Signposts of Fictionality: A Narratological Perspective," *Poetics Today* 11:4 (Winter 1990): p. 782. On the basis of this "direct" referentiality, but even more as a result of its generic agreement to refer, historical writing manages to do without the kind of truth-creating strategies employed by fictional narratives. Truth need not be created when it is seen to be out there for the taking. This is not to say that truth-creation in historical narratives has no textual dimension, only that the practice of footnotes or the presentation of quotations or appeal to general historical knowledge is a fairly uncomplicated textual strategy.

[18] White's main emphasis is, of course, that historical discourse is intra-referential in the same manner as literature. As he writes: "historical discourse is 'intensional,' i.e., is systematically intra- as well as extra-referential. This intensionality endows the historical discourse with a quality of 'thinginess' similar to that of the poetic utterance." White, *Content of the Form*, p. 24. This emphasis on textuality should, I believe, be read in the context of his general intention of overcoming naive thoughts of objectivity and textual transparency among many practising historians at the time.

suitable subject for narrative representation, the historical narrative is even in this first stage, tied to a movement from world to text. This limitation is clear even when the historian wishes to present this observation for a moral purpose or in order to illustrate a more general point. Where a fictional narrative becomes effective through its ability to create truth and immerse readers in the plausibility of ways of thinking and behaving that were previously foreign to them, the strength of the historical presentation is thus not in its universalizability or its strikingness on an abstract level but in its strictly particular and concrete nature. To illustrate this briefly: however charming or curious a fictional description of, for example, the ability to bluff one's way into influential circles as in the case of the protagonist in John O'Farrell's *This is Your Life*, its appeal as an example – as opposed to a theory – of the potential of the human condition would always be heightened by its being true rather than being merely plausible.[19] Simply put, then, a historical narrative marks our otherness and particularity whereas a literary one absolves us of such experiences.

– IV –

Even though it is true that the historical past cannot by definition be present in a historical narrative (i.e., it is indeed past and thus inaccessible to us), this absence is itself transformed into a concrete presence through the textual markers that define historical writing as referential. The *presence* within the text is not, then, that of the past but of a surrogate created for our historical imaginings in the text by its commitment to remain within the realm of the real rather than that of the imaginary. This dynamic has consequences that distinguish the historical text from the fictional narrative. The historical narrative is involved in a justification – or a pretense – of referentiality through the sleight-of-hand of introducing extratextual truth to a narrative rather than engaging in textual truth-creation. For this reason, the historical narrative remains, from a literary theorist's point of view, a formally inferior literary artifact. From an opposing point of view the faith placed by the historical narrative in its ability to convince without resorting to linguistic trickery may be taken as a sign of honesty. To take this one step further, it might be said that the narrative that refuses to lead us on is involved in an unconscious denial of representation.

The most important thing to note concerning the issue of presence in the text is that it shows us two alternative approaches to representation. The historical text is not, I would argue, involved in mimetic representation. It does not intend to conjure up a reality in our reading of it, nor does it claim to present the world it attends to *within* its representational discourse. Rather, its aim is to *direct* us to the artifacts that remain of a past reality and thus to *refer* us to something outside itself. The literary text, on the other hand, provides no reality of its own that we might refer to independently of the text. In the case of literary fiction we are referred only to our personal experiences of the world. Of course, there are instances where literary fiction does not proceed in such a self-sustaining manner: the case of the historical novel often provides the stumbling block for approaches that attempt to make a for-

---

[19] This should not be misunderstood, however, as arguing that referential discourse could lead to emotional identification with the protagonist as easily as literary dramatizations. In this instance, effectiveness is a matter of truth, not presentation. Phillips makes this same point in relation to biography as a model for historical writing, saying that "[i]n this new form the power of history resides in its actuality rather than its exemplarity." Phillips, "Histories, Micro- and Literary," p. 216.

mal distinction.The upshot of this argument, however, is that forms of discourse conventionally marked as literary rather than referential refuse to give control of interpretations to the reader. The dynamic they utilize in their meaning-production necessarily involves them in an overdetermining of their object to the extent that – although the reader may justifiably ask what something means with reference to his or her own life – the reader is unable to use the narrative as justification for changing his or her behavior. Granted, this is a result of the different ontological spheres these narratives inhabit. For the purposes of practical efficacy, then, there is much to be said in favor of a narrative that maintains its position in the ontological sphere of the real – even with the criticism heaped by traditional historians on historical narratives that lead to presentist thinking.

Handing responsibility for the construction of meaning over to the reader, the "committed" and self-aware historical narrative permits a different kind of understanding to be formed: it is not an understanding of the subjective processes of being human or the ability to empathize with those who are different from ourselves as much as one of recognizing one's role as a concrete actor in a world where meanings are not predetermined – a world where meanings are as fluid and unstable as we make them.

$$- \text{V} -$$

The distinction between the use of references in the traditional classic realist mode of historical writing and the new parahistorical kind that White calls for in *Figural Realism* could well be seen in terms of a totalizing function on the level of their structural significance, the added "content of the form." It seems clear from White's arguments on the kinds of modernist narrative strategies employed by Virginia Woolf, for example, that this content is no longer in any significant way determined by the manifest contents of the text but is rather imposed on the story elements in much the same way as plot structure, albeit in a more involved way. The imposition of a "metaphoric significance" on the text becomes a difficult issue in this newer understanding of the process of figuration, however. If the text uses references in a kind of postmodern "pastiche" manner, it performs a dispersal of meaning that undermines the whole idea behind White's former structuralist emphasis on the interpretive content of the form. This new reading of White would deny the extension of the idea of structural content as being anything more than an issue of emplotment, selection of material or their expansion and condensation. There would be no closure through anything as involved as semiotic overdetermination. For interpretations of White's thinking this seems a most significant issue: we no longer have White-the-structuralist but now see him as invoking the idea of a postmodern dispersal of meaning in the very sense which his somewhat overly enthusiastic supporters and critics have already previously come to understand his work. The relativist tendencies implicit in the assumption of a film like *JFK*, for instance, as a paradigm for historical representation are a long way from the kind of structuralist reading offered by White of *The Education of Henry Adams*, for example.[20] The totalization implicit in White's earlier attributions of semiotic significance to structural as well as tropological elements of the text towards the formation of a coherent meaning is no longer present. Historical references would no longer be seen to work together in the manner of a

---

[20]   See White, *Content of the Form*, pp. 185–213.

collage, where they – by design[21] – direct a reading toward a coherent interpretation but rather a pastiche, where various elements are no longer even expected to be "read" as belonging to the same, or indeed even commensurate, ontological or temporal levels. Of course, White explains this by saying that present-day readers read such presentations with an acquired ease.[22]

Indeed, White argues that it is the particular and exceptional nature of the modernist event that leaves it resistant to conceptualization through typical representational forms. As he writes: "It is the anomalous nature of modernist events – their resistance to inherited categories and conventions for assigning meanings to events – that undermine not only the status of facts in relation to events but also the status of the event in general."[23] To properly understand this, it seems we should pay particular attention to White's emphasis on "inherited" ways of assigning meaning. Despite White's assertion that there is something fundamentally different about the modernist event, this seems to suggest that the underlying motive of his claim relates to our distance to these events rather than their nature.

Surely, to say that we have no recourse to "inherited" representational strategies means only that we are in search of suitable approaches now – as indeed White's whole endeavor testifies – and not that those events are unrepresentable. Understood in this way, we might say that modernist events and our experienced troubles with representing them are a result of our closeness to them. Put simply, we lack the means to deal with these experiences on a personal level, although we may well have linguistically and conceptually codified ways of handling similar events more distant to us. In addition our proximity to events of such great magnitude of course leads us to look for alternative ways of comprehending and representing them. The reason that these events do not seem to allow for interpretive closure is that they have not yet been – and, as White's ethical-political argument goes, hopefully will never be – assimilated to our cultural understandings of "how the world is." To refuse the connection between the "outside" of such events (our customary reading or story of them) and their "inside" (their reality) is simply to maintain our attitude of awe in the face of things we do not (wish to) understand. If this can be done through renewed or alternative literary means, so much the better.

For White, the continual displacement and dispersal of meaning as well as the apparently almost random slippage or "leakage" from one frame of reference to another typical to

---

21 Although White does not discuss the issue of intentionality with regard to textual overdetermination at any great length, it seems that in urging historians to write more complex and literary texts he grants authorial intentions a significant role. Given the difficulties with rehabilitating the idea of authorial intentions to textual approaches, it seems sufficient for present purposes to adopt the kind of "weak intentionalism" Mark Bevir advocates for approaching literary artifacts. In such an understanding of texts, meaning does not reside in the text but in the intentions read into it by the author or the readers based on their social and historical context. Thus meaning is not atemporal yet can still be anticipated and shared. As Bevir writes, this weak intentionalism "equates meanings with the ways particular individuals, whether they be authors or readers, understand utterances. The crux of intentionalism thus becomes the idea that meanings are ascribed to objects by the intentional or mental activity of individuals, rather than properties intrinsic to the objects in themselves. Weak intentionalism implies only that meanings have no existence apart from individuals. Utterances have meanings only because individuals take them so to do." Bevir, "Meaning and Intention: A Defense of Procedural Intentionalism," *New Literary History* 31:3 (2000): p. 387. And, because of their historical nature, utterances have meanings that are far from free-floating.

22 White, *Figural Realism*, p. 67 ff.

23 White, *Figural Realism*, p. 70.

the modernist novel provides a way of avoiding the kind of intellectual mastery of the event that he would have us refuse. Yet, at the same time, having become competent readers of "postmodern parahistorical representations," we should already have the ability for refusing such mastery. As White says, "precisely insofar as the story is identifiable as a story, it can provide no lasting mastery of such events."[24] Given the shift toward a more full-blown relativism that such statements suggest, the alternate route to a subversion of representation through referentiality sketched below seems quite promising.

– VI –

White's emphasis on the "postmodern parahistorical" representation in *Figural Realism* can be seen to signal a turn in his thinking. No longer as concerned with issues of epistemological accuracy as in his earlier work, White now increasingly foregrounds the question of representational force. Focusing more and more on the effects of representations, he argues that the adoption of these parahistorical forms can better do justice to the kinds of events he labels "modernist," those where the outside and the inside of the event have become inseparably intertwined.[25] By definition, such events are, of course, most suitably represented following modernist or postmodern advances in literary writing. Yet there remains the question of what such modernist events in fact are. How do they differ from events where our proximity to them hasn't changed our perceptions and anticipation of them? From events that have been distanced from our present by being linguistically codified in their transmission through historical accounts?

Despite an apparent change in his approach, the examples White employs suggest that his attention remains focused on the structures whereby meaning is constructed rather than with the referential contents these constructions convey. It seems, then, that his emphasis on the similarity of interpretation and narration has led him to a partial denial of both with much greater force than previously. Narration qua interpretation hinders an understanding of those events and processes that do not easily conform to a traditional story-form.

It seems, then, that White's thinking regarding interpretation and the role of epistemological considerations is radically different in the context of these "postmodern parahistorical representations." Where his earlier approach emphasized the political function of historical writing and the way literary means could be used to overcome the doubts caused by the lack of epistemological efficacy, his interest with contemporary forms of representation in *Figural Realism* is more to do with the reification and uncertainty these produce when not controlled. With, that is, the way that the new media has partially undone the need for narrative presentation while also leaving viewers unsure of the way that a particular content should be understood. He makes this point especially with regard to technological advances in relation to understanding the events they convey. His example of the *Challenger* explosion, for instance, shows how interpretation is replaced by repetition of the documentary footage of the event with little or no commentary or narrative involved.[26] Explanations are

---

[24] White, *Figural Realism*, p. 81.

[25] Cf. White, *Figural Realism*, p. 79.

[26] This suggests, of course, that the main difference in his thinking after the introduction of the idea of the modernist event is not in the nature of representational structures but more in the very attitude to reality. In order for the reality of historical sources in the form of archival material to become reality for the reader they need to be figured in language following common conventions. Since the material available to viewers of "events"

sought in the material itself, which is, of course, unable to provide answers as such. The role of the historian as interpreter is simply displaced onto the viewer of privileged material.

To me, the most productive approach to the problem of the historical representation of modernist events – events that we have no preconceived interpretive models for – is to extend the idea of emergence to the historical narrative and simultaneously affirm its representational specificity vis-à-vis reference. In other words, we should foreground the reality of the inside of the events we attempt to figure while at the same time allowing for an openness of form that would leave responsibility for the interpretation to the reader. As the significance of the narrative would then come about through its interaction with the life-world of the reader, these two aims clearly support each other. Although the idea of an emergent property is the same, the aspect that needs to be done away with, then, is that of conceiving of historical writing as a branch of literature since this is the position that leads us to problematize the questions discussed. For historical writing to be "literary" in the sense of permitting a dispersal of meaning is not for it to become fictional or poetic since the particular dispersal of meaning that takes place within the historical narrative is toward reality, not language. The meaning of an "event" can be displaced on the material this event consists of. In this way, the kind of presentation that White calls for might provide us with a replication of reality in the form of an apprehending consciousness rather than the fiction of a coherent, all-knowing point of view. Bringing historical writing closer to its investigative processes could, then, go a long way toward engaging the subjectivity of the reader and rendering the past present in a way that satisfies the phenomenological yearning we have for the world even within language.

---

such as the Challenger explosion is already unproblematic in that it is a "true" view with no linguistic figuration, it is best left alone, without comment.

II NARRATIVITY

Introduction to Part II

Narrativity

The crucial notion in the history/literature debate is that of "narrative." However, whereas both Hayden White and Paul Ricoeur take history and literature as their major examples of narrative, the so-called "narrative turn" in the humanities and social sciences has paid more attention to the role of narrativity in everyday life.

In the fifth chapter, one of Germany's most distinguished literary scholars, Karlheinz Stierle, analyzes the conditions that allow the world to be narrated. Coming from a long tradition of German hermeneutics, Stierle addresses the issues of narrativity and textual representation from an original point of view that combines the Gadamerian hermeneutic tradition and French structuralism. He also places Hayden White's work within the wider context of European thinking by noting the similarities between White and Georg Simmel. He concludes that "the availability of the world to narration (die Erzählbarkeit der Welt) is, like justice or property, an inevitable fiction which offers a basis for the social world as constituted in the imaginary."

If the narrativization of identity marks the move from pre-modern to modern identity, then one may claim that the move from modern to post-modern identity is characterizised by "the death of narratives." Matti Hyvärinen addresses this issue by probing the work of Paul Auster to discuss the role(s) and meanings of narrative in human life and action. Auster's novels seem to highlight the importance of narratives by describing "life without narrative," life that seems to be, as Hayden White has put it, in the form of pure sequence. Hyvärinen concludes by discussing the relevance of narrative for the human ability to act. The disappearance of narrative substituted by the reign of sequential understanding of life seems always to be connected to the end of action, voluntary or involuntary.

CHAPTER 5

Karlheinz Stierle

Narrativization of the World

The world of the infinitely large and the world of the infinitely small, which are accessible to us through increasingly sensitive instruments of observation and through progressively more subtle operations of thought, are not narratable. In his ingenious book of narrative balancing acts *Cosmicomiche*, Italo Calvino appears to oppose this, whereas in reality, one can see at every turn the hilarious absurdity of his attempt. Likewise, the extension of science fiction to increasingly inconceivable realms, while retaining the classical mode of storytelling, shows that the astronauts in their space shuttles bear the same basic anthropological disposition of telling stories right along with them. The farther along we find our way towards the borders of the principally cognizable, the more massively do cases of pure emergence appear that can be stated as such, but that can no longer be elucidated in terms of 'whither' and 'whence.'

Basically very different from this kind of world is the world that, in the first place, is probably determined through its capacity for being narrativized, the world which the phenomenologists called the *Lebenswelt* (the Life-World). The *Lebenswelt* is the world that is basically opened up in stories. Even if for a proponent of the exact sciences or of critical philosophy this world might seem to be once composed of fables or fiction, this world is expressly an impassable reality of its own, as such. Even the scientist who penetrates into the depths of the universe has a home address, must pay taxes, has a social status and is, as the phenomenologist Schapp says*, in Geschichten verstrickt* (entangled in the web of stories).

Telling stories in innumerably different modes, genres, and pragmatic functions is common to all cultures and is used from the smallest circles of families to the totality of a society as an indispensable medium of constructing coherence. In storytelling, time in particular appears as a mode of obtaining coherence. Before any event time exists as a ubiquitous current that carries everything with it. But in the world of stories, too, which is a world made of stories, we have to ask ourselves: what happens, when the story grasps the world and takes possession of it, or when it reaches out to imaginary worlds? Can a story, even recounted in the most accurate and careful way by a historian who wants to secure every detail, tell the past reality as it "actually was" (L. Ranke)?

In his *Confessions* St. Augustine remarks that memory does not retain the memorized matter as such but first has to transform it into a form which makes it memorable: "This same memory also contains the feelings of my mind; not in the manner in which the mind itself experienced them, but very differently according to a power peculiar to memory."[1]

---

[1] St.Augustine, *Confessiones*, .X, 14; transl. A. C. Outler. "Affectiones quoque animi mei eadem memoria continet non illo modo, quo eas habet ipse animus, cum patitur eas, sed alio multum diverso, sicut sese habet vis memoriae."

Just as the memory has to transform the matters that come to it in a memorable form, so, too, must storytelling transform the matter into a form that makes the matter narratable. The infinite plurality of things that belong to reality and the infinite variety of meanings attached to them, seen as a mere occurrence of emergent events, cannot be conceived or depicted. What happens must first be transposed into the conceivable mode of a story [Geschichte], in order to be discerned from the infinite current of events. This affinity between remembering and storytelling can be seen as a sign of the anthropological complementarity of remembering and narration. Remembering or a fiction of remembrance is necessary for the act of narrating, but the reverse also applies, storytelling with its specific inner principles is necessary for remembering, which in itself already transforms the matter to be remembered, so that it gains stability. Even the fragmentary piece of memory that suddenly pops up, a souvenir involontaire, seeks this kind of stability: as it is firmly fixed in the memory and as it is to be conveyed to the others, this happens through appropriation of the mode of a narrative. In Prousts *A la recherche du temps perdu* a piece of souvenir involontaire, that of tea and a madeleine pastry, becomes a part of the story concerning the search for a lost past.

Only when a memory is bound to the form of a story does it actually become memorable. This, too, indicates that storytelling as a mode of appropriation of the past is bound to memory in a special way. Indeed, one could even say that a special mnemonical quality is involved in the mode of storytelling. It is true that the standard model of classical mnemonics is spatial and consists of a space with a series of different stages to be traversed, but the time-space-model presented by narration seems to offer a far more appropriate alternative for remembering the complex constellations of matters to be memorized.

For the following discussion it is preferable to start with a written text and to leave out the problematics of the difference between oral and written forms of storytelling.

The classical narrative text draws its reader on with a stream of narrative time that strives page by page to reach its ending. The reader senses the suction of the story from inside, but he or she also perceives it by watching the pile of unread pages becoming thinner and thinner. The first page already introduces the reader into the world of the story and also calls forth a kind of initial expectation or suspense which holds on until the last, concluding sentence of the text. The skill of the narrator consists in arousing in the reader the expectations that are, or are not fulfilled until the great bracket between the first and final sentence is closed. Again and again negation plays a role in enhancing the dynamics of narration, either by introducing an element of uncertainty in the story or by disappointing those expectations. In these cases the subject of these operations can be one of the characters of the story, the narrator him/herself or the reader as well.

In addition to this, there exists almost nothing in the world of a narrative that cannot be interpreted as a sign of what will happen in the future. At each moment the reader is sketching out from the material that is available to him or her a horizon of the future that is ever tighter and more determined in its form. This is the horizon into which the story to be narrated will be written. The reader experiences a constantly changing but steadily approaching horizon of the future, until at the end of the story the 'now' without a horizon is reached.

However, at the same time the reader feels the presence of another kind of horizon. Every story is the central point of the world as set out by the story itself. At any given moment the story works with the same thematic core material, with a central character or some central character constellation and a constantly changing horizon, but at each moment a virtuality of infinitely more stories and thematic core materials becomes apparent. The particular aesthetic and cognitive pleasure of the reader of narrative texts is due to the fact that, in contrast to what is possible in ordinary life, while traveling through time he or she can be in a world in which relevance is united with temporality. Precisely this seems to be the unwritten contract between the author and the reader: that nothing which is included in the story between its beginning and its ending is without relevance, be it in relation to the past or to the future. The principle of relevance for a narrative form is also a principle of style. But whereas relevance is taken for granted by the reader during the process of reading, it has implicit bonds with the ending, so that the end seems to become the culmination point of the story's relevance. Here one may find the actual, original fiction in which every narration participates: every moment of the storytelling stands in a direct relation to its ending, even before the ending has been reached and has become an event. For the reader, the principle of style only reveals itself as the principle of relevance, which has determined the entire movement of narration by the end of the story.

At this point the reader who now has a grasp of the whole story may finish his or her reading, or s/he may start re-reading the text on a different horizon of expectations. One can generally state that literature is principally meant to be read more than just once and its characteristics, as such, are revealed only in the process of re-reading. Within the horizon of re-reading, the narrative text is detached from the original order of temporality and discloses its hidden dynamics towards the ending as a compositional rationality. On the horizon of the first reading, the "context on the left side" (the pile of the already read pages) grows continuously, and this is counterbalanced by the narrowing down of the empty context of mere expectations. In this way the reader creates, him/herself, the temporality which s/he experiences. On the horizon of re-reading, the narrative text loses the fascination that came from immediate temporality and reveals itself as a structural and compositional whole. In re-reading, the horizon lies stereoscopically between two complementary contexts which may be called 'the left side context' and 'the right side context.' Every moment of the narration is thus doubly situated and also has a double functional value in relation to the beginning and to the end. Only this clears the way to grasp the decisive fundamental fiction underlying all narrative forms: that narrating happens within a horizon from a beginning towards an ending, that the line of temporality is limited, and that the beginning and the ending stand to each other in a significant relation that is principally withdrawn from the realm of mere temporality.

For not only is the ending a function of the beginning, so, too, the beginning is a function of the ending. The qualitative leap from temporal continuity to the temporality characteristic of the narrative itself is based on the ending that is the last moment in the continuity of this temporality. On the other hand, however, the potential of the ending is seen only from the perspective of the beginning. The fundamental fiction of beginning and ending is constitutive for every form of narration, irrespective of whether the narrations serve the pragmatic functions of remembrance and sense-making or whether it is developed as a free play of possibilities. Already Aristotle saw in the myth an especially significant form of narration which consisted of a beginning, a middle, and an end and was determined by these three parts. What is valid in Aristotle's *Poetics* for the myth is principally valid for every narrative form. But when the beginning and the ending are seen to stand in a conceptual relationship to each other, the story is as if stripped of its linear temporality, and the conceptual construction or the aesthetic rationality thus makes its appearance.

At this point it is necessary to reintroduce some results of the structural study of narrative texts that were prematurely abandoned by a general skeptical attitude towards theory, or by the triumph of the deconstructive philosophy of texts. Whereas narrative theory following Genette is focused almost totally on the problem (or the pseudo-problem) of 'focalization' and simply drops the problematics of the constitution of a narrative, or abandons it as the target of deconstructive skepticism of language, already Roland Barthes and especially Algirdas Greimas in their structural theory of narration, study the basic conceptual structure of narratives. Even earlier, at the beginning of the 20th century, Georg Simmel in his important essay "Das Problem der historischen Zeit" (The problem of historical time) talks about the indispensability of the "foundation of an ideal line" (Hindurchlegen einer ideellen Linie)[2] that would make it possible, independently of a special narrative concretization, to depict temporal concepts of experience such as a battle. This applies to an even greater extent to the relation between the beginning and the ending that cannot be set arbitrarily but, instead, follows the "foundation of the ideal line" or a conceptual axis of narrativity.

It was Claude Lévi-Strauss, who in his path-breaking essay "The Structural Study of Myth," launched the idea of a double reading of myth from the point of view of narration and of its conceptual content, thus becoming the first to take seriously Aristotle's claim in a methodically earnest way that the myth is more philosophical than history.[3] Throughout his essay Lévi-Strauss stays within the context of an anthropological concept of the nature of myths and their dynamics of modification. We can here overlook the technical problems and speculations in Lévi-Strauss's essay and concentrate on the basic idea which is constitutive for every structural analysis of narrative: that a narrative text can be read as a temporal order but also has a conceptual structure that is to be seen as the deep structure of narration. The first person to reach this conclusion based on Lévi-Strauss's analysis of myths is A. Greimas who postulates for every narrative form a deep structure consisting of an a-chronic system of oppositional concepts, from which the temporal structure of a story can be generated. For Greimas the basic model of a narrative grammar is the correlation between two conceptual pairs of oppositions, which means a structure consisting of four terms.

Departing from this one can take the further step of simplification and set a basic conceptual pair of oppositions of A vs. B, from which, through temporalization, two elementary narrative structures are generated: A vs. B; B vs. A. If the basic opposition of the narrative axis is understood like this, so that the narrative axis of relevance is also determined by the difference between the two basic oppositional terms – a narrative can be relevant only if it deals with an important conceptual difference within – the narrative process between the beginning and the ending can be seen as the processing of this difference. It is, of course, also possible that the basic opposition will be varied, modified, or also ironically deconstructed. For example, the basic narrative constellation "A becomes B" can be connected

---

[2]   Georg Simmel, "Das Problem der historischen Zeit", *Zur Philosophie der Kunst. Philosophische und kunstphilosophische Aufsätze*. Herausgegeben von Gertrud Simmel. (Potsdam: Kiepenheuer, 1922), p.165.

[3]   Claude Levi-Strauss, *Structural Anthropology* (New York: Basic Books, 1963), pp. 202- 212.

with the inverse figure "B becomes A" so that this ends with the joint figure "A becomes B becomes A," or the basic figure can be multiplied in strands of the story, which makes the diachronic figures look like simultaneous figures of oppositions. Especially in narrative structures whose inner coherence is experienced as being very dense, such immanent relations of reflections are not uncommon.

In his *Analytical Philosophy of History*,[4] Arthur C. Danto suggests an elementary model of narration which, in a quite different context, very much resembles the basic figure of Lévi-Strauss's structural analysis of myths and Greimas's structural model of narration. This is particularly the case in relation to Aristotle's structural description of the myth as a three part schema of beginning, middle, and ending; in Danto's terms,

(1) x is F at t-I.

(2) H happens to x at t-II.

(3) x is G at t-III.

The propositions (1) and (3) are for Danto the explanandum of the story, in other words, the conceptually given difference between the beginning and the ending, and proposition (2) is the explanans, the road in time that mediates the opposition between F and G, not logically, but in the experience of a person who lives it. But exactly this is the reason why the model proposed by Danto cannot be valid only for the purpose of explanation; it is a model that is valid also for depicting happenings that are meaningful, exemplary, provoking or unforeseen. In this way semantic experiments and constellations and also conceptual clusters are created, which bring a new concreteness [Anschaulichkeit] and thus also new semantic energy into perceptual conceptions.

This can be illustrated by the example of Heinrich von Kleist's novella *The Earthquake in Chile*. The basic opposition in this novella is not difficult to demonstrate, as it is also expressly named several times in the text, which is common practice in classical literary texts. This is the opposition of fortune and misfortune, which threads through the story in different variations and emphasized forms and which sets up the beginning and the ending in a significant relationship vis-à-vis one another. In momentous, sudden turns, deriving either from a monstrous contingency of things or from guiding providence, moments of an extraordinary fortune and misfortune dovetail one another until, at the end of the story, it looks as though fortune and misfortune were moments of one and the same swinging movement. Thus, an enormous semantic intensity is channeled into the concepts of fortune and misfortune. The narrative concretization creates a concept of fortune and misfortune which act as ideal equivalents of the abstract concepts themselves.

In its significant narrative structure, Kleist's novella shows especially clearly what role the conceptual structure has as the ground onto which the colorful events of the story are woven, the structure of which is revealed only by the second reading of the text. This structure, then, also has the function of being the basis for an embedded aesthetic rationality of the narrative form. The process of narration, connecting the beginning and the ending, is, however, also a treatment of concept. The concept or the perceptual form is not merely a medium of narrative communication. Reversing the point of view, it can be stated that the concept and its saturation with concreteness, in other words, perceptions crystallized as concepts, can always also be the object of attention. Every narration is inevitably also a

---

4   Arthur C. Danto, *Analytical Philosophy of History* (Cambridge: Cambridge University Press, 1965).

semantic experiment that destabilizes the terminological borders of concepts and makes the adventurousness of the narrated world into an adventurousness of a conceptuality thrown out of its conventional systematic frame.

It looks as if the conceptual hurdle in narratives could, in their adventurousness, be understood as a special form of what Derrida calls semantic destabilization in deconstruction. However, the conceptual basis of the narration has a principally different character, because the order of the narrative has a freedom of combination over the whole conceptual structure. What would be won, when, for example, the particular, unique and overwhelming conceptual affinity of fortune and misfortune at the end of Kleist's *Earthquake in Chile* were reclaimed to be a case of conceptual deconstruction? The psychic energies that are condensed in the concepts through the process of narration are something more than the mere transgression of semantic borders or unfathomable nature of linguistic and logical aporia. A reader, who does not simply yield to the narrative text but consciously participates in the process of its realization, is obliged to work continuously on the concepts of the story. The conceptual work keeps his judgement in continuous movement, either in the sense of Kant's "determining judgement" [bestimmende Urteilskraft], as the reader searches the surface of the text for the concrete determining moments of the lexically central concepts of the text, or in the sense of the "reflective judgement" [reflektierende Urteilskraft], in which case the reader chooses for the concrete particulars a suitable concept that is implied but not named in the text.

In a different way from the author, the reader must find the suitable concrete particulars for the concepts and a concept for the things. For this process, the constant self-reflection of the narrative text itself, in which concepts alternately overwhelm others or are overwhelmed, in turn, by others, provides a matrix of great heuristic importance. The concepts of narration in their a-chronic connections and their diachronic development are not only the moments of an infinite postponement, of a differential chain of signification, but they are constructing tools of the world [welthaltig], sedimentations of Being-in-the-world [des In-der-Welt-Seins – Heidegger], that, in the narrative process, become loaded to a great extent with concreteness.

Even if the conceptual analysis of the structure of narrative texts can bring forth important results, these are neither sufficient in themselves nor the only relevant results scientifically. It was a fundamental error of the structuralist paradigms in the sixties to consider themselves alternatives to a hermeneutic interpretation of texts. The road from a text to its structure is only the first half of the whole road. From here the interpretation must find its way back to the real complexity of a narrative text in its numerous strata and perspectives. The road from the text to its conceptual structure and back to the text is the actual form of the hermeneutic circle, in which the relation between structuralism and hermeneutics is also a part.

The conceptual structure of the relation between beginning and ending is a prerequisite of narration, but it is not the narration itself. This is more than a mere allegory of its structure. The structure is a prerequisite of the text, but the nature of the story shows itself in that it is not only subordinate to the structure, but it also defines it. The story thus maintains a free relation to the conceptual structure which it can fill out in manifold differentiation. Every story is bound to its structure and at the same time shows resistance to it. Every sentence in a progressing story is, in a way, a conflict between the conceptual boundness and the unboundness of the narrative detail that always shows the principal contingency of the world, the density of the events resisting the power of narration and, at the same time, the fact that there might be an infinite number of other stories about the world.

The story follows at once a narrative rhythm which, by using the instruments of rest and motion, condensation and expansion, is able to produce the finest patterns and profiles of relevance emerging from its conceptual structure. This narrative rhythmization is bound to a three-part basic scheme of state, situation, and event [Zustand, Situation und Ereignis], which repeats recursively the elementary three-part scheme of the narrative whole: the beginning, the middle, and the end. If the story as a whole can be understood as dynamization and differentiation of its basic conceptual structure, this applies even more to the discursive realization of the story. Every story presupposes the existence of an ideal narrative instance, because it is only from this perspective that the story can be seen as a whole, from beginning to end. Only under this condition of all-embracing overview – irrespective of whether this is explicit or remains implicit – can something like narrative economy become possible, which motivates the selection of the matter narrated. At the same, this selection serves as the actual instrument of differentiation of narrative conceptuality. Concepts and their linguistic equivalents are no abstract schemata; they are *welthaltig* and could be defined as sedimentations of our Being-in-the-world. It is precisely in narrative texts that this *Welthaltigkeit* appears in a play of semantic differentiations. But in the language of the discourse that carries on the narrative from the beginning until the end, the specificity of the narrative voice is always perceivable: the voice imprints its specificity on the concrete discourse and thus makes the existence of a special narrating instance visible. No story is narrated neutrally, and even if there were such a thing as narrative neutrality, it would be a kind of narrative voice, too. Only as the conceptual structure develops into a story and the story into a discourse, does the narrative whole with its different layers and nuances emerge in all its narrative colour.

One could possibly employ here the concepts of *disegno* and *colore* of the 16th-century theory of painting in Italy. *Disegno*, in which the *gestalt* is sketched without colors, is actually nothing but the expression [Umschreibung] of a concept of painting. Only in coloring does a painting receive its character of being a depiction of experience. Similarly, only the narrative discourse, in which the semantics and the syntax playfully intermingle, gives a story its coloring. And just as the painter has his specific hand in dealing with colors, so, too, the narrator's voice in depicting the world through the medium of storytelling entails the specificity of making the text. Grasping this is however no longer the task of a structural analysis of the text, but that of a hermeneutic understanding that finds its expression in interpretation.

That telling a story refers back to the central perspective of a narrative instance, implies a fundamental and inevitable partiality of the narration. There can be no depiction of reality outside this prerequisite of all depiction. Like the language itself that carries the story, the story in itself is self-referential and open to the world. This is equally valid for both fiction and historical writing. For in historical writing, too, the basic fiction of a beginning and an end through which the ideal time of narration is constituted is not omitted, and in historical writing, too, there exists a perspectivism of relevance referring to the central point of view of the narrative instance. One must be reminded of the fact that the original meaning of fiction as implied in the Latin word fingere was ambiguous: *fictio* could mean in Latin a lie, a treacherous speech or a poetic fiction, but could also indicate the molding and shaping of that which is yet the unformed in the sense of rational, proper constructivity. The elementary act of *fingere* was to shape a figure out of the shapeless clay. Even historical writing is not free from this type of *fingere*; one could even say that historiographic writing could not even grasp its subject, 'history,' without it. Also history itself in the sense of historiography is both self-referential, subjected to its own leading concepts, and open to the world, tending toward history, its narrative form and its interpretation. After Georg Simmel it is Hayden White who, in his book *Metahistory*, makes this especially clear.[5] Fiction as creating a (pseudo-)autonomous world and historiography as the scientifically objective depiction of reality in the realm of the past are only ideal-typical constructions. The sentence by Aristotle, "Poetry is more philosophical and more serious than history, because poetry deals with the general, whereas historiography deals with the particular," is valid only for the chronicle-type, narratively unmediated historiographic writing. In reality, already in antique historiographic writing, every historian had his own philosophy of history that can be found in the conceptual layer of the historiographic narration. Moreover, even if no wisdom could possibly be extracted from historiographic writings that would be valid for the future – falling back into barbarity, as the most recent events show, cannot be inhibited by any historiography – history in the form of historiography still remains through its conceptual philosophical readability a magistra vitae.

However, one should add *Fictio magistra vitae* to *Historia magistra vitae*, because fiction in the narrower sense also stands in a relation to the world, due to the *Welthaltigkeit* of its conceptions and to the fact that its leading concepts refer to the world, whereby its self-referentiality is created on the horizon of the real world. No fiction exists without a relation to the world, just as there is no narrative relation to the world, not even in historiographic writing, in which fiction is not included. This is exactly why the actual space of narration is multitude of different modes and genres between fiction and the relation to the world, ranging from the most simple exemplary forms of fable, parable, anecdote, joke, fairy tale through the middle forms of novella, short story, and conte to the grand formations of the novel and historiographic writing, with their distinctive formal principles, structures of relevance, pragmatic goals, and modes of reference to the world. This infinite multitude of forms is matched by a scaling of conceptual processing, starting from the stereotypes of pulp fiction with their transparent structure to the most avant-guardistic experiments of narration to the figures of hypothetic formations of experience. More than any other form of text formations, narration serves orientation to Being-in-the-world, as Heidegger in *Being and Time* refers to the way that the world opens up as a *Lebenswelt* for a person.

Between the trivial, mechanic stereotypes and the play with border possibilities lies the broad field of narrative formations of experience that still largely escape unnoticed by literary scholars, even though it would be especially suitable for showing the significant historical differences in molding experience as this is mediated in narration. There is a correspondence between the infinite plasticity of man following his distinctive cultural features, but also his individual inclinations – not least the specific character of different stages of life –

---

5   Hayden White, *Metahistory: The Historical Imagination in Nineteenth-century Europe*. (Baltimore: Johns Hopkins, 1973).

and the infinite plasticity of narration and thus the never-ending training [Einübung] of Being-in-the-world in ever new ways.

However, there still remains the question of whether the form of narrative molding of experience can possibly be valid in a world that changes with an inconceivable rapidity following new insights in science and technology. Might this world not have become principally unavailable to narration; could not the narrative mode be bound to a past state of the world? This is the conception proposed by Walter Benjamin in his great essay "Der Erzähler" (The Narrator). In view of the horrors of the First World War, whose horrors do not outweigh the horrors of the wars to come later, Benjamin pinpoints the appearance of a tendency that had already been long incoming: the hollowing of experience in the modern world:

> With the world war a phenomenon started to make its appearance that has not ceased since. Had one not noticed after the end of the war that people came back dumb stricken from the frontier? Not richer – poorer in experiences that could be mediated to others. What flowed into the war books ten years later was everything else, but the experience passed from mouth to mouth. And this was no surprise. Never had the lessons of experience been proved so completely wrong as the strategic experience of the war in the trenches, the economic ones by inflation, the corporeal ones by through mass battles, the moral ones by those exercising power.[6]

The *nouveau roman*, and still more the *nouveau nouveau roman* actually made an attempt to get rid of the narrative schema and explore new forms of molding experience [Erfahrungsbildung]. Actually it has become apparent that the efforts to break the narrative schema have been unsuccessful and that those of the nouveaux romans – that can no longer actually still retain the privilege of being 'new' – have to a great extent been able to resist the aging which combined their new dimension with some of the traditional modes of narrative moulding of experience. Whereas a gigantic industry of information that already covers our planet is exploding the world into an infinite mass of incoherent details, the form-giving of experience through narration is more necessary than ever. Even if the new experimental form of narration has immensely enlarged the field of narrative forms, the laws of remembering that give form to the possibility of narration are still valid. Thus the narrative forms have not lost their pragmatic function.

In a world that has lost its faith in the stability of form, formlessness is not yet the final word. Even though the idea of substantial forms cannot have validity any longer, form itself is an inevitable fiction that belongs to the cluster of the indispensable, essential fictions without which no social coherence is possible. Communication cannot be replaced by suspicion. Even in modernity, and late modernity, the world remains a world available to narration, at least as long as trust in our own mode of Being-in-the-world remains. The paradigm of narration might, together with its frontiers, come closer to other discursive formations, especially the essay and description and also the complex modes of lyrical texts, but this does not shake up the trust in the power of the narrative schema to organize the *Lebenswelt* and thus to make the world available to narration. The world's potential for narration [die Erzählbarkeit der Welt] is part of the innermost nature of the cultural world and belongs to what one might call the anthropological fundamentals. The availability of the

---

6   Walter Benjamin. *Gesammelte Schriften, vol. II.* Ed. Rolf Tiedemann and Hermann Schweppenhäuser (Frankfurt am Main: Suhrkamp, 1980), p. 230.

world for narration [die Erzählbarkeit der Welt] is, like justice or property, an inevitable fiction which offers a basis for the social world as constituted in the imaginary.[7]

Translated by Liisa Saariluoma

---

[7] Due to technical reasons this essay is almost without footnotes. The last passage is inspired by Cornelius Castoriadis' *L'institution imaginaire de la société* (Paris: Seuil, 1975). Part of my arguments refer to previous papers: "Geschichte als Exemplum, Exemplum als Geschichte" in *Geschichte / Ereignis und Erzählung* (Munich: Fink); "Erfahrung und narrative Form" in *Theorie und Erzählung in der Geschichte* (Munich: Deutscher Taschenbuchverlag, 1979); and "Das Beben des Bewußtseins. Die narrative Struktur von Kleists *Das Erdbeben in Chili*" in *Positionen der Literaturwissenschaft* (Munich: Beck, 1985).

CHAPTER 6

Matti Hyvärinen

Life as Sequence and Narrative: Hayden White Meets Paul Auster

Hayden White, in his *Content of the Form*, poses the question of my article: "Does the world really present itself to perception in the form of well-made stories, with central subject, proper beginning, middles, and ends, and a coherence that permits us to see "the end" in every beginning? Or does it present itself more in the forms that the annals and chronicles suggest, either as a mere sequence without beginning or end, or as sequences that only terminate and never conclude?"[1]

In posing this question, White clearly has "historiography" and "literature" in mind as his paradigmatic examples of narrative. In a similar way, Paul Ricouer's program in his *Time and Narrative*[2] was to find common ground for narrative theory between these two broad categories of narrative. Between literature and historiography there still resides the huge terrain of personal or ordinary narratives: from stories we tell about daily events and happenstances to personal histories and life stories. Radical narrativists who argue for a strong continuity between "life," "experience" and "narrative," typically take these personal stories as primary example of narrative in their theorizing.[3] However large the difference between these two perspectives on narrative might seem to be, it is worth noticing that when Hayden White talks about how "world" presents itself to us the narrativists prefer to discuss the relationship between "life" and "narrative." I will return to some implications of this difference in terms at the end of my article.

Agreeing with the narrativists, I find the third category of narratives relevant if we are to say anything about the "real" experience of life. Yet I am not sure if the phenomenological theorizing on "our" experience of time, music, and life is enough to cover the whole track from the experience of temporality to "world" as a narrative.[4] If you ask *my* intuitions, I can

---

[1]   Hayden White, *The Content of the Form. Narrative Discourse and Historical Representation* (Baltimore and London: The Johns Hopkins University Press, 1987), p. 24.

[2]   Paul Ricoeur, *Time and Narrative, I-III*. Transl. by Kathleen McLaughlin and David Pellauer (Chicago and London: The University of Chicago Press, 1984, 1985, 1988). In his *Oneself as Another*, translated by Kathleen Blamey (The University of Chicago Press, 1992), Ricoeur discusses more thoroughly the relationship between "semantics of action" and narrative.

[3]   Within this group, I include primarily Alasdair MacIntyre, David Carr and Stephen Crites. See: Alasdair MacIntyre, *After Virtue. A Study of Moral Philosophy*. Second Edition (Notre Dame, Indiana: Notre Dame University Press, 1984/1991); David Carr, *Time, Narrative, and History* (Indianapolis: Indiana University Press, 1986); Stephen Crites, "The Narrative Quality of Experience." In Hinchman, Lewis P & Hinchman, Sandra K. (eds.), *Memory, Identity, Community. The Idea of Narrative in the Human Sciences* (Albany, NY: State University of New York Press, 1997).

[4]   David Carr's structure of argumentation in *Time, Narrative, and History* is telling in this issue. He begins with the temporal structure of "passive" experience, proceeds to show the teleological and narrative aspect of simple acts ("serving in tennis"). He shows how everyday life is full of storytelling. In a way, he is truly convincing in showing how much narrative structuring there is in everyday life. But instead of "world" or "human

easily accept both of the opposing understandings and still feel uncomfortable. To proceed to more of a concrete discussion, I take Paul Auster as my co-theorist of narrative and read his work, both as a thought experiment and as empirical material to discuss "life as se-quence" and "life as narrative."

There is no question that the issues of living out a narrative and living without a narra-tive permeate Auster's work, both fiction and interviews. Auster trusts in stories and it is stories he wants to tell in his books: "When I write, the story is always uppermost in my mind, and I feel that everything must be sacrificed to it. All the elegant passages, all the curious details, all the so-called beautiful writing..."[5] To put it another way, Auster does not take story only as a *form* to be experimented with, but as an obvious and recurrent *theme* of his books. Yet, if we need to take the next key concept abounding in his work it apparently would be "chance." His novels seldom portray "a concept of a self whose unity resides in the unity of a narrative which links birth to life to death as narrative beginning to middle to end."[6] Instead of this unity, he sees the fragments. "Like everyone else, his [A's] life is so fragmented that each time he sees a connection between two fragments he is tempted to look for a meaning in that connection. The connection exists. But to give it a meaning, to look beyond the bare fact of its existence, would be to build an imaginary world inside the real world, and he knows it would not stand."[7] Stories, yes, but not the smoothly storied, continuous existence David Carr and Alasdair MacIntyre want to theo-rize.

In all his emphasis on story, Auster seems suddenly very close to White. "In philosophi-cal terms, I'm talking about the powers of contingency. Our lives don't really belong to us, you see – they belong to the world, and in spite of our efforts to make sense of it, the world is a place beyond our understanding."[8] We are clearly back in Hayden White's world.

But why resort to literary fiction in the first place? Why not go to the "real" persons and listen to their stories, as proper social scientists should do? For one thing, actual life stories seldom register such moments of change of story which Auster is keen to study: the hegem-ony of current perspective and current story often blurs the moments when earlier stories break down and new ones emerge. In comparison with philosophical ponderings, Auster is more empirical; in comparison with empirical life stories, his work is more fictional and philosophical.

In what follows, I proceed by looking for moments when Auster's main characters are (or at least come close to) experiencing their world in the form of sequence, and their life without a narrative. What can we learn from these moments? Which parts of the story and the character's life do they constitute?

plurality," he subsequently introduces the historical "we persons," again with joint objectives, shared histories and traditions of storytelling.
5 Paul Auster, *The Art of Hunger: Essays, Prefaces, Interviews* (Harmondsworth: Penguin, 1997), p. 283.
6 MacIntyre, *After Virtue*, p. 205. *City of Glass*, for example, has most often been characterized as a book about multiple and changing identities. See William Lavender, "The Novel of Critical Engagement: Paul Auster's City of Glass," in Harold Bloom (ed.): *Bloom's Modern Critical Views* (Philadeplphia: Chelsea House, 2004); and, Stephen Bernstein, "The Question is the Story Itself. Postmodernism and Intertextuality in Auster's *New York Trilogy*," in Patricia Merivale & Susan Elizabeth Sweeney (eds.), *Detecting Texts. The Metaphysical De-tective Story from Poe to Postmodernism* (Philadelphia: University of Pennsylvania Press, 1999).
7 Paul Auster, *The Invention of Solitude* (Harmondsworth: Penguin, 1988), p. 147.
8 Auster, *The Art of Hunger*, p. 289.

The walking eye

City of Glass is a book about multiple personalities and change of identity. The story resists the unity of life by way of introducing radically new storylines to live on. In the beginning, the main character Mr. Quinn writes detective stories under the pen name of William Wilson, before he by chance decides to impersonate detective Paul Auster, in order to become himself like his previous hero Max Work. The fact of writing detective stories is by no means marginal, quite the contrary. Quinn thinks, echoing Paul Auster himself, that "in the good mystery there is nothing wasted, no sentence, no word that is not significant."[9] Mystery stories - the world of significance and center.

Before the story really gets started, the narrator gives a short background account of Quinn's prior life, in a rather suppressed and matter-of-fact style. Like: "We know that he had once been married, had once been a father, and that both his wife and son were now dead."[10] We learn that Quinn had since left his friends, and no one but his agent knew the identity of William Wilson.[11] Earlier, he had been a more ambitious writer, but he had left all of it behind. Quite casually, it is mentioned that "he did not sleep with the lamp on anymore" and that he did not "think about his son very much anymore."[12] How did he live, then? By writing his mystery books, reading, looking at paintings. But the most important part of his life was walking. And here, I think, we come close to the experience of sequence:

> More than anything else, however, what he liked to do was walk (…) New York was an inexhaustible space, a labyrinth of endless steps, and no matter how far he walked, no matter how well he came to know its neighborhoods and streets, it always left him with the feeling of being lost. Lost, not only in the city, but within himself as well.[13]

This condition of being lost, however, is not a problem, it is the very reason for walking:

> Each time he took a walk, he felt as though he were leaving himself behind, and by giving himself up to the movement of the streets, by reducing himself to a seeing eye, he was able to escape the obligation to think, and this, more than anything else, brought him a measure of peace, a salutary emptiness within. (…) By wandering aimlessly, all places became equal and it no longer mattered where he was. On his best walks, he was able to feel that he was nowhere. And this, finally, was all he asked of things: to be nowhere.[14]

All places became equal, so there was no trace of the significance a good mystery book provided with every word. There was no plan, and a view here did not anticipate or prefigure some later space. This means that the whole vocabularies of action and thought are re-

9   Paul Auster, *City of Glass. The New York Trilogy* (London: Faber and Faber, 1987), p. 8.
10   Ibid, p. 3.
11   As often noticed, the name comes from Edgar Allan Poe, and hints at doubled personality. Aliki Varvogli has written one of the most systematic presentations of Auster's legacies in his *The World that is the Book. Paul Auster's Fiction* (Liverpool: Liverpool University Press, 2001). See also Stephen Bernstein, "The Question is the Story Itself."
12   Auster, *City of Glass*, p. 5.
13   Ibid, pp. 3-4.
14   Ibid, p. 4.

placed by motion and behavior: "Motion was the essence, the act of putting one foot in front of the other and allowing himself to follow the drift of his body."[15]

Quite obviously, Auster outlines here a moment without narrative, a moment when the world indeed presents itself in the form of casual sequence[16]. Undoubtedly, this exceptional state of mind is a relief to Quinn, and he keenly looks for it. The other thing, however, is that this state of oblivion is far from easy to reach, let alone automatically available. Getting rid of narrative meant for Quinn nothing less than "leaving himself behind" and being lost "within himself" as well. To see the world just as a sequence implicates a radical loss of selfhood, and it is looked for precisely in order to leave the self and his own history behind. One reason for these exercises is the loss of his wife and son, the original trauma that is never elaborated in so many words, but which crops up, painfully, and is repeatedly referred to in the story.

Traumatic loss frames several of Auster's stories: take the air crash in *The Book of Illusions*, the disappearance of a brother in *In the Country of Last Things*, to name just a few. As a child, the hero of *Mr. Vertigo* was found on the streets of Saint Louis, as an orphan, because he was "no better than an animal" and "a piece of human nothingness," as his future teacher and mentor had it.[17] In *Moon Palace*, the young Marco Stanley Fogg is knocked off of the balance by the sudden death of his Uncle Victor, the last known member of his family. After Victor's funeral, Marco realizes that his funds will not take him properly past his college education. He ponders what to do, and comes to the conclusion: "I decided that the thing I should do was nothing: my action would consist of a militant refusal to take any action at all."[18] Like Quinn, he chooses to tell friends complex lies to hide the actual state of affairs. Step by step, stubbornly avoiding any self-generated initiative towards earning and surviving, he loses contacts to his friends. It is a story of obsession, echoing Knut Hamsun's *Hunger*, a book about which Auster wrote an appreciative essay in 1970.[19] Auster characterizes Hamsun's artist tellingly: "He loses everything – even himself."[20] The beginning of *Moon Palace* concerns similar disappearance:

> …the future stood before me as a blank, a white page of uncertainty. If life was a story, as Uncle Victor had often told me, and each man was the author of his own story, then I was making it up as I went along. I was working without a plot, writing each sentence as it came to me and refusing to think about the next. All well and good, perhaps, but the question was no longer whether I could write the story off the top of my head. I had already done that. The question was what I was supposed to do when the pen ran out of ink.[21]

---

[15]   Ibid, p. 4.

[16]   Walking is a recurrent theme in Auster. In *The Invention of Solitude,* p. 122, for instance, journeys "are equivalent to mental movements, an walking becomes actualization of cognition itself," as Tim Woods has it. Even more than Woods, I would emphasize the *different* functions and *different* forms of walking in Auster's work. Tim Woods: "Looking for Signs in the Air": Urban Space and the Postmodern, in Dennis Barone (ed.), *Beyond the Red Notebook. Essays on Paul Auster* (Philadephia: University of Pensylvania Press, 1995), pp. 105-128.

[17]   Paul Auster, *Mr Vertigo* (London and Boston: Faber and Faber , 1994), p. 3.

[18]   Paul Auster, *Moon palace* (Harmondsworth: Penguin, 1989), pp. 20-21.

[19]   Auster, *Art of Hunger*, pp. 9-20.

[20]   Ibid, p. 14.

[21]   Auster, *Moon Palace*, pp. 41-42.

"If life was a story." With these few words Auster invites a whole range of theoretical is-sues. But even the keenest of subscribers to this idea would hesitate with what follows: "…and each man was the author of his own story." MacIntyre agrees only partially here: "Now I must emphasize…the fact that we are never more (and sometimes less) than the co-authors of our own narratives."[22] Paul Ricoeur leaves Uncle Victor's company even earlier. He agrees that "we are justified in speaking of life as a story in its nascent state, and so of life as an *activity and a passion in search of a narrative*."[23] Yet, it is about here that Ri-coeur wants to draw the line. By way of reading literature, he says, "we learn to become the *narrator* and the hero of our own story, without actually becoming the *author of our own life*."[24] Perhaps Uncle Victor's thought was just a popularized version of David Carr's search for authorship.[25]

Fogg the narrator accepts the metaphor of life as a story, at least ironically, but only to stretch it to its utmost extreme. Fogg the character rejects the idea of a plot; he resists other intentions than not to act, not to do anything with his life. He no longer "lives out" his story in the sense MacIntyre uses the term; he rather resembles a secretary who perfunctorily writes down every sentence of his life at the moment of its occurrence. There is not much left of a temporal structure of life, there is only the passive acceptance of any moment as it comes. In this form the story seems to be little more than fictive re-presentation: "I was making it up as I went along". Even this fictional function was at risk due to the material conundrum: the ink of the pen was running out, he was at the verge of disappearing.

If it is true that Fogg fought against emplotment and intention, does it mean that he re-ceived his life in the form of a sequence? Explanations, theories, and newspaper stories still swirled in his mind. But even these ideas, emotions, and great vision seem to surface co-incidentally, as in a serial or sequential manner, not as a part of an intentional thought, ac-tion, or narrative. Finding daily sustenance and shelter sustained his story's short-term in-tentionality and momentum. It was only when his "head was particularly blank" that he found pleasure in "dull and obsessive games," as the older narrator Fogg has it: "Counting the number of people who passed a given spot, for example, or cataloguing faces according to which animals they resembled…."[26] Even these "dull and obsessive games" were only temporary experiences, and organized themselves through sheer obsession. Eliminating plot and intention was not yet enough to arrive at the full experience of life as sequence.

In both of these novels, the state without a story was occasioned by trauma, despair, and obsession. The trauma made the earlier story too heavy a burden to live on as such, too full of painful memories to think about. The eclipse of story helps neither Quinn nor Fogg out of his dilemma, but in both cases it precedes the change of storyline. Yet it is not that the traumatic experience, as such, had pushed them into this storyless state; instead, both of them had to decide first - and then focus on the obsessive project. In both cases, the state included withdrawal from the vocabulary of action, intention, and communication. What-ever these moments are, they are neither automatic, general, nor routine.

---

[22] MacIntyre, *After Virtue*, p. 213.
[23] Paul Ricoeur, "Life in Quest of Narrative." In David Wood (ed.), *On Paul Ricoeur*, London and New York: Routledge (1991), p.29.
[24] Ibid, p. 32, italics by Ricoeur.
[25] Carr, *Time, Narrative, and History*, pp. 82-92.
[26] Auster, Moon palace, p. 63.

World as a sequence

Both Quinn and Fogg had chosen to shut out storied life. In Auster's *In the Country of Last Things*, this setting changes entirely: now it is the enormous push of the surrounding world that makes living out narratives a difficult and dangerous business. Anna Blume has left for this odd country by the last charity ship that ever went there, in order to search for and bring back her brother William, who went there earlier as a journalist and disappeared.[27]

The outlook of the city where Anna has landed is dismal: "These are the last things. A house is there one day, and the next day it is gone. A street you walked down yesterday is no longer there. Even the weather is in constant flux."[28]

This picture may lead to the conclusion that the book would characterize dystopia. This is the option that Auster himself has openly rejected; he insists that the book is entirely about 20th-century history.[29] The siege of Leningrad, the Warsaw Ghetto, Cairo, and contemporary New York are the closest references. Rather than a dystopia, the novel "in many ways resembles a fairy-tale," as Aliki Varvogli[30] puts it. But just like the tales of the Brothers Grimm, the tale has its darker shades: "When you live in the city, you learn to take nothing for granted. Close your eyes for a moment, turn around to look at something else, and then the thing that was before you is suddenly gone."[31]

These few words outline a world reigned by contingency-as-dependency. This has almost nothing to do with the chance-as-opportunity that is often found in Auster's work in the form of a windfall or a new identity.[32] Hunger, for example, is a constant element of life in the city. Nothing new is produced, thus the city resembles a huge but crumpling recycling system, in which burning the dead is one of the few remaining profitable enterprises.

These conditions of life shift the balance among planning, intention, and observation, respectively. Constant alertness is a necessity of life, and quite surprisingly it seems to require a similar denial of narrative that Quinn and Fogg had experienced. Once, Anna had a friend, Isabel, who told her how to survive on the streets:

> We didn't do much talking in the streets, however. That was the danger Isabel warned me against many times. Never think anything, she said. No musings; no sadness or happiness; no anything but the street, all empty inside, concentrating only on the next step you are about to take.[33]

If Quinn and Anna were observers of the sequence on the streets, they performed this task for different reasons and in different states of mind. Quinn and Fogg looked for the bliss of preoccupation, a luxury which could have killed Anna in no time. For Quinn, no place mattered more than any other; for Anna, every single place and view could make all the difference. Quinn and Fogg struggled out of the story; Anna had to resist the story to struggle for life.

---

[27] Paul Auster, *In the Country of Last Things* (Harmondsworth: Penguin, 1988).

[28] Ibid, p.1.

[29] Auster, *Art of Hunger*, p. 320.

[30] Vbarvogli, *The World that is the Book*, p. 75.

[31] Auster, *In the Country*, pp. 1-2.

[32] See Maureen Whitebrook, Identity, Narrative and Politics (London and New York: Routledge, 2001), pp. 87-100.

[33] Auster, *In the Country*, p. 57.

It is no wonder then that there is nothing of politics proper in the *Country*. People are too starved, too focused on their next step, too keen on the next meal. Facing this surge of occurrences, Anna finds herself incapable of acting. This has a paradoxical consequence: "Because you cannot act, you find yourself unable to think."[34] For Auster, politics, action and narrative belong to the same vocabulary. It is thus chilling to find out that losing this narrative vocabulary and storied thread of life also implicates a loss of one's very ability to think. But alas, the idea is too convincing: facing the continual chaos of the surroundings, feeling the impact of contingency as a series of unrelated occurrences leaves scant prospects for organizing thought.

Anna's letter is an attempt to capture something of the chaos of the city, or as it were, of the perception of the world as sheer sequence. At the beginning, Anna indeed has a clear plot in mind: go and find William, take him home. But she never finds a trace of him. Not only has the editorial office disappeared, but the whole street and whole neighborhood is demolished, leaving just rubble. Eventually, even the last fragment of the storyline is lost: after Isabel's death Anna decides to return home anyway, only to realize that the city is blockaded by the *Sea Wall Project*, and no one is allowed out. The end of the story: "I had to give up the idea of going home."[35]

But it is too early to suppose that the city was entirely devoid of stories, quite the contrary. Even if the storied life has mostly disappeared, the ideological representations of city life abound. For example, Anna learns that an epidemic had hit the area where William's office had been. The city government had intervened, blocked the area and burned it down. Anna continues, however, that there is no way of knowing if there is any truth in this story, because:

> It's not that people make a point of lying to you, it's just that where the past is concerned, the truth tends to get obscured rather quickly. Legends crop up within a matter of hours, tall tales circulate, and the facts are soon buried under a mountain of outlandish theories.[36]

Ideological stories, unreliable stories, tall tales spread in the city. They are oddly independent and self-referential stories: there is no way of checking how reliable they are, and they do not point to any particular narrator. Then there are stories Anna rejects outright. The small, escapist sects of the city each nourish some sort of peculiar story. "But when hope disappears, when you find that you have given up hoping even the possibility of hope, you tend to fill the empty space with dreams, little childlike thoughts and stories to keep you going."[37]

It is here that Anna reminds "you", the reader of her letter, how she used to tell stories as a kid, how important the stories were then. A cruel paradox grows out of the names of the childhood stories: *The Castle of No Return*, *The Land of Sadness*, *The Forest of Forgotten Words*. Something went wrong, and now she is in the Country of Last Things, an odd combination of these old stories. Here, her attitude is clear: "Now I am all common sense

---

[34]   Ibid, p. 20
[35]   Ibid, p. 89.
[36]   Ibid, p. 18.
[37]   Ibid, p. 9.

and hard calculation. I don't want to be like others. I see what their imaginings do to them, and I will not let that happen to me."[38] (op. cit., 11)

Within this episode, Anna's hard calculation is contrasted with the wishing sessions, the storytelling of her childhood, and her imagining. Imagining, as Marshall Gregory points out, is one of the major effects of narrative.[39] The disappearance of the world of stories does not only implicate the narrowing down of empathy and compassion, it also cuts the possibilities of action due to the limited sphere of understanding: "First-hand experience is too slow, too limited, too repetitive, and too monotonous."[40] This picture aptly characterizes Anna's situation in her solitary struggle with the anything-but-monotonous city. Without ordering narratives, the all-embracing chaos and contingency threatens to make life just a repetition, both repetition of alertness and repetition of reactions.

However much Anna feels like having evolved into a state of hard calculation and common sense, she is far from being protected from her world by it. Gregory's triad of detail, image and story work its effect on Anna in the streets. The problem is that one cannot just observe at and remain coolly outside of what one sees. What is it to see a dead child on the street? In contrast to all of her manifest purposes, Anna creates an image, a detailed image of a dead girl, "crushed and covered with blood": "That is what I mean by being wounded: you cannot merely see, for each thing somehow belongs to you, is part of the story unfolding inside you."[41]

There is still *the story unfolding inside you*. The world may indeed present itself to perception in the form of chaotic sequence, but the last remains of humanity, after all common sense and hard calculation, keep working to find and tell a new story.

The Historiography of the Last Things

The conditions of the *Country* attack the possibilities and the whole sphere of narrative in a number of ways. Things, streets, and people are not the only entities that disappear. Memories and words disappear as well. When Anna finds out that there are no more ships out of the city, she asks about airplanes. The city official does not understand her question at all, and asks her to explain what she is talking about:

> That's ridiculous, he said, giving me a suspicious kind of look. There's no such thing. It's impossible. Don't you remember? I asked. I don't know what you're talking about, he said. You could get into trouble for spreading such kind of nonsense.[42]

The crumbling of collective memory, and the whole sphere of collectively shared stories helps the work of the government. The ideology is to forget, neither to remember nor to tell about the past. The world where words and memories disappear, of course, has nothing to do with the worlds spirited by strong traditions and collective narratives, outlined by MacIntyre and Carr. Neither, however, do these horrific conditions of life ground the leftist

---

[38]   Ibid, p. 11.
[39]   Marshall Gregory, "The Sound of Story: Narrative, Memory, and Selfhood". *Narrative, Vol. 3*, No 1, January 1995, p. 36.
[40]   Ibid, p. 48.
[41]   Auster, *In the Country*, p.19.
[42]   Ibid., p. 87.

criticism of narrative as suspicious ideology.[43] As Hayden White has it in his recent work, by unmistakably revising his earlier position: "Therefore, it is absurd to suppose that, because a historical discourse is cast in the form of narrative, it must be mythical, fictional, substantially imaginary, or otherwise 'unrealistic' in what it tells us about the world."[44] In the absence narratives, the inhabitants of the *Country* are devoid of the necessary tools to understand or to resist.

One day, Anna escapes a food riot, and ends up in the National Library. There she tries two locked doors in vain, while she manages to open the third, as often happens in fairy tales. To her surprise, she finds a group of Jewish men sitting in a room. The gate to a new story opens up from a surreal but familiar discussion:

> "I thought that all Jews were dead," I whispered.
> "There are a few of us left," he said, smiling at me again. "It's not so easy to get rid of us, you know."
> "I'm Jewish, too," I blurted out.[45]

After Isabel's death, this is the first friendly exchange of words. It is this exceptional quality of conversation which creates the feeling of sanctuary. The fact of being a Jew never meant anything on the streets. It is as if Anna suddenly rediscovers her past identity.

With the help of these men, Anna meets Samuel Farr, the journalist who was sent to look for William, but even Sam has no information on William. However, he had not given up his calling as a journalist: he interviews the inhabitants in order to write a history of the "Troubles," as these hard times are called. Sam has over three thousand pages of notes for the book, and a plan to get the "preliminary work" done in five or six months, except that his funds are about to finish. Anna decides, in her matter-of-fact style, to stay with him, share her money with him and to work as his secretary. Soon they also share a bed, and she falls in love with him.

At first the book project was an obstacle for Anna and her common sense. Sam will get himself killed before the book is ready, she reckons, thus there are thousands of better ways of using the remaining money. Who will read the book anyway? Sam thinks differently: "I can't stop. The book is the only thing that keeps me going. It prevents me from thinking about myself and getting sucked up into my own life."[46]

Sam has the Austerian obsession: he has to write his book whatever the practical problems, and he will take his manuscript back home and get it published. The unfinished manuscript is thus the very script of his life. Sam is the exceptional person who is not only behaving, but acting and working as well. As time goes on, Anna comes to understand this point, because "Sam's book became the most important thing in my life. As long as we kept working on it, I realized, the notion of a possible future would continue to exist for us."[47]

As for the debates on narrative, this setting is ironic enough. Sam and Anna are working on the oral history of the *Country*. Indeed, oral histories "are not lived" and "[s]tories are

[43]   Richard Kearney refers by the term to authors like Benjamin, Barthes and Baudrillard, in contrast to right-wing critics like Harold Bloom. In Kearney, *On Stories* (London and New York: Routledge, 2002), p. 10.

[44]   Hayden White, *Figural Realism. Studies in the Mimesis Effect* (Baltimore and London: The Johns Hopkins University Press, 1999), p. 22.

[45]   Auster, *In the Country*, p. 95.

[46]   Ibid, p. 104.

[47]   Ibid, p. 114.

told or written, not found," as White has it[48]. But collecting and writing these stories grants Sam and Anna a new future and a new storyline to live on. Perhaps we can go as far as saying that Anna really *finds* a story, Sam's story, when she gradually begins to understand the role of the project. But I am not sure if there is any point to emhasize that this story would be more "real" than stories in general: it was not a story as a thing, out there, autonomously living and working its way slowly forward. But it was a story that organized Sam's and Anna's life, a story that gave meaning to what they were doing – writing a book about a *Country* that was not the least bit interested in history any longer. Before this story, there was not much meaning left in Anna's life, which – up until the time she met Sam - was just a struggle for survival.

Thus writing the impossible book in the impossible situation marks a new beginning. Anna is acting again, not just reacting. Those were the happiest days of her whole life, as she recounts this period of her life in the letter. Serving both as an image and as a highlight of the exceptionality of their joint project, Anna becomes pregnant. Anna has never seen either children or pregnant women in the whole city, which had long ago lost its fertility, the capacity to create anything new.

But there is no escaping back into MacIntyre's secure teleological world, where people have the right to properly live out their narratives, either with or without contingencies. Isabel's most crucial advice for behavior on the streets was to never think anything, never to have any feelings. But now Anna is happy and she is slipping away from the hard realities into her and Sam's joint story. Then, happy to solve a practical problem, she allows herself to be conned into entering a human slaughterhouse. She just barely survives, throwing herself through a window, but loses her baby.

To make matters worse, a fire breaks out in the library. The whole manuscript of Sam's book is destroyed, and Anna cannot get any information about him or his fate after her own recovery. This is a tough reminder of Auster's philosophy of life: our lives do not belong to us, they belong to the world. It is the world that tests, crushes, or elevates the storied projects that people live out. To what extent normal everyday life is ever storied or organized by a narrative order, as Carr and MacIntyre have it, the world is not storied.

Still, Anna has luck. She is found by a private charity, and receives shelter and care in their hospital, recovers slowly, and later on starts working for the same Woburn House. Again, the whole rationale of charity work is challenged by Anna as an empty gesture in the face of this sea of misery. Why give people food, temporary shelter, and understanding – indeed to teach them to behave carelessly – and then push them back into the city without the requisite harshness they needed to survive there? As it turns out, Sam eventually walks into the place in a very poor condition, but recovers. At the end of the book, the day comes when all of the resources of the charity operation are exhausted, and the small remaining group plans to escape the city by car. Everything is ready, and they can leave any morning.

Since the fire, Anna's letter is the only document witnessing the city. No grand and all-encompassing historiography seems to be possible. Anna's reasons for writing are not clear even to herself, beyond the fact that accounting for her condition became a necessity.[49] Anna had bought a notebook for Isabel, who was not able to speak by that time any more.

---

[48]   White, *Figural Realism*, p. 9.
[49]   Auster, *In the Country*, p. 3.

Quite by chance, Anna finds the notebook in the Woburn House and starts writing down her letter. This record is unreliable, or thoroughly uninformed: [50]

> I've been trying to fit everything in, trying to get to the end before it's too late, but I see how badly I've deceived myself. Words do not allow such things. The closer you come to the end, the more there is to say. The end is only imaginary, a destination you invent to keep yourself going, but a point comes when you realize you will never go there.[51]

The end is imaginary, she is sure, but still she is not giving up. Anna's letter is a testimony of dark times and finished at night. We are again at the crossroads of hard calculation, wishful thinking and necessity to act anyway. She does not believe the letter will ever reach "you," and yet she cannot stop writing. Aliki Varvogli renders the letter as a journal: "Anna's journal/letter becomes not only a document of this desolation [of the city], but also a means of survival, a way of maintaining her humanity amidst the corruption of every value she grew up with."[52] Somehow this estimate misses the point, the unreliability of the document. Anna found the notebook just weeks or days before the end of story.[53] She was already living safely in the Woburn House with Sam when she started the notebook, about three years after arriving in the *Country*. This is a far cry from a daily journal. Neither is her life any more the bare hard calculation of the streets, thus she is able to find the relevance of her story. It is no longer Sam's story she is living for, it is her own story. Rather than maintaining, she is regaining her humanity and her capacity to act.

There is a parallel between Sam's book and Anna's letter. Sam interviewed people to write his book, and Anna's work in Woburn House consists of interviewing the newcomers. As a matter of fact, she got all the needed background information within a few minutes. However, "[T]hey all wanted to tell me their stories, and I had no choice but to listen. It was a different story every time, and yet each story was the same."[54]

Give them a safe place, a break from the chaos of the streets, and people start telling their stories. The problem fall as in therapy, on the one who bears to listen to all of them. The streets are a hazardous place to live out such stories, but the hard life out there creates an intense and overwhelming need to express them at the first opportunity.

How does all of this reflect back upon the original question about observing the world? Anna is indeed observing the *Country* in the form of a sequence: "Our lives are no more than the sum of manifold contingencies."[55] But this is also a world of horror which robs one of any decent chances for acting and thinking. It is quite evident that the world does not present itself in the form of "well-made stories, with central subject, proper beginning, middles, and ends, and a coherence that permits us to see 'the end' in every beginning," as White puts it ironically.

In criticizing "theorists like Mink and White," David Carr argued that their problem "is not that they postulate the possibility of such meaningless sequence, but that they turn things upside down: they place it at the heart of human experience, giving us as sad and

---

[50] The concept comes from Dorrit Cohn, "Discordant Narration.." *Style, Summer 200, Vol. 34*, Issue 2.
[51] Auster, *In the Country*, p. 183.
[52] Varvogli, *The World that is the Book*, p. 89..
[53] Auster, *In the Country*, p.182.
[54] Ibid, p. 143.
[55] Ibid, p. 143.

depressing (and inaccurate) picture of human reality as we can imagine."[56] At first sight, Anna Blume could easily be put to in the company of Mink and White. The second notion might be about phenomenological universalism, "the heart of human experience" and "human reality" versus the *Country* as a *historical* picture of some of the most problematic moments of the 20th century.

Yet Anna Blume is resolute in taking every opportunity to escape the horrors of the *Country*. Here, indeed, the stories that are not only told but lived out mark her way to human contact, trust, and action. Stories with Isabel, the book with Sam, the whole history of Woburn House, the letter to "you," and finally the plan to escape the *Country* are all narrative projects, with the purpose of creating a meaningful storyline to live on. As an agent, Anna senses a huge pull towards the teleological world of MacIntyre and Carr, as a sceptic, full of common sense and hard calculation, she resists the seductive image of believing in such a world. She is such an optimistic figure precisely because she is able to act and take the initiative, in spite of her meager trust in teleology.

Opposing White, I believe that there is a remarkable sense in using the idiom "living out narratives." Quinn, Fogg and Anna Blume each have shown how difficult it is to eliminate the storylines to be lived out. Opposing MacIntyre, I would acknowledge the fragmentary and changeable character of these narratives: there is no way of living out the world or contingency. Even though a plethora of narratives is lived out all the time, it does not make these stories "true" or "real" from the perspective of historiography. Stories are decisive for action, and they indeed have been around a while before any historiographer begins his or her work. "We are justified in speaking of life as a story in its nascent state, and so of life as an *activity and passion in search of* a narrative," as Paul Ricoeur has it.[57]

With her last words, the sceptic and non-believer Anna Blume is still giving a promise, stretching her hand and words towards the future:

> Anything is possible, and that is almost the same as nothing, almost the same as being born into a world that has never existed before. Perhaps we will find William after we leave the city, but I try not to hope too much. The only thing I ask for now is the chance to live one more day. This is Anna Blume, your old friend from another world. Once we get where we are going, I will try to write to you again, I promise.[58]

[56] Carr, *Time, Narrative, and History*, p. 89.
[57] Ricoeur, "Life in Quest of Narrative", p. 29.
[58] Auster, In the Country, p. 188.

III HISTORY AS LITERATURE

Introduction to Part III

History as Literature

The third part of this book includes three studies that, each from their own point of view, challenge the view that histories could be purified from all fictive and rhetorical elements.

In his essay, an Australian writer and artist Andrew Burrell looks at points of interaction between fiction and non-fiction, memory and perception, the collected object and the formation of personal histories. The essay opens and closes with some small sections of narrative that both illuminate and question some of the issues raised within the essay. A brief discussion of some historical fake object, including a missing link and a furry trout, lead into an investigation of the role of the fake as both a narrative device and "character" within Umberto Eco's most recent novel Baudolino. Burrell then returns to analyze the (impossible) attempt to create a single linear narrative of one's own personal history by using the 'fake' to fill in the 'gaps' within a personal narrative.

Fiona McIntosh-Varjabédian studies the literary pattern of vraisemblance that gives shape to the historians' sense of probability. In which cases does the probability or the verisimilitude of an event compete with other standards of judging, such as testimony and material evidence? Are the most violent events in history likely to be untrue just because they are morally improbable or just because they shatter to pieces the historian's mental picture of what the past should be and thus endanger his authority as a narrator? McIntosh-Varjabédian examines the role of probability in the building up of an authoritative figure and its interplay with the classical notion of verisimilitude in 18th-century historical writing (especially Voltaire and David Hume).

"Viewed simply as verbal artifacts, histories and novels are indistinguishable from one another," Hayden White has famously claimed. In her essay, Claire Norton explores the manner in which audiences recognize and construct the fiction/non-fiction or literature/history dichotomy by analyzing the reception of Ottoman accounts of the Habsburg siege of the strategic border castle of Nagykanizsa (1601). The status of these almost identical narratives as fiction or non-fiction, folk stories/literature or history has been constantly contested over the last 400 years. Norton argues that the use of particular narrative strategies and the adherence to various protocols, as constructed by the interpretative community, determine the (non)fictional status of a work rather than its content, its intrinsic nature, or a putative correspondence with reality or the past.

CHAPTER 7

Andrew Burrell

Narratives of the Fake: The Collected Object, Personal Histories and Constructed Memory

> *My brother was under the water, face upturned, eyes open and unconscious, sinking*
> *gently; air was coming out of his mouth.*
> *It was before I was born but I can remember it as clearly as if I saw it...*
> Margaret Atwood, *Surfacing*

Preamble

This paper investigates a few of the diverse areas of interest that have engaged my research in both my artistic and theoretical pursuits. This research weaves together a broad range of elements, creating new ways of looking at, and reading both the philosophical and poetic associations between memory, narrative, collecting and the object.

In my work, the direction of which is shaped by my practice as a new media artist, I have always been interested in positing a range of questions, and addressing these through the juxtaposition of ideas and thoughts – both my own and those of others. This process of interrogation is generally conducted through narrative, especially those narratives which take the forms of memories and personal histories.

In the development of this work I have used the collected object, and the very process of collecting as a metaphor for a way in which personal memory could be seen to work. While this may seem a superficially poetic relationship, the act of collecting is very much tied to the act of remembering. The further I investigate this connection, the more I am convinced that they are explicitly interrelated.

This paper follows the dual narratives of collected object and memory, yet also contains within it the dual narratives of text and notes. The structure of the paper will follow several occurrences of the fake, each in itself a discrete narrative that when combined, may at first appear somewhat disparate, but will slowly come together as the texts of this paper evolve. These narratives, which range from the personal to the historic, could be seen as subjective constructs. Yet as progress through them, we will see that the gaps between subjective and objective perception within these constructs mediate between the blurry edges of what is read as real and what is recognised as being fake. Privilege is not given to any particular form of narrative, each being a fragment of something much larger, with the selection presented being but one of many possible combinations. The reader is invited to take advantage of the opportunity to invoke his or her own understandings between the gaps in these fragments, and bring into play their own autonomy in interpreting what is real and what is fake.[1]

Allow me to begin with a narrative of my own which takes the form of a childhood memory.

Where I recall A Pair of Red Mittens with White Cross-stitch Patterning and a Train Full of Monsters

For some reason, for as long as I can remember, I have had a memory that has constantly played on my mind. I wonder, is it because I have replayed it over and over so many times that it is so vivid, or has it always been so? This memory is somewhat problematic, for, as you will see... it leads me to believe in monsters.

I do believe in monsters! I have to, otherwise I can't trust my own memory, and without a memory that I can believe in, there isn't much point in anything.

Once, when I was very young, my father took me to see a steam train that was going to pass by on the lines at the top of our street. We were quite close to the railway lines, but far enough back to be at a safe distance. I was sitting on my father's shoulders so that I could get a good view. A couple of other people from the street had gathered and the children amongst them all seemed as excited as I was. The sun was behind clouds that day, there was quite a strong wind blowing, and I was wearing red mittens with white cross-stitch patterning. Somebody yelled out "It's coming!" We all looked down the tracks to where a man was pointing. I could see smoke, lots of smoke. A whistle blew, it kept blowing. I was scared. I started to scream. I grabbed onto my father's head and screamed louder. I could see the great, ever increasing pall of smoke getting closer. I drove my fingers into my father's scalp; I could not take my eyes off this terrible, loud, dark thing that was approaching. Then as the smoke enveloped us, and I could see the train itself, I SAW MONSTERS!

That steam train full of monsters is one of my most vivid memories from childhood. Not just one or two monsters, but hundreds of them, all hanging from the side of the train, crawling on its roof, and hanging out of its windows. Each one of them different, each one

---

[1] There is much scholarship that explores the themes presented in this paper, and the reader may be interested in the following selection, which although not extensive, will provide further illumination. For example, the role of the collections acting as an intermediary between the gaps between the tangible and the intangible see, Krzysztof Pomian, *Collectors and Curiosities: Paris and Venice 1500-1800* (Cambridge, U.K. Cambridge, Mass., USA: Polity Press; Basil Blackwell, 1990). For discussions on the relationship between the object, nostalgia and memory see: Susan Stewart, *On Longing: Narratives of the Miniature, the Gigantic, the Souvenir, the Collection* (Durham: Duke University Press, 1993); Celeste Olalquiaga, *The Artificial Kingdom: A Treasury of the Kitsch Experience* (London: Bloomsbury, 1999); and John Boardman, *The Archaeology of Nostalgia: How the Greeks Re-Created Their Mythical Past* (London: Thames and Hudson, 2002). The psychological and emotional impact of this paper's themes is evident in the highly contentious issue of *false-memory*, the debate surrounding which I am but an observer. For a broad discussion of this debate of recent years refer to: Lenore Terr, *Unchained Memories: True Stories of Traumatic Memory Lost and Found* (New York: Basic Books, 1994); Martin A. Conway, *Recovered Memories and False Memories, Debates in Psychology.* (Oxford; New York: Oxford University Press, 1997); and Frederick C. Crews, *The Memory Wars: Freud's Legacy in Dispute* (New York: New York Review of Books, 1995). For a discussion of *false-memory* in memoir see Susan Rubin Suleiman, "Problems of Memory and Factuality in Recent Holocaust Memoirs: Wilkomirski/Wiesel," *Poetics Today* 21, no. 3 (2000). And of course on the narrativization of history, see the work of Hayden White and the scholarship surrounding it, to which this volume is dedicated.

of them nasty and vicious and ready to jump off the train at any moment and eat me or my father.

There were monsters on that train.

I choose to believe this memory, and therefore I choose to believe in monsters. If I were to distrust this memory, then what of the next, and the next, and the one after that? I have come to the conclusion that all memory is true, and if it is not, then no memory is true.

I DO believe in monsters… At least I try very hard to…

A Case of Constructed Memories.

I have often tried to convince people that I can recall my second birthday party. While I know this is obviously not possible (or perhaps it is) I have vivid memories of several very striking images of this event. When these memories are recalled in my mind, they are little more than static and quite fragmentary images – quite probably mnemonic renditions of photographs I have seen, although I have no recollection of actually ever seeing any photographs of this event. I have always assumed that the memories stem from the event itself.

For years, as I was growing up, our glassware cabinet contained a tartan ribbon that was wrapped around an egg painted to look like Humpty Dumpty. Each time I saw this ribbon in the cabinet I would remember the egg sitting on the edge of my birthday cake that was decorated to look like a wall – the very cake that I can remember so well from my second birthday party.

A Case of Fabricated Memories.

In relation to memories which have either no origin in fact and which have been altered through perceptions mediated through a trusted other, Jean Piaget, in a work on developmental psychology,[2] details a fabricated memory of his own. This memory had been created in his own mind through the narratives he had heard repeated many years earlier as a young child.

He narrates one of his earliest memories, where as a child his nanny was pushing him in his pram along the *Champs Elysées* in Paris when a man tried to kidnap him. Piaget recalls this moment,

> I was held in by the strap fastened round me while my nurse bravely tried to stand between me and the thief. She received various scratches, and I can still see vaguely those on her face. Then a crowd gathered, a policeman with a short cloak and white baton came up, and the man took to his heels.[3]

This became an important memory for Piaget which appeared to be grounded firmly in personal experience. Years later, however, the nanny returned a watch she had received as a reward on this occasion. In an accompanying letter she stated that she had become a member of the Salvation Army and was confessing past misdeeds – she had made up the entire

---

[2] Jean Piaget, *Play, Dreams and Imitation in Childhood* (New York: W .W. Norton, 1962).
[3] Ibid. pp. 187-88.

story and had inflicted the wounds upon herself. Piaget, it turns out, had created the memory of the event from stories he had heard his parents repeating, and, in his own words, "therefore, must have heard, as a child, the account of this story, which my parents believed, and projected into the past in the form of a visual memory, which was a memory of memory, but false."[4]

It is interesting to note the importance of the visual representation of physical objects in both this and my own memories, described previously – the pair of red mittens with white cross-stitch patterning, the Humpty Dumpty sitting on my birthday cake made from a real egg, the policeman with a short cloak and white baton. These images of objects that have been so strongly imprinted as part of a memory, are perhaps the easiest thing to pull out and describe verbally, much easier, than, for example, describing the fear felt as a steam train passes by.[5]

The Case of The Missing Link That Never Was.

In his introductory essay in the catalogue of the British Museum exhibition *Fake? The Art of Deception*, editor Mark Jones writes,

> [...] perception itself is determined by the structure of expectations that underpins it. Present Piltdown Man to a palaeontologist out of the blue and it will be rejected out of hand. Present it to a palaeontologist whose predictions about the 'missing link' have been awaiting just such evidence and it will seem entirely credible.[6]

The discovery of Piltdown Man was announced in 1912, and besides filling in the so-called 'missing link,' it also conveniently placed the origins of humankind, as we know it, in the United Kingdom. Pieces of what turned out to be a human skull (perhaps dating from the Middle Ages) with part of an ape jaw bone with its teeth filed down to simulate characteristic human wear patterns, were reported to have been found in a field in England by Charles Dawson – an amateur archaeologist. Despite the fact that Dawson had been involved in a long list of seemingly dubious and outright fraudulent discoveries, it took until 1953 for these items to be exposed as fakes and not to be taken, by some members of the scientific community, as significant evidence of a link in the chain of the lineage of humankind. Some of the "discoveries" that Dawson had also been associated with include the first example of cast iron, a transitional boat design known as the Behill Boat, a transitional horseshoe, a new race of human – with an extra dorsal vertebra – that was found among the skeletons at the Royal College of Surgeons and a mammal with traces of its reptilian roots.[7] It would seem that our Mr. Dawson was intent on filling in the gaps of the historical narrative with pieces of evidence that would seem to fit perfectly, but upon closer inspection turned out to be fake.

---

[4] Ibid. p. 188.

[5] These objects can also act as triggers to the recall of memories, be they 'real' or 'fake'; whilst they are readily available parts of a memory that can be used to describe a recollection verbally, they also provide an entry point to a recollection – as when I saw the ribbon in our glassware cabinet, or when I see another piece of tartan ribbon that reminds me of that first ribbon – my memory of the events associated with that object are recalled. Consider also Proust's madeleine cake, probably the most famous example of an object (experienced through taste rather than sight) bringing a memory narrative into the present.

[6] Mark Jones, ed., *Fake? The Art of Deception* (London: British Museum Publications, 1990), p. 11.

[7] Ibid., p. 94.

While most credible sources seem unwilling to completely commit themselves to claiming that Dawson was wholly responsible for the fraud, it does seem obvious that he was either involved or was so keen to find the "missing" link from within archaeology, a field in which he was so passionate, that he was able to suspend his belief, or look the other way, so to speak, rather than follow a rigorous scientific approach to his discoveries. Indeed, one of the main reasons put forward for why this fake was so readily accepted by so many was that it fit so neatly with what theories on evolution at the time expected of a missing link. Rigorousness was not necessary because the 'results' fitted so well with the popular theory.[8]

The Case of a Fake, Fake, Furry Fish.

Often the narratives that surround a fake item are so strong and so set in place that it is very hard to shake them even when it is proven beyond a reasonable doubt that the object involved is a fake. Take, for example, the narrative of the Furry Trout.[9]

Rumors seem to have existed in the United Kingdom that there existed in Canada a fish, which had evolved a furry hide that provided it with warmth in the depths at which it dwelt. The rumor is said to have started with a grammatical misunderstanding when a Scotsman in the seventeenth century wrote home saying that Canada had an abundance of "furried animals and fish." He was asked to provide an example of this wonder, which he did.

In the 1970s a member of the public brought one of these fish, which at the time were being made for a gullible or good-humored tourist trade in Canada, to the Royal Scottish Museum, where it was recognized as a fake and rejected by the museum. But it would seem that the museum's hand was forced, as the story of this fish's existence had already gotten out, and due to public demand the museum had to create a fake of the fake to display, in order to appease popular demand.

Where History is Faked by the Author who Places His Faith in Fakes.

In Umberto Eco's fourth novel *Baudolino*, we find reference to another form of fake – that of the faking of the unique object, of which, by its very nature, there can only ever be one. In this novel we encounter the faking of many such unique objects including the Grail, and a variety of other religious relics. When questioned as to the authenticity of one of at least two known heads of John the Baptist, one of the characters replies:

---

[8]   Mark Jones provides a basic introduction to the Piltdown fake. An essay devoted to the Piltdown fake, entitled "Piltdown Revisited," in Stephen Jay Gould, *The Panda's Thumb: More Reflections in Natural History* (New York: Norton, 1980), argues that one of the main reasons that the Piltdown fake was so successful was that it fitted with the hopes and expectations of the culture at the time. For further surveys of this fake, see John Evangelist Walsh, *Unravelling Piltdown: The Science Fraud of the Century and Its Solution* (New York: Random House, 1996), and Richard Harter, "Piltdown Man" [online], http://home.tiac.net/~cri_a/piltdown/piltdown.html [June 6, 2003].

[9]   The version of the story of the Furry Fish of Canada is recounted in Jones. This fake also appears in the film *Brotherhood of the Wolf*: the hero presents a French nobleman with a new kind of trout he has discovered in Canada which appears to be covered in fur. Here the fake is used to signify the importance of impartial scientific investigation. Finally, Alex Boese cites another story which alleges that the trout's habitat is North America in general, and states that another form of its story ascribes its fur to the spilling of hair tonic into the Arkansas River. Jones, ed., *Fake? The Art of Deception*, p. 87; *Brotherhood of the Wolf*, Universal Pictures 2002, directed by Christophe Gans; and Alex Boese, *The Museum of Hoaxes* (Camberwell, Australia: Penguin, 2002), p. 83.

Holy things must not be spoken of in human terms. Whichever of the two relics was given me, I assure you that in bending to kiss it, I would sense the mystical perfume that it emanates, and I would know it was the true head.[10]

Allen B. Rurch calls the novel "Eco's book of lies"[11] and indeed we are presented with multiple layers of falsehoods and interpretations that appear to add up to a credible reinterpretation of history. As with Eco's other novels we find much emphasis placed on the validity of the evidence used to write and create histories. We find historic figures and purely fictional characters placed side by side in such a way that it might be difficult to argue his narrative was any less 'real' than that of a traditional history on the subject. These characters, be they historic figures or fictional creations, are presented as ghostwriters, as characters, as observers, as narrators, as novelists, as historians and ultimately as liars, albeit well-intentioned liars, who at the same time have been given the responsibility of recording history for posterity (the very history being critiqued throughout the novel).

The novel mixes historical 'fact' with fiction, but in such a way that it would be hard to prove or disprove many of the falsifications. Baudolino, through his ghostwriter Niketas,[12] tells how as a young child, from a poor family, he became the protégé to Emperor Frederick Barbarossa. Through the clever use of lies he manages to become extremely powerful within the empire. We find that he was actually behind many of the events we now see to be historically important, including the re-emergence of the Grail myth around that time. We find Baudolino is as savvy as the creators of the Piltdown Fake. When he is in need of an object with which to fake the Grail, he works with people's expectations and beliefs of what such an object would be like. In the end he chooses an old, worn wooden cup that had belonged to his father – and so an "original" faked religious relic is born.

What we find here is again testament to the fact that a trend exists associated with fakes, which is that when something that one wants to believe in, or something which is in line with expectations, is falsely presented as authentic, it is more likely to be believed genuine, despite evidence to the contrary.[13]

To this day there is a trade in religious relics, often tiny pieces of cloth that are cut from a larger piece of cloth which is said to have come into contact with another known relic. Whether this is an example of the Fake or not would really depend on the faith and belief of the owners of the relic and their desire for the intangible elements "stored" within such an

---

10   Umberto Eco, *Baudolino*, trans. William Weaver (Sydney: Random House, 2002), p. 267. This dialogue reminds one of a passage in Umberto Eco, *Travels in Hyperreality*, trans. William Weaver (London: Pan Books, 1987), p. 16, in which Eco is discussing the Ripley's *Believe it or Not!* Museums; "The authenticity the Ripley's Museums advertises is not historical, but visual. Everything looks real, and therefore it is real; in any case the fact that it seems real is real, and the thing is real even if, like Alice in Wonderland, it never existed."

11   Allen B Rurch, "Eco's Book of Lies – Baudolino" [online],
http://www.themodernworld.com/eco/review_baudolino.html [February 26, 2003].

12   Niketas Choniates, author of *O City of Byzantium: Annals of Niketas Choniates*, is a major primary source of the period. Eco has used Choniates' written history as source material in combination with his own narratives in creating the plot of the novel *Baudolino*.

13   This also rings true of beliefs associated with memory narratives, as highlighted by Lenore Terr in her discussion of the current *false-memory* debate. She states, for example that "a false memory is even more likely to come about when the therapist is an acknowledged expert in trauma who sees incest victims almost exclusively. Here the patient expects from the beginning to retrieve incest memories from childhood in the course of treatment." Terr, *Unchained Memories*, p. 160.

item. It is customary for the reliquary or container of the relic to be sold and the actual relic given as a "gift," to bypass canon law restricting sales of relics, and perhaps to allay the seller's guilt if the relic is indeed a fake.

Reflections

While this is not an original notion, I have come to look at an individual's life narrative as being something that is made up of a person's collected memories, and it is through this narrative that a person forms an idea of himself or herself as a discrete entity. This narrative becomes extremely important as it is proof of individuality and from a poetic and perhaps psychological standpoint could be seen as making me, me – or you, you. There are, however, gaps that form in these narratives and it is in these gaps that the so-called fake memories slip in unnoticed, or noticed, or, in some instances even welcomed with open arms.

So it is with the Piltdown Man, where the desire for a "gapless" narrative of history led to the acceptance of a fake, despite evidence to the contrary, because the evidence provided by the Piltdown Man fitted with the expected criteria for such a thing. Gaps that have formed through desire (such as the desire to connect with a memory of my second birthday, or the desire to connect with an intangible god through tangible means) can lead to the faked replacing the actual, creating strong mnemonic images of this birthday, or an unshakable faith that an item is truly a relic from religious history.

As I now muse upon the situation of remembering my second birthday, I can also recall asking my mother about the tartan ribbon on many more than one occasion. I would ask the question to which I already knew the answer: "Mum, where did that ribbon come from?" and she would reply (if time permitted) by telling me the story of my second birthday party, perhaps each time in a slightly different version. So I find that it is possible that my memory serves me well when I say that I have never seen photos of that event, and that I do actually remember my second birthday, albeit not through my own recollections, but through those of a trusted other – my mother. If on the other hand, these memories do in fact stem from photographs I have seen then, as suggested by Susan Stewart, what I am experiencing when I recall my second birthday may be an abstract object of nostalgia relating to generic feelings of my childhood, that I have misinterpreted as a memory of a specific event.[14]

As Bertrand Russell points out, we rely on memory to confirm our memory, looking "for reasons tending to show that what we recollect was what was to be expected."[15] This highlights and further complicates the issue at hand, in that if I believe I remember my second birthday, but use photographs or my mother's testimony to confirm these memories, I have no way other than relying on my memory to tell whether I remember the event, or simply the photograph or testimony. This very reliance on confirmation jeopardizes the reliability of memory I am seeking.

---

[14] Stewart, *On Longing*, p.138.

[15] Bertrand Russell, *An Inquiry into Meaning and Truth* (London: Allen and Unwin, 1940), p. 157. Russell provides us with an example demonstrating our reliance on memory to confirm our memory. He asks the reader to suppose they remember seeing a very bright meteor the previous night, and find a note in their handwriting on their desk confirming this memory. "But if you are discarding memory as a source of knowledge, you will not know how the note got there. It may have been made by a forger or yourself as a practical joke" (ibid.). The note cannot then function as a confirmation of the memory.

As for the case of the furry fish, personal narratives although known to be fake can become more desirable than the actual desire to preserve a strictly 'real' memory, as in the obviously extreme case of the monsters on the steam train. In Jean Piaget's foiled kidnapping we see that the repeated narratives of someone so close as a parent, although not lining up strictly with a personal experience, can overwrite a 'real' memory with a 'fake.' We find that it is preferable to keep a life narrative intact than to have a conflict between one's own experience and the narrative told by the trusted other. The memory is confirmed, but in this, as in our other cases, falsely.

Epilogue

To conclude, I would like to look at an example of my own artistic practice, a piece which is thematically tied to some of the ideas I have been working with both here and in my practice as a new media artist. The work is entitled "This is Not a Love Story."

An enclosed and darkened space with sixteen floating panels of light and a constantly evolving soundscape is controlled by the interaction of the viewer. Each lit panel contains fragments of an allusive monologue, detailing a mysterious encounter. The text is reminiscent of the approach used by a diarist, but also suggests the genre of the detective novel – each fragment a clue to a larger story. But these are only fragments and the viewers must fill in many of the gaps themselves.

Each time the viewers raise a hand to one of the lit panels, they create changes and layers within the soundtrack. The combination of the fragmentary text and the audio is all the viewer has to work with to piece together the narrative as a whole. The audio is purposefully dramatic, taking obvious quotes from film, in order to build up a cinematic atmosphere. This happens through careful construction of the layers in the sounds by using iconic audio samples and constructed sounds that, through cultural training, we associate with different emotions and feelings. For the audio in this work I drew quite heavily on cinematic conventions of constructed soundtracks. Through association these sounds are able to summon up memories of feelings, emotion and imagery related to the viewer's own personal history, even though this is purely through convention and the fakery of the cinema.

The written text on the lit panels on the walls is based on a series of meetings with a stranger in a small town. It is based on actual events, but the 'real' narrative has also been doctored and changed, not much, but just enough so that it is no longer 'my own' narrative. Perhaps I have rewritten parts of it to go the way I would have preferred them to, or for the sake of a little extra drama have added an anecdote or two. Also much has been removed from the narrative, only highlights are presented, and there are many gaps in the story, gaps which leave room for the viewer to provide their own interpretations, and create their own connections within the narrative. All that the viewer has outside of these fragments is the audio that is constantly shifting as they intersect with the work, and as we have seen even the audio has been created in such a way that it will control the way a viewer reads the texts, that is, through the conventions of the cinematic soundtrack. In the end, the viewer, who has believed that he or she is being invited to share part of my own personal narrative, is left with fragments of the real narrative, filled out with their own layers of interpretation, which if they were to project back onto me as the storyteller, would become unreliable and faked, yet directed and having interpretations influenced by this very storyteller.

As an anecdote and as a comment to close, which highlights and punctuates issues I have been dealing with here, I would like to point out that the person around whom this narrative centers, became known simply as K. within the narrative of the artwork. As I worked on this piece I completely forgot his real name, and I now only know this person from my past as K. He has become the character from the narrative that I wrote for the work, and I no longer know how much of what I know of him in my memory is fake, and how much of it is real...

CHAPTER 8

Fiona McIntosh-Varjabédian

Probability and Persuasion in 18th–Century and 19th–Century Historical Writing

To try and define the role played by probability in historical writing is to pry into the innermost workings of the narrative; it is to ponder on the means by which the historian aims at recreating the past in a satisfactory manner, both for himself and for his would-be readers. For, notwithstanding the epistemological turning point of the late 17th century and its sequel, History remains a speculative art, in which facts and likelihood guide the historian and the reader towards an always-elusive truth. The conquering assertions of the enlightened philosophers such as Hume, who sets History on the tracks of science at the beginning of the second volume of his *History of England*,[1] encounter a lasting impediment. The historian's hypotheses are made at the expense of an *abridgement*, which means, to quote Hume, that the narrator will have to "drop all the minute circumstances, which are only interesting during the time, or to the persons engaged in the transactions " (HE, II, 3-4).[2] What kind of image of the past can the historian then give, if it does not correspond to the experience of the people engaged in the events? To which extent must the historian depart from this experience? He may gain a certain form of hindsight that enables him to overcome the blindness of those who took part in the action, but while setting aside some facts according to more or less clearly defined criteria, he loses one of the main guidelines in experimental science, that is to say, that an interpretation is true as long as the facts do not contradict it and, therefore, that the validity of a conclusion and of an inference has to be constantly put to the test. This inherent contradiction between the declared aims of modern historical writing and its means, which is made conspicuous by Hume, although unconsciously, is only one of the many epistemological flaws that burden the historical narrative and which chain it, as it were, to the field of imagination: thus of literature.[3]

During the 18th and the 19th centuries, two main strategies appear in historical writing so as to counteract this defect. Indeed, the historians seem to hesitate, sometimes during the same narration, between exposing its mere probability and creating the illusion of a self-contained reality. Thus I shall try and examine the role of likelihood in the building up of a

---

[1] David Hume, *The History of England from the Invasion of Julius Caesar to the Revolution of 1688*, based on the Edition of 1778, with the Author's Last Corrections and Improvements, Foreword by William B. Todd, (Indianapolis: Liberty Classics, 1983), vol. II, p.3 : "Most sciences, in proportion as they encrease (sic) and improve, invent methods by which they facilitate their reasonings." Henceforward cited as HE.

[2] Hayden White stresses the same point while commenting upon Hegel. See Hayden White, *Metahistory, The Historical Imagination in Nineteenth-Century Europe*, (Baltimore & London: The John Hopkins University Press, 1973), p. 91.

[3] See Fiona McIntosh, "Histoire, littérature, rhétorique, à partir de données écossaises," in Jean Bessière éd., *Savoirs et littérature, Literature, the Humanities and the Social Sciences*, (Paris: Presses Sorbonne Nouvelle, 2002), pp. 195-204.

mainly fictive authoritative figure and its interplay with the classical notion of verisimilitude. Last I shall study how historians such as Carlyle and Michelet resort to metaphors and
enumeration so as to impose new chains of events.

In the often polemical context of the Enlightenment, the building up of an authoritative
voice inside the narrative is part and parcel of the historian's method. It means that the historian must show where he stands and must impose his own version of the events, against
preceding versions or, on the contrary, thanks to the authority of his predecessors. He may
intervene more or less obtrusively, he may give a seemingly exact and comprehensive account of his avowed sources or of the objects of his criticism, like Gibbon, or make more
fleeting allusions which, for all their allusiveness, serve to define the narrator and to reveal
the nature of his standards. This last operation is certainly crucial to understand Voltaire's
references. René Pomeau, among many other critics, underlined Voltaire's seeming flip-
pancy and frequent inaccuracies, but here, exactitude is less important than the pertinence
of the argument, as is the case when Voltaire invokes Father Gaubil to prove the validity of
the Chinese chronology, but altered the missionary's observations.[4] Gibbon rebuked Voltaire for his sweeping and unsupported assertions,[5] but nevertheless, behind his own moderate practice, his character is at stake in a manner which does not greatly differ from Voltaire's writings. Gibbon's tone is that of stifled witticisms and his notes serve to make the
point just as the Frenchman's own faulty references, while his own self-restraint agrees
with the figure of the modern historian he wishes to give: "But the temper, as well as
knowledge, of a modern historian require a more sober and accurate language"(DF, 55).

Thus the writer hierarchizes his sources according to their credibility and so evinces his
own *precision* and *perspicuity*, that is to say, his ability to convey the facts "clearly to the
minds of others"[6] together with great accuracy of detail. He draws subtle boundaries between the *ingenious historian* (DF, 181), who for all his ingeniousness may presume too
much on his fancy (DF, 231), the *judicious* one (DF, 177), the learned one but endowed
with *a heated imagination* (DF, 181) and the *careless writer* (DF, 200). He sets aside the *ill-
worded narration* (DF, 190), the *obscure chronology* (DF, 201) or the improbable and contradictory relation.[7] By thus pruning the stories of the past, he asserts his own rights to es-

---

4
   Voltaire, *Essai sur les Mœurs*, ed. by René Pomeau (Paris: Garnier, 1990), vol. I, p. 205 ; henceforward cited
   as EM.
5
   Edward Gibbon, *The History of the Decline and Fall of the Roman Empire*, ed. David Womersley, (London:
   Penguin, 1994), Vol. I (corresponds to the first volume, 1776, and the second, 1781), p. 54. Henceforward
   cited as DF.
6
   For the crucial notion, see Hugh Blair's *Lessons of Rhetoric and Belles Lettres* (Basil: James Decker, 1801),
   Vol. I, chap. X : "Style, Perspicuity and Precision," p. 210.
7
   The act of divesting some of the traditional historical narratives of the myths and legends that encumber them
   is of course one of the historian's main tasks. Nevertheless, I would like to soften down the opposition Hayden
   White establishes between Vico and the other historians of the Enlightenment. According to White (*Metahistory*, p. 51), Vico was the only historian of the period to seriously take myths into account and to interpret
   them so as to decipher what was ultimately behind the corrupted image of the past they gave and to analyze
   what caused these mythical representations. However Voltaire's Euhemerism also assumes such a corruption.
   The theme is also commonplace in Fontenelle's "De l'origine des fables" and even the catholic D'Herbelot's
   Dictionnaire Oriental (see Fiona McIntosh, "Désymbolisation et resymbolisation du mythe oriental au XVIIIᵉ
   siècle: quand la religion devient elle-même un mythe," ed. Véronique Gély, Jean-Marc Moura, *Les Mythes de
   l'Orient* (Villeneuve d'Ascq, UL3, forthcoming). Voltaire examines Egyptian, Persian, and Indian Myths in
   his *Essai sur les mœurs* in order to undermine the supposed primacy of the Old Testament. However, if the

tablish the facts and to make his own assumptions according to the very same laws he enforced on his predecessors.[8] These operations are of course to a great extent illusory, if one takes into account that they are simultaneous: a historian may be discredited because of an improbable narration, but such narration may be judged improbable because of the suspicious character of the narrator himself. The argument is mainly circular and thus called forth when needed by Hume, Voltaire and Gibbon, especially against those *monkish historians* who are the butt of all their criticisms.

It may be useful to bear in mind the nature of their reproaches, since it will enable us, by matter of contrast, to define the ideal image of the modern historian that Hume and Gibbon wish to promote. Indeed, they reject both their predecessors' "bombast and inaccurate style"(HE, II, 88). More forcibly, they discard their moral assertions, arguing that they are prejudiced and false and that, because of their seclusion, their misunderstanding of human nature and of man's needs is glaring. Consequently, David Hume follows some of the main events of Bede's *Ecclesiastical History of the English People*, subscribes to the latter's main explanation of the Saxons' defeat, i.e. that they had abandoned arms, but ridicules the idea that luxury might have corrupted them (HE, I, 24)[9] and thus questions Bede's political judgement. More astonishingly perhaps, Hume and Gibbon cast off their predecessors' economic computations, strongly refuting those who were nearer to the scene of action. The Scottish historian considers as a general law that "the sums mentioned by ancient authors, who were almost all monks, are often improbable and never consistent"(HE, II, 24). Behind the barrenness of the sums, Hume, Gibbon and Voltaire discard the exaggerations transmitted by tradition, the superstitious legends these exaggerations convey and above all, Voltaire, when he makes his own demographic estimations, rejects the biblical revelation itself (EM, 86). All facts may be put to the test insofar as they seem to have been inflated.

These elements are known but since all tradition is liable to be closely examined by the historian, his authoritative voice must assert itself all the more forcibly and, by making his targets explicit, the writer requests the reader to recognize the legitimacy and the validity of the procedures, as when Voltaire asks provocatively: "Strabon dit que les Perses épousaient leurs mères; mais quels sont ses garants?"(EM, 43) In a sense, each time the historian discusses his sources, refers to different possible meanings, and puts them to the test, far from

---

analysis of these mythologies represents a major argument in the debunking of the Bible, Fontenelle and Voltaire seem more prudent than Vico because they consider that it is impossible to completely reveal the truth that is hidden behind the fables of the imagination. See "De l'Origine des Fables" (1724), p. 192. Fontenelle, *Œuvres Complètes*, t. 3, éd. Alain Niderst (Paris: Fayard, 1989). Thus, I would like to point out this paradoxical statement, that the best recognition of the fictive nature of all narratives comes from those who believe that there is a *terminus ad quem* in the possibility of disclosing the whole truth behind the figments of the imagination. Irony may be a kind of ultimate reassessment of the power of fiction, that is to say, to quote White, (*Metahistory*, xii) "there are no apodictically certain theoretical grounds on which one can legitimately claim an authority for any one of the modes over the others as being more 'realistic'". However, this pessimism that also pervades more Romantic writers, albeit in a more subdued manner, must not hinder the historian from endeavoring to trim the facts as far as it is possible to do so.

8   See Arnaldo Momigliano for a judgement on Gibbon's method: very critical at first, referring to what he calls a very superficial comparative assessment of his sources, Momigliano recognizes his extraordinary knowledge of these same sources, a few lines later: *Problèmes d'historiographie moderne*, trad. Alain Tachet (Paris: Gallimard, 1983), pp. 321 and 323.

9   See F. McIntosh, "Les Saxons dans l'Histoire d'Angleterre de Hume: sauvages ou défenseurs de la liberté à l'ombre de Tacite," pp. 30-31. *Discours sur le primitif*, ed. by F. McIntosh (Lille: UL3, 2002).

exposing his weakness, he re-establishes his privileged links with the reader and even reinforces them because, by expressing his doubts or the mere probability of such-and-such
event, he makes the reader participate in his deductions and computations. Thus, in many
respects, the reader becomes another self with whom the historian may share certain values.
Since exaggeration endangers this relationship and makes the historian an object of suspicion, it must be sieved and sifted through. But the point is, how does one recognize that
facts have been exaggerated? How can the historian justify his amendments?

The historian's extreme wariness is most conspicuous when he refers to war crimes.
While evoking the great slaughter after the battle of Falkirk, Hume rejects the testimonies,
which spoke of tremendous losses on the Scottish side under the pretence that they come
from the "populace"(HE, II, 130) and for this reason they are deemed legendary. The idea
that authority prevails over testimony is so deeply ingrained into his implicit procedures
that Hume feels obliged to explain why, on another occasion, he goes against the rule. But
this cannot be done without a highly perceptible reluctance and uneasiness, because it
means that the historian is contradicting previous choices and thus undermining their validity, because the same argument could have been invoked previously for the great slaugh-
ters:

> The circumstances, which attended Bruce's first declaration, are variously related; but we shall rather follow
> the account given by the Scottish historians; not that their authority is in general anywise comparable to that of
> the English; but because they may be supposed sometimes better informed concerning facts, which so nearly
> interested their own nation. (HE, II, 137)

Indeed, moderation founded on human nature is the prevailing principle. However this general assumption contends with the overwhelming image of the crimes and horrors man may
inflict to man out of superstition, enthusiasm and excessive ambition, which, from Voltaire
to Carlyle is a longstanding topic in historical writing – all the more so since the topic
proves the moralizing aims of the narration[10] – and the modern reader is sometimes at a loss
to understand why some revolutions and acts of violence are considered as the core of history and others not. So while Hume, Robertson and, to a lesser extent, Gibbon try to keep
barbarism in the margins, assuming that that kind of History is totally untrustworthy and
cannot teach the modern reader,[11] these restraints imposed by civilization seem greatly inadequate to account for the past. The literary criterion of verisimilitude predominates, the
classical phrase according to which "le vrai n'est pas toujours vraisemblable" seems to be
reversed because instead of serving as a guideline in fiction or in rhetoric, it plays a part in
History – which should seek for truth, since it pertains to science. But as such, historical
writings should also endeavor to persuade and persuasion cannot go without probability and
thus the creation, or the constant reassertion, of a common ground, between the writer and
his reader, which is greatly indebted to the idea that such-and-such an event *must* have
taken place in such-and-such a manner.

---

[10]   Gibbon, DF, p. 102: "history; which is, indeed, little more than the register of the crimes, follies, and misfor-
tunes of mankind."

[11]   See William Robertson, *The History of Scotland* (1794), éd. Sher, Smitten et Philipson (London: Routledge,
Thoemmes Press, 1996), p. 1: "The first ages of the Scottish history are dark and fabulous. Nations, as well as
men, arrive at maturity by degrees, and the events, which happened during their infancy or early youth, cannot
be recollected, and deserve not to be remembered."

The modern reader may start at these inconsequences and reject the enlightened historian's complacency as belonging to the infancy of historical studies. However if we examine the writings of more positive authors, we discover that the same moderate argument is at work, for instance in Rawson Gardiner's *History of the Great Civil War*: "A reader has, no doubt, to be on his guard against stories of Cavalier outrages, especially upon women, which are probably for the most part as imaginary as are, I hope, the stories which were told in Ireland of both sides as habitually carrying babies on the ends of pikes [...]."[12] Here, a mere wish prevails over testimony and extreme scenes of violence and of cruelty are treated as a sort of collective delusion. This similitude, between Hume and Gibbon on the one side and Gardiner on the other, tends to confirm that the spectacle of horror and the bloody chronicles of the past endanger the writer's authority as a moderate, sensible and discerning historian as well as his ability to unveil the implicit rules in action on the historical scene and – last but not least – invalidate his explanations.

In this instance, one can refer to Gérard Genette's analysis of Balzac's narratives,[13] in which he showed the importance of gnomic assertions in order to justify the dynamics of the story. Although the facts that are narrated are fictitious on the one side and historical on the other, one is entitled to draw an analogy between these so-called rules Balzac constantly invoked and the ones expressed by Gibbon, all the more so since, in both occurrences, they justify the chain of events itself. Assuming that "the attachments of the multitude are capricious and inconstant" (DF, 97), Gibbon paves the way – carefully and at a very early stage – for the many disruptions in the succession to the imperial throne which will take place after Commodus. The Romans' prejudice against monarchy explains why inheritance, the easiest mode of succession according to the historian, never prevailed in spite of its advantages, and consequently accounts for the disruptive violence which predominated, for "[i]n elective monarchies, the vacancy of the throne is a moment big with danger and mischief"(DF, 98). Thus thanks to the regular use of gnomic assertions, the events are clearly associated with general rules which endow the narrative with coherence and meaning. As it were, horror and crimes must be encompassed by a mechanical causal chain, in which each factor reinforces the next. If such an operation is impossible because the implicit rules are blurred and cannot be accounted for, then these savage scenes are rejected beyond the pale of normality and of all likelihood, except if they can be "attested by grave and contemporary historians"(DF, 168), as is the case with Elagabulus' vices. Consequently, if they cannot be attested in such a manner, then the circumstances must be *sifted, softened* (DF, 190) or even set aside when too improbable.

Indeed, the historian picks and chooses amongst the various accounts at his disposal so as to decipher the motives and the features of the actors on the historical scene. However, from these multifarious but fleeting indications, he may hint at different possible meanings, defining a field of probability, instead of privileging one meaning only. Leo Braudy showed

---

[12] Rawson Gardiner, *History of the Great Civil War, 1886-1891*, introd. Christopher Hill (Adlestrop: The Windrush Press, 1987), Vol. I (1642-1644): VII.

[13] Gérard Genette, "Vraisemblance et motivation": *Figures* II (Paris: Editions du Seuil, 1969), pp. 79-86. See also how Hayden White (*Metahistory*, pp. 11-12) comments upon such "putative laws": "the commonsensical or conventional nature of these latter generalizations, does not affect their status as the presumed major premises of nomological-deductive arguments by which explanations of events in the story are provided."

how this technique was inspired by the novel and by Fielding in particular.[14] At first, this method seems to undermine one of the writer's chief aims, that is to say, according to Gibbon, to give an "unbroken thread of narration" (DF, 253). However, these probable conjectures are perhaps less disruptive than they may seem, since they flourish essentially when the causal structure is strong. First, to avow one's failures is to assert more forcibly one's power to unravel the facts and to establish clear-cut links on other occasions. In Chapter X, Gibbon warns the reader that conjectures are not facts, but at the same time, he explicitly places the "knowledge of human nature" and "its fierce and unrestrained passions" among the various prerequisites for the historian who must *collect, compare* and *conjecture* (DF, 253), thus founding his narrative on moral likelihood.[15] Second, as shown above, to emphasize a lesser degree of truth – especially when the facts are appalling – preserves the character of the writer and the narration as a whole.

When the writer ceases to underline altogether that the events are merely possible, or probable or even likely, the implicit hierarchy on which the narrative is built becomes more blurred. Nowhere is the expression of probability less conspicuous than when Gibbon is at a loss to explain the expansion of Christianity on human grounds.[16] Here the English writer encounters two difficulties, which may account for the obstacles met by later historians like Michelet and Carlyle. He is relating mass history instead of describing the actions of two or three leaders. On the one hand, he must consider the people as a whole and, on the other, he must treat each individual as a more or less independent member of the group. The same uneasiness is perceptible to a lesser degree when the number of rivals, pretenders, and local tyrants are multiplied in the Roman Empire: "To illustrate the obscure monuments of the life and death of each individual, would prove a laborious task, alike barren of instruction and of amusement" (DF, 288). If the author followed each destiny, he would provide us with a broken narrative which would follow each actor successively. Thus the thread of narrative can only be preserved at the cost of oversimplification. In order to avert this oversimplification, later historians dealing with the history of the masses resort to what we can call more evanescent chains of causality and endeavor, through metaphors and enumeration, to impose another image of the historical scene – beyond probability, as it were.

Let us consider Guizot, Michelet, and Carlyle, who have dealt either with the English Civil war or with the French Revolution. François Guizot is an interesting case as he represents a sort of intermediate step in historical writing, keeping some of the traits of Gibbon's *Rise and Fall* which he translated in 1828, but shifting from a more traditional narrative in which a limited number of actors are defined (the king vs. The Commons) and general laws are determined (ambition, faith, the English spirit of liberty) to a more complex frame in which groups are circumscribed, balanced, and eventually redivided. Thus, in the first pages of his *Histoire de la Révolution d'Angleterre*, he states more traditional political explanations, stressing on the various, but limited, contending forces, whereas, as he progresses, he refers more and more to rumors, to misunderstandings, and finally to the blindness of the

---

[14]   Leo Braudy, *Narrative Form in History and Fiction* (Princeton : Princeton University Press, 1970), p. 216.

[15]   See Michel Baridon, "Le Style d'une pensée: politique et esthétique dans le *Decline and Fall*," ed. Pierre Ducrey, *Gibbon et Rome à la lumière de l'historiographie moderne* (Genève: Librairie Droz, 1977), pp. 88-89.

[16]   Patricia Craddock, "Historical Discovery and Literary Invention in Gibbon's Decline and Fall," 585, *Modern Philology* (May 1988), p. 85.

miscellaneous actors in order to explain the capricious progress of the events, just like Michelet and Carlyle.[17] Thus the evolution of his narrative seems to confirm the link between mass history and the disruption of the traditional causal sequence and likelihood.

Indeed, compared to Gibbon's gnomic assertions, these factors founded on mere thoughts and suspicions should be considered as forming more evanescent explanations, since they can make history sway one way or the other. Their effect is often erratic, because, according to the common phrase, masses are unpredictable and because, against the general mechanistic rule, the same cause may entail sometimes opposite consequences. To a certain extent, Carlyle, Michelet, and Guizot each share Hegel's dialectic pattern, which may be understood as the overthrow of the Scottish mechanistic frame,[18] all believing, like Carlyle, that "actual events are nowise so simply related to each other as parent and offspring are; every single event is the offspring not of one, but of all other events, prior or contemporaneous, and will in turn combine with all others to give birth to new."[19] Guizot, in particular, insists on the fact that the actors on the historical scene are unwittingly the agents of Providence. In this respect, even the great man sees his previsions baffled so that his true action on the events differs from what he contemplated (HRA, 45). Consequently, as it is more difficult to determine the exact responsibility of each actor on the scene, it becomes redundant to define the probability of such-and-such a motive, because the chain of causality itself has been diluted and undermined. Since all see their intentions frustrated, psychological plausibility can only play a minor role in the narrative.

Michelet, in his *Histoire de la Revolution française*, makes conspicuous this weakening of responsibility: "La responsabilité même, entre ceux-ci, n'était entière à personne."[20] Instead of focusing on the king and on his main opponents from the States General, he uses the pronoun (*on*) on a very large scale, for both parties, i.e. the court and the revolutionaries.[21] The French locution is known for its indeterminacy and its generality – it is generally translated in English by the passive form. Among these loosely defined groups, now he lays the stress on a party as a whole, now on its inner divisions. Being constantly redivided, the group can only appear as an unreliable actor, prone to fickle change and to violent outbursts. The court hesitates and double-crosses the people and the members of the National Assembly. The people are suspicious and overreact to the faintest rumor. "*On*" also expresses this mixture of facts and hearsay, which also characterizes Carlyle's history of the French Revolution. Now if reality and suspicion mingle, then proof and evidence are no longer first and foremost. The latter's sources only belong, as it were, to the marginalia be-

---

17 See how hesitations, vague rumors and more or less likely defections serve to introduce Guizot's picture of the divisions and of the various insurrections during the Civil War: "les hésitations du roi, les bruits de complots, les défections aperçues ou pressenties dans l'armée et le Parlement réveillaient toutes les alarmes," *Histoire de la Révolution d'Angleterre*, ed. Laurent Theis, (Paris : Robert Laffont, 1997), p. 164. Cited henceforward as HRA.

18 I am referring to the Scottish School of Historiography.

19 Thomas Carlyle, "On History", *Critical and Miscellaneous Essays*, (London: Chapman & Hall, 1889), Vol. II, p. 257.

20 Jules Michelet, *Histoire de la Révolution française* (Paris: Robert Laffont, 1979), p. 171.

21 See Michelet speaking of the revolutionaries: "On était en pleine crise, dans un combat plus douteux encore. On ne pouvait trouver une trop haute montagne pour y planter le drapeau." HRF, p. 190. The same, referring to Necker, to the court, the queen and even to the parliamentarians: "On avait compté, trop compté sur cette incapacité ; autrement on n'eût hasardé de faire ce grand mouvement." HRF, p. 96.

cause they are neither discussed in the main narrative nor weighed according to their probability,[22] and even though I do not question their seriousness, they merely play the part of a
punctual warrant. To take Carlyle's words as he is referring to hangings that probably took
place in jail: "Brief is the word; not without significance, be it true or untrue!"[23]

Thus, symbols, emblems[24] and mere beliefs have also become part and parcel of the historical process.[25] To a certain extent, they seem more important, because they are more
striking, than the actual facts or than the barren truth itself. This explains why Carlyle
stresses mere coincidences or random encounters, instead of suggesting that there might be
a causal link of some sort: each actor has become entrapped, as it were, in the events and
reacts at the spur of the moment: "Cholat the wine-merchant has become an impromptu
cannoneer. See Georget, of the Marine Service, fresh from Brest, ply the King of Siam's
cannon. Singular (if we were not used to the like): Georget lay, last night, taking his ease at
his inn; the King of Siam's cannon also lay, knowing nothing of him, for a hundred years.
Yet now, at the right instant, they have got together, and discourse eloquent music." (FR,
201) These highly improbable, because fortuitous actors symbolize the general revolutionary rage and for this reason Carlyle quotes their names and sometimes enumerates them,
even though they are unimportant by themselves, in order to recreate the spirit of the age.
Once again, the historian aims at disorganizing the traditional form of historical narrative,
in which actors are cited according to their actual political weight or to their real and determined influence. Hence, even though he does not reject the idea of a necessary abridgement,[26] he eludes to one of the principal faults laid by philosophical historians on testimonials, that justified their amendments, that is to say, these testimonials provide a whole bulk
of details and circumstances that rapidly becomes of no interest.

Moreover, by laying stress on the simultaneous nature of things rather than on a linear
succession of events (*On History*: 257), Carlyle undermines the *post hoc propter hoc* pattern which generally predominates in historical writing. Causality explodes because the
remote past is *big with* the present and with the still unknown future. Carlyle and Michelet
insist on the fact that the crimes of the nobles are long-lasting and can be traced back to
antecedent generations. In such a manner, responsibility itself is lost in the sins and errors
of the forefathers.[27] Since innumerable and sometimes long-forgotten elements play an ill-
defined but, nonetheless, real part in the historical process, the traditional relation of direct
cause and effect must be replaced by metaphors and images in order to symbolize what can

---

[22] I disagree here with Murray Baumgarten, "Writing the Revolution," *Dickens Studies Annual* (Vol. 12, 1983),
p. 167.

[23] Thomas Carlyle, *The French Revolution* (Oxford, Oxford University Press, 1989), p. 190. Henceforward cited
as FR.

[24] e.g. *Dubarrydom*: 5, *Sansculottism, Furies, human Solecisms*, pp. 216-217. The list is very far from being
exhaustive!

[25] FR, 185: " As indeed man, with his singular imaginative faculties, can do little or nothing without signs."

[26] "On History Again", *Critical and Miscellaneous Essays*, (London: Chapman & Hall, 1891), Vol. IV, p. 217.
Henceforward cited as HA.

[27] FR, pp. 60-61: "Nay answer the Courtiers, it was it was Turgot, it was Necker, with their mad innovating; it
was the Queen's want of etiquette; it was he, it was she, it was that. Friends! It was every scoundrel that had
lived, and quacklike pretended to be doing, and been only eating and *mis*doing, in all provinces of life, as
Shoeblack or as Sovereign Lord, each in his degree, from the time of Charlemagne and earlier. All this (for be
sure no falsehood perishes, but is as seed sown out to grow) has been storing itself for thousand of years; and
now the account-day has come."

no longer be directly expressed, that is to say, the multifarious factors at work. Let us examine *the French Revolution*, Chapter I, Book III. The chapter is called "Dishonoured bills" and hints at those former iniquities that call for vengeance and must be paid for. However, this realistic and practical image is temporarily set aside so as to refer to Physics and Geology that impose their own mechanical chain of causality (volcanoes must explode sooner or later) which, with the image of sulphur, is fraught with demonic undertones.[28]

> While the unspeakable confusion is everywhere weltering within, and through so many cracks in the surface sulphur-smoke is issuing, the question arises: Through what crevice will the main Explosion carry itself? Through which of the old craters or chimneys; or must it, at once, form a new crater for itself? In every Society are such chimneys, are Institutions serving as such: even Constantinople is not without its safety-valves; there too Discontent can vent itself, – in material fire; by the number of nocturnal conflagrations, or of hanged bakers, the Reigning Power can read the signs of the times, and change course according to these. (FR, 65)

The superimposition of these various motifs must render the complexity of the historical process, since they reappear regularly in the narrative and are constantly recombined. The plausibility of the metaphors is more important than the probability of the facts themselves. That is the reason why we can consider that Carlyle and even Michelet have tried to go beyond probability and beyond the causal chain it implies and its very reassuring and, as it were, urbane guidance. But at the same time, these compact and complex images avoid the disintegration of the cause-and-effect narrative itself, for time and causes are "*infinitely divisible.*" (HA, 217)

Probability is linked to the historian's desire to create a common ground and to justify his own choices in the reader's eyes. However, when this confidence is shattered, when the traditional mechanistic chain is unable to account for the past, the probability of the events, their implicit hierarchy can no longer be mirrored in the narrative because the boundary between actual facts and mere beliefs is blurred. The vocabulary changes, the historian no longer examines what is likely or probable, but what is merely possible. Thus a new range of experience has to be taken into account by other means than by an "unbroken thread of narration," founded on a cause-and-effect temporal pattern, i.e., by analogies and enumeration that aim at giving a picture of Time both as a whole and as an accumulation of partial facts.[29]

---

[28] Once again, I am following Hayden White (*Metahistory*, p. 143) in the main lines. Nevertheless, it seems exaggerated to assert that "The Romantics repudiated *all formal systems of explanation* [I stress here] and tried to gain an explanatory effect by utilizing the Metaphorical mode to describe the historical field and the Mythos of Romance to represent its process." Carlyle's notion of "Chaos of being" (*Metahistory*, 144) can also be understood in a more ironical mode (in Hayden White's sense of the word), since it also stresses the historian's limitations. Furthermore, the subject of the narrative itself greatly influences the undermining of the "Scottish mechanistic frame." Mass phenomena need new modes of explanation, but when Michelet narrates the major events of the Middle Ages his style remains more canonical and more critical and resembles that of his predecessors, whereas when he draws the outlines of his "Picture of France," a geographical account of the history of France, analogies prevail. See Michelet, *Le Moyen Âge*, présentation Claude Mettra (Paris: Laffont, 1981), pp. 186-227.

[29] See Carlyle, "On History," p. 259.

CHAPTER 9

Claire Norton

Fiction or Non-fiction? Ottoman Accounts of the Siege of Nagykanizsa

Introduction

The Habsburg-controlled castle of Nagykanizsa in present-day Hungary was captured by the Ottomans in 1600 after a three-month siege. The following year, in 1601 the Ottoman commander Tiryaki Hasan Pasha successfully defended the castle when it was besieged by a Habsburg led coalition. A detailed account of Hasan Pasha's defense during the second siege is given in a corpus of twenty-five manuscripts dating from 1616 to 1815. These manuscripts are not identical copies of each other, but neither are they distinct individual works. Rather they are sufficiently similar to warrant classification together as an interrelated corpus. The common consensus in contemporary Ottoman scholarship is that *gazavat-name* (campaign narrative) manuscripts such as these represent a hybrid genre; less than history yet more than fiction. It is frequently argued that although historical material concerning past battles may be embedded in these narratives they are recounted within a framework of popular literary traditions and therefore historical realities are subordinated to epic and religious motifs.[1] Thus they conform more to the genre of epic than history and are consequently classified and analyzed as [popular] literature not history.[2] However, both the rubrication and reception of these manuscripts and other re-inscriptions over the past four hundred years suggests that they have not always been received thus and that their (non-) fictional status is more complex.

This article will explore the manner in which audiences recognize and construct the dichotomies of fiction/non-fiction and story/history through an examination of the contested fictional status and genre of these Nagykanizsa narratives. In particular, I will foreground the role framing, rubrication, intertextuality and fictional 'non-fiction' sources have in determining the received status of the narrative. Through such a discussion a number of the problems inherent in traditional representationalist explanations of fiction and genre classi-

---

[1]   See Colin Imber, "Ideals and Legitimation in early Ottoman History," in *Süleyman the Magnificent and his Age: The Ottoman Empire in the Early Modern World*, edited by Metin Kunt and Christine Woodhead. (London and New York: Longman, 1995), pp.142-44.

[2]   Franz Babinger, *Geschichtsschreiber der Osmanen und Ihre Werke* (Liepzig: Otto Harrassowitz, 1927), p.156 n. 2 describes the corpus of *gazavatnames* mentioned above as "folk books" which are "considerably divorced from the truth." Agah Sirri Levend, *Gazavat-nameler ve Mihaloğlu Ali Bey'in Gazavat-namesi* (Ankara: Türk Tarih Kurumu Yayınlarından / XI. Seri, No. 8 Türk Tarih Kurumu Basımevi, 1956), pp. v and 1 also refers to *gazavatnames* as 'literary texts' and *hikaye* (story). In contrast, Christine Woodhead, "Perspectives on Süleyman" in *Süleyman the Magnificent and his Age: The Ottoman Empire in the Early Modern World,* edited by Metin Kunt and Christine Woodhead (London and New York: Longman, 1995), pp. 171-2 describes *gazanames* (the singular of *gazavatname*) as historical works and campaign monographs.

fications will be exemplified. In conclusion, an alternative, less problematic explanatory model predicated upon a different epistemology, one which explains how audiences actually construct and recognize the genre and fictional status of a work, will be elucidated. In particular, I argue that although 'fiction' is generally understood as meaning something akin to 'invented story' or 'imaginary narrative', such a classification is not made by audiences in terms of external referentiality, but is rather determined by reference to specific community-defined protocols and interpretative strategies employed by both author and audience.

The *Gazavatname*s: History and Story

Titles possess a complex notational status; they describe, denote, exemplify, advertise and contain potential readings. Nomination identifies the work as a particular script and by positioning it within a known frame constructs or modifies audiences' horizon of expectations and thus their consequent reception and interpretation of the work.[3] Modern cataloguers and scholars have categorized the twenty-five *gazavatname* manuscripts within a typographic model as instances, or copies, of one work and have given this now unique work a single title: *Gazavat-i Tiryaki Hasan Paşa* (The Campaigns of Tiryaki Hasan Pasha). The small variations between the manuscripts are subsequently glossed as evidence of scribal incompetence or residual orality. This collective rubrication positions the work as a campaign narrative and assigns it to a single genre, that of *gazavatname*, thereby conditioning the expectations of modern audiences to respond to the work not as history, but as fiction. So great is the lure of the typographic model and its insistence on a single title and genre that when scholars have encountered alternative titles on these twenty five manuscripts they have ignored them or argued that the scribe or rubricator made a mistake.[4] However, of the eighteen manuscripts which have a title or incipit, most do not describe the work as a *gazavatname*: five describe it as a *hikaye* (story), five as *tarih* (history), two as *menakibname* (narrative of exemplary deeds), one as *risale* (treatise) and only four use the term *gazavat* or *muharebe* (campaigns or battle).[5]

---

3   See Deborah Tannen, "What's in a Frame? Surface Evidence for Underlying Expectations" in *Framing in Discourse*, edited by D. Tannen (Oxford: Oxford University Press, 1993), p.20 quoting the research of Bransford and Franks "The Abstraction of Linguistic Ideas," *Cognitive Psychology* 2: pp. 331-350, and Bransford and Johnson "Consideration of some Problems in Comprehension" in *Visual Information Processing*, edited by William G. Chase (New York: Academic Press, 1973). See also Dennis Jarrett, "Pragmatic Coherence in an Oral Formulaic Tradition: I can Read Your Letters/Sure Can't Read Your Mind" in *Coherence in Spoken and Written Discourse*, edited by Deborah Tannen. (Norwood, New Jersey: Ablex Publishing Corporation, 1986), p.160, and Thomas, L. Berger, "'Opening Titles Miscreate': Some Observations on the Titling of Shakespeare's Works" in *The Margins of the Text*, edited by D.C. Greetham (Ann Arbor: The University of Michigan Press, 1997), p. 155.

4   Hilmi in his catalogue *Fihristü'l-Kütübi't-Türkiyyeti'l-mevcadeti fi'l-Kütübhaneti'l-Hidiviyye* (Egypt: 1306 [1888-9]) entry 231, describes manuscript No. 235, Dar-al-Kutub, Cairo, as having the title: *The Gazavat of Hasan Pasha*, despite there being a title coterminous with the inscription of the actual manuscript on fol.1b, which reads: *Recounting the war and campaign of the deceased Gazi Hasan Pasha which happened in the siege of Kanije Castle*. Pal Fodor also notes in a personal e-mail dated 25 June 2001 that he was informed by a colleague that manuscript, Magyar Tudományos Akademia Konyvtara, Budapest, O.216 is probably erroneously rubricated as *Risale-i Divan Efendisi* (*Treatise of the Court Official*), despite this being the actual title written above the text.

5   Many of the manuscripts have a number of titles, some contemporaneous with the original inscription and some added at a later date. Here I am only citing those titles or incipits which appear to have been written by

Why have Ottoman scribes chosen to label these extremely similar narratives variously as *tarih*, *hikaye* or *gazavatname*? These different nomination practices are more explicable if the typographic model with its concomitant assumptions of authorial originality, textual stability and the figuring of the scribe as a vital printing press is abandoned in favor of one which recognizes that many manuscripts were not produced and consumed within a discourse of authority, but were part of a more fluid discourse which embodied different concepts of style, language, authorship and text. Such an approach does not explain the small, but significant differences in rubrication, framing, and narrative description as a consequence of orality or the technological limits of chirographic reproduction. Instead it argues that such manuscripts should be understood as re-inscriptions or performances by scribe-authors who read, interpreted and re-wrote the manuscripts to account for, and reflect, alternative religious and political perspectives and different textual functions.[6] Within this model the various rubrics can be understood as reflecting how the scribes perceived the genre and fictionality of the narrative and wished to position it for their implied audiences. Different titles therefore do not necessarily signify incorrect rubrication by ignorant scribes, but rather the diverse ways in which scribes responded to and categorized the narrative: as *tarih*, *hikaye* or *gazavatname*.

Although, the term *hikaye* is generally understood as connoting a tale or story and thus implying a fictional aspect, it is also applied to narratives with a historical theme and a greater degree of realism than those of other Ottoman literary genres such as epico-religious narratives. On the other hand, *tarih* is usually applied to narratives agreed to be about historical events, but this does not preclude the introduction of more imaginative elements, if required in order to convey the desired message or moral.[7] Moreover, for some, but not all,

---

the scribe at the time when the manuscript was written. The manuscripts that describe it as *hikaye* (story) are; British Library, London O.R.12961, and O.R.33; Bibliothèque Nationale, Paris, Nr. 525; Arkeoloji Müzesi, Istanbul, No. 374; and Preußische Nationalbibliothek, Berlin, A. Oct. 34. Those that describe it as a *tarih* (history) are; Millet Kütüphanesi, Istanbul, A. E. Tar.187, A. E. Tar.188, and A. E. Tar.189; Bayerische Staatsbibliothek, Munich, O. R. 393; and Preußische Nationalbibliothek, Berlin, Oct. 3442. Two manuscripts rubricate the narrative as the *Menakib-i Tiryaki Hasan Paşa* (*The Exemplary Deeds of Tiryaki Hasan Pasha*) thus categorising the text as being of the *menakibname* (narrative of exemplary deeds) genre: İl Halk Kütüphanesi, Manisa, No.5070; and National-bibliothek, Vienna, H.O.71d. Magyar Tudományos Akademia Konyvtara, Budapest, O.216 is rubricated as *risale* (treatise) while Biblioteca Universitaria, Bologna, Bub.3459; Bibliothèque Nationale, Paris, Sup.Turc.170; National-bibliothek, Vienna H.O.71b; and Staatsarchiv, Vienna, Nr.508 all classify the narrative as a *gazavatname* (battle narrative) through their use of the word *gazavat* (campaigns) in the title. For the title of Dar-al-Kutub, Cairo, No.235, which does not use any of these phrases, see endnote 4, above.

6 Tim William Machan, "Editing, Orality, and Late Middle English Texts," in *Vox Intexta: Orality and Textuality in the Middle Ages*, edited by A.N. Doane and Carol Braun Pasternack (Madison: The University of Wisconsin Press, 1991), pp. 236-7. John Dagenais in both *The Ethics of Reading in Manuscript Culture: Glossing the Libro de Buen Amor* (Princeton, N.J.: Princeton University Press, 1994), and "That Bothersome Residue: Toward a Theory of the Physical Text" in *Vox Intexta: Orality and Textuality in the Middle Ages* (as above) also argues for the application of reader-centerd models of analysis to certain corpuses of manuscripts.

7 The Ottoman historian Naima describes a seven-point ideal for writing history: to tell the truth and substantiate it; to disregard false tales current among the common folk; to not be content with 'simple annals,' but to enable the reader to draw the moral for himself; not to be partisan; to use plain language; to limit oneself to strictly appropriate embellishments; and to discuss astrology only when it can be proved that astrological causes had certain results. Quoted in Lewis Thomas, *A Study of Naima*, edited by Norman Itzkowitz (New York: New York University Press, 1972), p.116.

Ottoman audiences the term *tarih* more appropriately signifies the genre of chronicle history which relates the events of a sultan's reign year by year. For such audiences descriptions of specific military campaigns are more properly classified as *gazavatnames* and can contain more or less imaginative or rhetorical sections. The different titles on the Nagykanizsa manuscripts thus foreground the fluidity that the terms *tarih, hikaye* and *gazavatname* possessed for distinct Ottoman discourse communities: by variously rubricating these nearly identical manuscripts the scribes reflect different Ottoman understandings of the above genre classifications as well as different conceptions of the accuracy or fictionality of the Nagykanizsa narrative.

Katib Çelebi: Framing Story as History

The seventeenth-century Ottoman scholar Katib Çelebi reproduced the Nagykanizsa *gazavatname* narrative virtually *in toto* into his history of the Ottoman Empire *Fezleke al-tevarih* [*Epitome of History*].[8] Despite this almost verbatim incorporation, and in contrast to the *gazavatnames* which are today read as 'story,' the *Fezleke* has been received since the seventeenth century as true factual knowledge.[9] The concomitant bestowal of authority occasioned by this re-classification as non-fiction positions the work as 'history' and has permitted its use as a potential historical source by present-day historians. An analysis of the few variations between the *gazavatname* narratives and the *Fezleke* account can explain this dramatic shift in fictional and epistemological status and genre classification. Although some of Katib Çelebi's alterations function to situate the narrative in a more politically and religiously orthodox framework many seem designed to control the reception of the narrative as history. The framing, rubrication, vocabulary, intertextual references and the status

---

[8]   The work was originally written in Arabic with the title *Fazlaka akval al-ahvar fi 'ilm al-tarih va'l-ahbar*. Katib Çelebi subsequently translated it into Ottoman Turkish. I have employed two manuscripts of this work; Bodleian Library, Oxford, Rawl.or.20 and Sale60 and the nineteenth century printed version; Katib Çelebi *Fezleke-i Katib Çelebi* (Istanbul: Ceride-i Havadis Matbaası, 1286 [1869-70]). All references, unless otherwise stated, will be to the latter version. Dates for works published in the Ottoman era (up until 1923) have been given according to the *hicri* calendar (AH) with C.E. dates given in square brackets. I have argued in chapter two of "Plural Pasts: The Role of Function and Audience in the Creation of Meaning in Ottoman and Modern Turkish Accounts of the Sieges of Nagykanizsa" (Ph.D. Diss., University of Birmingham, 2004), that the wholesale unacknowledged inclusion of the work of other writers by Ottoman authors should not be viewed as plagiarism, evidence of unoriginality, residual orality or the result of a stunted literacy. Instead it should be understood as a device or means to legitimize and situate the work into an existing system of knowledge. In contrast to twenty-first century academic citation practices which function as integration and legitimizing procedures by diachronically and teleologically connecting a work to a specific field or body of knowledge, Ottoman scholars authorized and integrated their work through the specific inclusion of precedents, the incorporation of previous works, and the diffuse use of a shared vocabulary rather than through explicit citation practices. See C. Berkenkotter and T. Huckin, *Genre Knowledge in Disciplinary Communication: Cognition/Culture/Power* (Hove, UK: Lawrence Erlbaum Associates, 1995), pp. 46-7. G. Piterberg *An Ottoman Tragedy: History and Historiography at Play* (Berkeley: University of California Press, 2003), pp.53 and 119, also discusses Ottoman historians citation practices and the importance of not interpreting them in accordance with modern academic expectations.

[9]   For example, Suraiya Faroqhi in *Approaching Ottoman History: An Introduction to the Sources* (Cambridge: Cambridge University Press, 1999), pp.152-3, argues that Katib Çelebi in the *Fezleke* exemplifies the writing of history as a branch of scholarship rather than as a literary genre.

of the author all intersect and label or signal the account to audiences as non-fictional history.[10]

Among such indicators of the genre history is the inclusion of the *hatt-i hümayun* (imperial rescript) sent by the sultan to Tiryaki Hasan Pasha conferring upon him the position of vizier. The reproduction of such an official document, in effect, a primary source, confirms and authorizes the narrative and legitimizes the work as history and Katib Çelebi as a historian. Similarly, the inclusion of two different narrative versions of the 'flight of the servant' incident suggests that Katib Çelebi had access to and researched a number of different sources which again positions the work as history not fiction.[11] This is reinforced by his incorporation of direct and indirect references to the works of other Ottoman historians such as İbrahim Peçevi, Ahmed Hasan Beyzade and Abdülkadir Topçularkatibi.[12] Likewise, the explicit identification of the narrator with the author together with an erasure of all evidence of enunciation and subjective presence, with the exception of 'I' as historian, organizer of the text, and arbitrator of alternative narratives, figures the work as history. This contrasts with the *gazavatname* narratives where there is no such conflation and 'I' is often figured as an eyewitness or as a transmitter of the tale but never as a historian.

Katib Çelebi's use of more complex grammatical forms and Persian and Arabic vocabulary together with a decontextualized discourse also signals academic or historical writing to various audiences.[13] The subheadings are in Persian which, as a language of *authoritas* for the Ottomans, imbues the work with gravity and also positions it intertextually with the great classical histories of Islamic civilizations and empires. Katib Çelebi decontextualizes the narrative through an increased use of subordinate, as opposed to additive grammatical structures, relative clauses and intensifiers, and through the inclusion of linguistic features such as chronograms. This decontextualization is particularly pertinent for modern audiences whose horizon of expectations surrounding academic scholarship, and specifically the distinction between 'factual' history and 'fictional' historical literature, is intimately associated with the presence of expository prose, possibly the most decontextualized type of discourse.

Furthermore, the structuring of the narrative also conveys the genre of 'history' to audiences. It is broken into discrete sections by headings that are distinguished from the body of the text, either spatially or graphically. While the section titles in Bodleian Library, Oxford, Rawl.or.20 are illuminated in red ink, in the printed edition they are spatially distinct. These headings summarize the following paragraph and thus not only act as explanatory introduc-

---

[10]   Cf. Margreta de Grazia, *Shakespeare Verbatim: The Reproduction of Authenticity and the 1790 Apparatus* (Oxford: Clarendon Press, 1991), p.11.

[11]   Katib Çelebi, p. 163.

[12]   Katib Çelebi, p.170, directly quotes İbrahim Peçevi, *Tarih-i Peçevi* vol.2 (Istanbul: 1283 [1866-7]), p. 241, and also indirectly incorporates material from the works of Abdülkadir Topçularkatibi, *Tevarih-i al-i Osman* (Österreichische National-bibliothek, Vienna, Mxt. 130), cf. pp. 136-7 and fol.131a; and Ahmed Hasan Beyzade, *Talhis-i Tac al-tavarih* (Arkeoloji Müzesi, Istanbul, no. 234), cf. p.140 and fols 467a-b. Piterberg chapter 2 provides an introduction to Ottoman history writing and brief biographies of the Ottoman historians mentioned above.

[13]   See Deborah Tannen, "Relative Focus on Involvement in Oral and Written Discourse," in *Literacy, Language and Learning: The Nature and consequences of Reading and Writing*, edited by David R. Olson, Nancy Torrance, and Angela Hildyard (Cambridge: Cambridge University Press, 1985), pp. 137-8, for a discussion of the decontextualised nature of expository prose and its use in academic scholarship.

tions but in effect construct each event as a discrete phenomenon or incident. They also delineate the work as history through their chronological arrangement. The narration of the Nagykanizsa sieges does not form a discrete narrative unit, but is interspersed with descriptions of other events happening simultaneously in the Ottoman Empire. It is therefore read diachronically, as part of a continuous unfolding history, as one event among many in a war. In contrast, the *gazavatnames* are structurally subdivided, and events are managed, by the use of narratorial interjections such as the phrase *ez-in-canib* which literally translates as "from this side." These interjections do not identify specific events such as "the capture of the castle," or the "flight of the servants" as do the headings in *Fezleke*, but indicate scene changes when the action shifts from one person or place to another. The *gazavatname* narratives are therefore presented more synchronically which to modern audiences again positions them more as fictional stories than as histories.

A further contrast between the *Fezleke* and the *gazavatname* narratives which impacts upon the perceived fictional status and genre classifications is evident in the dating practices. While the *gazavatnames* occasionally refer to the day of the week on which key moments of the siege occurred, Katib Çelebi gives the calendar dates.[14] This use of the calendar locates and fixes events in a known world and time and asserts the realism of history, not fiction. Lastly, the *gazvatname* narrative is incorporated into a work which is already framed and understood by Ottoman and modern audiences as a history. The title *Epitome of History* immediately signals its genre and the reputation of the author as a scholar also precedes and conditions audiences' expectations.

The power of the re-framing of the *Fezleke* as non-fiction is illustrated in the subsequent acceptance as fact, by Ottoman and modern historians, of Katib Çelebi's fictional additions. His uncorroborated description of the Nagykanizsa garrison's successful attempt to manufacture more gunpowder during the siege is likely to be a fictional addition as it occurs in no earlier description of the siege.[15] Similarly he has embellished certain other incidents quite dramatically, most notably the gunpowder explosion in one of the towers which ostensibly occurred during the first siege. Of the three Ottoman historians who were present at the first siege of Nagykanizsa in 1600, only İbrahim Peçevi and Abdülkadir Topçularkatibi refer to an accidental explosion of gunpowder in the Habsburg held castle and they disagree as to when it occurred. İbrahim Peçevi states that it occurred before the enemy relief army appeared whereas Abdülkadir Topçularkatibi argues that it happened after the defeat and flight of the enemy army.[16] Hasan Beyzade, who participated in the siege and composed the *fethnames* [victory letters] distributed afterwards does not mention any explosion nor do any other European sources.[17] In the *Fezleke* however, these vague allusions to an accident have become exaggerated into a deliberate act of sabotage and heroic sacrifice by an Ottoman prisoner who, by throwing a lighted fuse into the gunpowder store, blew up the tower

---

[14] Katib Çelebi, pp.151-2.
[15] Katib Çelebi, p.161.
[16] İbrahim Peçevi, p.233 and Abdülkadir Topçularkatibi, fol. 138a.
[17] Cf. Knolles, *Generall Historie of the Turks...* (London, 1621); Nikolaus Istvanffy, N. *Historiarum de rebus vngaricis*, (Cologne, 1622); and W.P. Zimmermann, *Eikonographia aller deren ungarischer Statt Vostunge Castellen und Hauser welche von Anfang der Regierung Rudolphi des anderen Romischen Keyser biss auffdas 1603...* (Augsburg, 1603).

in which he and his fellow prisoners, including '*women, youths and especially virgins*', were imprisoned.[18]

Namık Kemal and the Fictional Fa'izi

Namık Kemal is best known as a journalist, novelist, and playwright, but his nineteenth-century work *Kanije* has generally been received as historical non-fiction. *Kanije* is largely based on the *Fezleke* but Namık Kemal also claims that much of it is derived from a now lost manuscript, the *Hasenat-i Hasan* by Fa'izi who was ostensibly an eyewitness participant in the siege and a close friend of the commander, Tiryaki Hasan Pasha: "in the heart of the treatise many things have been taken from the book of Fa'izi which has the title Hasenat-i Hasan."[19] Despite the fact that all other references to Fa'izi and his manuscript postdate the publication of Namık Kemal's *Kanije* they have become reified to such an extent that the *Hasenat-i Hasan* is frequently cited as a primary source for the siege.[20] The existence of both the author and manuscript has been uncritically accepted as fact, not fiction, by scholars and cataloguers such as Levend, Bursalı Mehmed Tahir, and Babinger.[21] However, I argue that Fa'izi is in fact a fictionalized narrative construct and thus offers an instructive paradigmatic case of the influence of framing on genre classification and fictional status.

There is no corroborative source for the existence of Fa'izi and his work. Although some scholars have tentatively identified him as Kafzade Fa'izi, records show that he would only have been twelve at the time of the siege and none of the contemporaneous Ottoman writers who discuss Kafzade Fa'izi's life and works mention that he was present at the siege of Nagykanizsa or that he later wrote about it.[22] There are also no extant manuscripts of the *Hasenat-i Hasan* and no mention of it in Ottoman bibliographical works of the seventeenth century.

A consideration of the possible narrative functions of Fa'izi further strengthens the argument that he was a literary device employed by Namık Kemal to frame his work as non-fictional history. Firstly, Fa'izi validates *Kanije* as history through being figured as an extraordinary primary source, an eyewitness account. In addition, potentially controversial assertions, and the introduction of fictive characters, events and interpretations not found in any other sources are presented as quotes from Fa'izi.[23] In this manner their reception as indicators of fictionality is contained and limited to the work of Fa'izi, allowing Namık

---

18   Katib Çelebi, p.138.
19   Namık Kemal, *Kanije* (Constantinople: Matbaa-i Ebuzziya, 1311 [1893]), p.3.
20   See Vahit Çabuk, *Tiryaki Hasan Paşa'nın Gazaları ve Kanije Savunması* (Istanbul: Tercuman 1001, Temel Eser, 1978), p. 7, and H. Ziya Ersever, *Kanije Savunması ve Tiryaki Hasan Paşa* (Ankara: Türk Asker Büyükleri ve Türk Zaferleri Seri no.12, Genelkurmay Askeri Tarih ve Stratejik Etüt Baskanlığı Yayınları Gnkur. Basımevi, 1986), p. 78.
21   Levend, pp.101-2, Bursalı Mehmed Tahir, *Osmanli Müellifleri* vol. 2. (Istanbul: Matbaa-i Amise, 1333 [1914-15]), p. .386; and Babinger, pp. 155-6.
22   Levend, p. 102, Babinger, pp. 155-6, and Bursalı Mehmed Tahir, p. 386. Levend, p. 102, mentions a number of contemporary Ottoman writers who do not mention Fa'izi's presence at the siege.
23   Potentially controversial statements include: the 18,000 enemy heads brought in front of Hasan Pasha; and the enemy's vision of the green-headed ghost fighters, Namık Kemal, pp.118 and 126. For fictive characters and events see the character of Abdulrahim who questions the wisdom of the grand vizier; and Sokullu Hasan the soldier who criticized Hasan Pasha for lying under oath, Namık Kemal, pp. 34 and 56-7.

Kemal's *Kanije* to still be read as non-fictional history. Likewise, enemy speeches and other examples of direct speech are framed as quotations from Fa'izi to constrain their fictionalizing tendencies. The inclusion of direct speech contextualizes and brings a sense of immediacy and passion to a narrative by permitting a greater degree of identification with the participants through the use of the first person. However, as a consequence this tends to shift the perceived genre from that of history to literature. Analogously, Namık Kemal can both portray Hasan Pasha as a mystical holy warrior and ensure his work is still received as history by presenting references to the fictionalized miraculous abilities of Tiryaki Hasan Pasha as direct quotes from Fa'izi: his descriptions of the eighty-seven-year-old Hasan Pasha being tied onto his horse, then leading the attack against the enemy, leaping into the trenches, personally filling in breaches in the castle walls, and sustaining numerous sword wounds as a result of the raging battle are figured as excerpts from Fa'izi's *Hasenat-i Hasan*.[24] In this manner Namık Kemal does not transgress the conventions inherent in the secular, enlightenment-influenced approaches to history prevalent at that time and thus ensures the continued reception of his work as non-fiction.

Analysis

What can these examples of the effect of framing on the fluid fictional status and genre of the Nagykanizsa narratives tell us about the fiction/non-fiction, story/history dichotomies? Conventionally, these categories are elucidated by representationalist, also known as foundationalist or realist models, which argue that non-fiction is distinguished from fiction by the presence of facts expressed as propositions which are made true as a result of their isomorphic correspondence to, or accurate representation of, a mind-independent reality. Such explanations rely upon the Kantian metaphysical axis of appearance-reality in that they distinguish between a non-description-relative world free from value judgments and human interests, and our perception and interpretation of this world, where in Platonic fashion the former acts as the truth maker of facts and guarantor of knowledge in the latter.

In a similar manner, history since the nineteenth century has been frequently described as epistemologically distinct from story or fiction. It claims the status of knowledge or justified true belief because of its representation of the 'actual' through the inclusion of verifiable facts; facts made true by their direct correspondence to the past. However, the development of language-based modes of criticism in the twentieth century have made explicit "the fictions of factual representation" and exposed both transparent language as rhetorical voice and facts as constructed artifacts.[25] This has led to an understanding that fiction and non-fiction, story and history share modes of narrativity and representation and that "[v]iewed simply as verbal artefacts," they are "indistinguishable from one another."[26] Consequently, many historians such as Appleby, Hunt, and Jacob have concluded that because all narrative requires a degree of fictionalizing, complete mimesis between their narratives and the objective world of fact is impossible and have instead argued for a high degree of

---

[24] Namık Kemal, pp.61-3 and 67-8.

[25] Hayden White, "The Fictions of Factual Representation," in Hayden White, *Tropics of Discourse: Essays in Cultural Criticism* (Baltimore and London: The Johns Hopkins University Press, 1978), p. 121.

[26] Nancy Partner, "Historicity in an Age of Reality-Fictions," in *A New Philosophy of History*, edited by Frank Ankersmit and Hans Kellner (London: Reaktion Books, 1995), p.24 and Hayden White, p. 122.

probability or "some correspondence" between people's perceptions of the world and the world itself in order to guarantee the non-fictional and epistemologically distinct status of history.[27] However, this idea of "some correspondence" based upon a combination of the theories of practical realism and pragmatism, rather than providing a heuristically beneficial synthesis is still susceptible to the problems inherent in any explanation which relies upon the concept of a mind-independent world as truth-maker.

It is argued that the most significant problem with the representationalist explanatory model is its emphasis on representation, correspondence, and the appearance-reality distinction which ultimately cause it to collapse into extreme skepticism or relativism. From where can we distinguish appearance from reality, the scheme of our perceptions from the content, the subjective from the objective, the noumenal from the phenomenal? How can we verify the accuracy of the correspondence between reality and our perception of it in order to guarantee the truth of our facts or propositions? In addition to these theoretical problems there are more practical concerns. The representationalist explanation of genre and fictional status does not describe tangible *praxis*, it does not delineate how audiences actually construct and recognize these categories. It also forces changes in fictional status and genre to be explained using the vocabulary of error: if there is one true picture of the world then past or alternative classifications must be incorrect or false.

I want to elucidate an alternative explanatory model to explain how and why the Nagykanizsa narratives have been variously received as fiction or non-fiction, story or history, one which abandons the vocabulary of metaphysics and the correspondence theories of truth and meaning for a pragmatist theory of justification based upon our practice. Rorty argues that knowledge claims do not need to be justified by correspondence to an ontologically grounded extra-social authority, but rather they can be authorized in terms of a justificatory responsibility tied indexically to our community and social practices. In other words, it is the protocols or standards of warranted assertibility determined by the community which validate and justify our beliefs and knowledge and thus distinguish fiction from fact.

The importance of these protocols in historical *praxis* and in determining fictional status and genre is evident from Partner's argument that language-based modes of criticism have had no practical effect on actual historical academic practice. Historians continue to adhere to the integrity of method manifested through disciplinary protocols which govern the finding and handling of evidence and methods of argumentation, not because it ensures correspondence with a real past, but because this is what writing academic history in the twenty-first century consists of. Non-adherence to these protocols opens historians to charges of fraud or shoddiness and excludes their work from the genre of history.[28] It is this semiotic scaffold established and maintained by "communities of the competent," not correspondence to a mind-independent true past that signals the genre, fictional status, textual intention and truth claims of the work to audiences.[29] These practices constitute a readable code which states that sentences susceptible to verification can be verified according to the norms of historical practice and that interpretative sentences have been constructed following generally accepted rules of reasoning.[30]

---

27 Cited in, Richard Rorty, *Truth and Progress* (Cambridge: Cambridge University Press, 1998), pp. 73-4 n. 11.
28 Partner, p. 22.
29 Phrase is from Thomas Haskell, following Francis Abbot, cited in Rorty, p. 74 n. 11.
30 Partner, p. 23.

In more detail, the protocols for twenty-first century academic history writing include the use of standard models for the ascription of cause, effect, and contingency; the physical framing of the work as history through the employment of a critical apparatus, or the icons of scholarship, such as the acknowledgements, explanatory introduction, footnotes, bibliographical references, appendices, and indexes; invocations of authority such as the identification of the narratorial voice with the known author and the attribution of information to cited sources; coherence, both intra- and intertextually, including intersubjective agreement among historians; inclusiveness – the narrative should explain coherently all the evidence available; a decontextualized tone achieved through the use of expository prose which requires less interpretative engagement by the reader; and an explicit explanatory purpose or function.[31]

Thus, it is neither correspondence with the past 'as it is in itself,' nor referentiality with an extrinsic reality, but the degree of a narrative's adherence to the particular set of protocols or desiderata stipulated by current academic historical *praxis* that allows audiences to both distinguish between history and story, fact and fiction, and also to critically evaluate particular histories or stories as good or bad. The distinction between genres and fictional status, between history and historical fiction or literature, does not therefore lie in different structures of factuality verified through correspondence to the past, but in different patterns of *praxis* and justification. Moreover, while everyone may agree that factual narratives such as histories describe actual events, the decision as to what counts as an actual event is determined by community-based norms of interpretation rather than referentiality with an external world. The epistemic status of a narrative, its status as fact or fiction, true or false is thus not inalienable and fixed forever. Rather it shifts with situational, disciplinary and other contextually variable factors: criteria internal to interpretative communities and their needs, not external to them.[32] When we describe something as true, factual or non-fictional we are not commenting upon its relation to a non-linguistic reality; rather, we are endorsing it within a particular framework, for a specific audience and function. It is the fluidity of these protocols or interpretative strategies that can explain the impact of framing on the shifting status of the Nagykanizsa narratives from fiction to non-fiction and vice versa.

The *gazavatnames* are rubricated as *hikaye, tarih* or *gazavatname* because this is how they were judged by the differing protocols of diverse Ottoman audiences. For some scribes the *gazavatname* narrative contained 'fictional' elements which positioned the work as *hikaye* whereas for others the realistic depiction of the historical events figured it as *tarih*.

---

[31]   See Partner, pp. 22-3 and 26; Paul Armstrong, *Conflicting Readings: Variety and Validity in Interpretation* (London: North Carolina Press, 1990), pp.13-6; Matt Oja, "Fictional History and Historical Fiction: Solzhenitsyn and Kis as Exemplars," *History and Theory*, Vol. 27, No 2 (May 1988), pp. 119-21; Michal Zellermayer, "An Analysis of Oral and Literate Texts: Two Types of Reader-Writer Relationship in Hebrew and English," in *The Social Construction of Written Communication*, edited by B. Raforth and D. Rubin (Norwood N.J.: Ablex Publishing Corp., 1988), pp. 299-300; Tannen, "Relative Focus...," pp.137-8; and Robert F. Berkhofer, *Beyond the Great Story: History as Text and Discourse* (Cambridge, Mass.: The Belknap Press of Harvard University Press, 1995), pp. 51-2.

[32]   The notion of an 'interpretative community' is derived from Stanley Fish, "Introduction, or How I Stopped Worrying and Learned to Love Interpretation," in S. Fish, *Is There a Text in this Class* (Cambridge Mass.: Harvard University Press, 1980), p.14: "Interpretative communities are made up of those who share interpretive strategies not for reading, but for writing texts, for constituting their properties"   and "An interpretive community is [....] a bundle of interests, of particular purposes and goals."

The *gazavatnames* are read as fictional story today, because they not only lack the framing structures necessary to twenty-first century academic history: the critical apparatus, the explicit reference to sources, an identification of author and narrator, and a decontextualized tone; moreover, they also include criteria which signal fiction or story such as: a preponderance of direct speech, obvious exaggeration, and the presence of miraculous events. However, a closer analysis of the Nagykanizsa *gazavatnames* reveals a high degree of intersubjective coherence between them and other sources for the event which may ultimately result in their reclassification within a framework of twenty-first century academic historical scholarship as having at least some historical validity or accuracy.

The reception of Katib Çelebi's re-framing of the 'fictional' *gazavatname* narrative as non-fiction illustrates the importance of protocols in determining the reception and status of the work. There are no extra facts in this account which allow it to correspond more closely with a mind-independent past reality, rather the narrative, through references to other historians and eyewitnesses, the incorporation of primary sources, the diachronic structuring of events and a more decontextualized discourse, is framed in such a way that it accords with the protocols of modern academic history. Ultimately, therefore it is judged to be non-fictional history because it looks like non-fictional history.

The acknowledgement that the 'fictional' *gazavatname* account was incorporated into the *Fezleke* does not necessarily cause a reclassification of the latter as legendary narrative or bad history. Indeed such is the reputation of Katib Çelebi as a forerunner of modern historians among current Ottomanists that this observation is more likely to result in a re-categorization of the *gazavatname* narratives as history. Similarly, the identification of a number of 'fictional' elements in Katib Çelebi's narrative does not, in effect, alter present-day categorizations of his work as history because the majority of the work continues to abide by modern history-writing protocols and standards. Indeed, the slight variation in norms and protocols signaled by the presence of these 'fictional' additions, instead simply foregrounds the fluidity of the genre 'history' and makes explicit the differences between Ottoman and modern academic understandings of the term: for many Ottoman interpretative communities an essential criteria of 'history' was not an isomorphic correspondence to a mind-independent past reality, but rather that it conveyed the appropriate message. This is illustrated by Naima's addition of a fragment of verse into his virtual *verbatim* incorporation of Katib Çelebi's Nagykanizsa narrative into his own history of the Ottoman Empire written at the end of the seventeenth century. Immediately after the section giving two different versions of the 'flight of the servant' incident he writes: "It may be that some call the beloved, cypress and some elif The aim of all of them is one, but the telling differs."[33]

The explanatory force of this diptych works on a number of levels, but essentially, just as the cypress tree and the Arabic letter *elif* which have different referents are both used to signify the beloved, the two distinct 'servant' narratives can be read as signifying the same thing and serving the same function historically. The poem therefore can be read as evidence of one Ottoman perception of the function of history: that it is not necessarily, or solely, about accurately representing the past or telling *the* truth about what *really* happened, but that it also has a didactic or exemplary function.

---

[33] Naima *Ravat ül-hüseyn fi hulasat-i ahbar il-hafikayn* more commonly called the *Tarih-i Naima,* (3rd ed. Istanbul: Matbaa-i âmire, 1281-3 [1864-6]), p. 277.

Lastly, later audiences' reification of Fa'izi and his manuscript has occurred not because of any correspondence to reality, but because Fa'izi and his role in Namık Kemal's *Kanije* make the same pattern that non-fiction makes; he looks real or factual. Thus, ultimately fiction can and does become non-fiction, history becomes story and vice versa, when we agree t does.

IV LITERATURE AS HISTORY

Introduction to Part IV

Literature as History

The fourth part of this book takes seriously literature's claim for historical knowledge. It includes readings of some literary narratives that address the historical past of the 20th century: campaigns against the war in Vietnam, urbanization in the Caribbean Islands, and recovery from the traumatic experience of Hiroshima. In all cases, literary writing furnishes some new tools that flesh out the historical record and provides a more complete picture of our past, a picture that also takes into account its subjective, material, and traumatic nature.

Markku Lehtimäki creates an imaginary dialogue between Hayden White's theories and Norman Mailer's self-reflexive "nonfiction novel" The Armies of the Night (1968). Lehtimäki shows how Mailer uses the subjective point of view and different literary techniques in order to "correct the errors" that traditional historiography produces. Referring to structuralist narratology, Lehtimäki also charts certain theoretical shortcomings as well as some of the more illuminating aspects in Hayden White's work, and proposes how his general remarks about narrativization might eventually profit by focusing even more on complex cases of literary narrative, fictional or nonfictional.

Concentration on written documents tends to marginalize those groups who have no access to power, and many Third World authors feel that it is their duty to give voice to those histories that have survived only in either oral memory or material traces. Olabode Ibironke's essay is an attempt to understand the obsessive presence of the past in the Caribbean novel, especially in Patrick Chamoiseau's Texaco. Using analytical tools provided by Michel Foucault and Henri Lefebvre, among others, he argues that a unique sense of the past is constituted in this novel precisely through its account of transformations of space or "the tactics of the habitat." The article concludes that the theory implicit in Chamoiseau's Texaco is significant for how it experiments with and opens up the possibility of constructing an alternative history of a community, one which is based on the transformations of home, its architectures and monuments.

In the last chapter of the book, Lara Okihiro brings into focus the question of how to represent the past, particularly in a way that will meet the terms of a horrific, traumatic event and transmit it to the audience. Taking Robert Lepage's play Les sept branches de la rivière Ota (1996) as the central focus of the presentation, Okihiro examines three issues regarding what it is to remember the traumatic historical event of Hiroshima. First, she considers how historical referents are subject to the potential of being emptied of their particular significance. Second, in examining the relationship between the play and history she asks how a visual medium supports or suspends historical narratives, notably in terms of the contradictory theme of blindness or the admission of not having witnessed the bomb. Finally, she reflects on how Lepage's play inherits the history of Hiroshima through a topographical theme of the river Ota in a way that neither remembers nor loses sight of the event. Where mapping and storytelling converge, she argues, moments coalesce that break or suspend habitual and automatic memorial responses.

CHAPTER 10

Markku Lehtimäki

History as a Crazy House: Norman Mailer, Hayden White, and
the Representation of a Modernist Event

In Norman Mailer's works of literary nonfiction, conventional forms of storytelling are no
longer valid in representing a mysterious modern event, be it the first moon flight or the
assassination of President Kennedy. This notion about new modes of representation required by specific *modernist* events comes very close to Hayden White's thesis, especially
in his more recent writings from the 1990s. One of the basic ideas in White's theories is that
narrative discourse is not a neutral medium for the representation of historical events and
processes but a significant mode that endows those events and processes with plot, coherence, and meaning. As White argues in connection with such paradigmatic events of the
modern age as the Holocaust and the Kennedy assassination, the form and content of textual
representation become almost indistinguishable from each other, so that "cultural modernism has to be seen as both a reflection of and a response to this new actuality."[1] According
to my reading of both Mailer's literary work and White's theoretical work, a kind of modernist event does not lend itself to explanation and understanding in terms of conventional
categories and techniques. What most clearly links these two figures together is that both
emphasize the importance of new, self-reflexive, and experimental ways of historical *representation*, both in verbal and visual form, whereby both appear to reflect on how literary
modernism is partly influenced by the developments and revolutions in the visual media in
the twentieth century.

White's thesis about making history meaningful through literary shaping and emplotting
apparently comes close to such poetics of postmodernism as represented, among others, by
Linda Hutcheon, who argues that "the meaning and shape are not *in the events*, but *in the
systems* which make those past 'events' into present historical 'facts.'"[2] As Hutcheon herself reflects, to take this position does not mean a dishonest refuge from truth, but an ac-
knowledgment of the meaning-making function of human constructs. When discussing
White's theories, we should note his strong emphasis on narrativization, and according to
him, the most crucial concern for the narrative historian appears to be the telling of a story
and the finding of the most plausible story form that can be told about the documented
events of the historical past. As regards the much-discussed "impossibility" to represent the
Holocaust, White does not believe that there are any actual limits on the kind of story that
can truthfully and responsibly be told about these phenomena, but he rather suggests that

---

[1] Hayden White, *Figural Realism: Studies in the Mimesis Effect.* (Baltimore and London: The Johns Hopkins
University Press, 1999), p. 41.
[2] Linda Hutcheon, *A Poetics of Postmodernism: History, Theory, Fiction.* (New York and London: Routledge,
1988), p. 89.

"its representation, whether in history or in fiction, requires [--] *the modernist style.*"[3] This means that the representation of historical events (like the Holocaust) must be made in such a way as to make those events *believable* to readers who have no experience of such events.[4] White's conclusion here is that "the stylistic innovations of modernism [--] may provide better instruments for representing modernist events,"[5] and what ultimately counts are not the facts themselves but the different story forms that help to make those facts meaningful.

In this essay, then, I will construct a tentative comparison with two distinct figures, Norman Mailer and Hayden White, suggesting certain similarities in their thinking. While Mailer's innovations in the mode of 'literary nonfiction' or 'the nonfiction novel' have caused much critical debate, even more can be said of the critical response to White's well-known thesis of narrativization and emplotting of historical events. There is a somewhat dangerous implication in White's theory that "anything goes" in terms of the representation of historical events, and still White seems to problematize one of his main tropes, *irony*, as a seriously political basis for a world-view. Similarly Mailer, on the basis of his private philosophy (or mythology), argues that our fashionably postmodernist sense of irony and absurdity inadequately captures the ultimate sense of *tragedy* in contemporary (American) history. In this essay my focal texts are White's theoretical writings, on the one hand, and Mailer's works of 'literary nonfiction,' on the other. Especially, I will focus on *The Armies of the Night* (1968), Mailer's novel/history about the March on the Pentagon, and *Oswald's Tale* (1995), his documentary account of the ultimate "American mystery," the assassination of John F. Kennedy and Lee Harvey Oswald's possible participation in it.[6] In addition to Mailer's Oswald version, I will make some comparative notes to Don DeLillo's novel *Libra* and other representations of this paradigmatic "modernist event" as discussed, among others, by Hayden White.

The Filtered Vision: Mailer's History of the March on the Pentagon

In order to recognize what kind of "modernist style" is suggested by Mailer in his self-conscious literary nonfiction, we might begin by reflecting on the specific form and aim of his major work. *The Armies of the Night*, with its subtitle *History as a Novel/The Novel as History*, signifies a modernist text's self-consciousness of existing literary conventions and the aims of breaking those conventions. Both personal and textual "schizophrenia" seems to

---

[3]   White, *Figural Realism*, p. 42; my emphasis.

[4]   As regards a realistically "believable" portrayal of death camps, the book entitled *Fragments* written by a man called Binjamin Wilkomirski raised much critical controversy after it was revealed to be a false memoir. See, for example, Susan Rubin Suleiman, "Problems of Memory and Factuality in Recent Holocaust Memoirs: Wilkomirski/Wiesel." *Poetics Today* 21:3 (2000), pp. 543-559.

[5]   White, *Figural Realism*, p. 82.

[6]   In the text, I will refer to the following editions of Mailer's books and use the following abbreviations: *The Advertisements for Myself* (New York: G.P. Putnam's Sons, 1959) [AM]; *The Armies of the Night: History as a Novel/The Novel as History* (London: Weidenfeld and Nicholson, 1968) [AN]; *Oswald's Tale: An American Mystery* (London: Abacus, 1996 [1995]) [OT]; *Pieces and Pontifications* (Boston: Little, Brown, 1982) [PP]; *The Prisoner of Sex* (Boston: Little, Brown, 1971) [PS]; and *St. George and the Godfather* (New York: Signet Books, 1972) [SGG].

define some of Mailers nonfiction, very self-consciously so.[7] The narrative text of *The Armies of the Night* as a whole is divided into two parts, as the subtitle of the book also suggests. Book One of *Armies*, "History as a Novel: The Steps of the Pentagon," is more like a novelistic narrative in its style and intent, describing the character Norman Mailers involvement in the March on the Pentagon, a demonstration against the Vietnam war, in Washington, D.C., in October 1967. Book Two, "The Novel as History: The Battle of the Pentagon," attempts to describe the same event by using the tools of journalism and historiography, at least seemingly changing the subjective, participatory viewpoint of the first book onto the level of a detached, "objective," as if panoramic vision. Throughout the book it is implied, and occasionally made explicit, that the "mysterious" and "ambiguous" event itself requires these different viewpoints, techniques, and generic styles.[8]

When trying to represent his subject, the March on the Pentagon in *The Armies of the Night*, Mailer is forced to contemplate the difficulty of historical writing which is that "the *history* is interior – no documents can give sufficient intimation," and therefore "*the novel* must replace history at precisely that point where experience is sufficiently emotional, spiritual, psychical, moral, existential, or supernatural" (AN, 255; my emphases). In Mailer's book the historical event becomes represented as a "paradigm" of the contradictions of the twentieth century, "an ambiguous event whose essential value or absurdity may not be established for ten or twenty years, or indeed ever" (AN, 53). This inherent complexity, indeterminacy, ambiguity and contradictoriness of the event cannot be approached and understood from the "objective" and "factual" viewpoint of the established media or those people, like organizers of the march, who were "the real principals":

> For that, an eyewitness who is a participant but not a vested partisan is required, further he must not only be involved, but ambiguous in his own proportions, a comic hero, which is to say, one cannot happily resolve the emphasis of the category – is he finally comic, a ludicrous figure with mock-heroic associations; or is he not unheroic, and therefore embedded somewhat *tragically* in the *comic*? Or is he both at once, and all at once? These questions, which probably are not much more answerable than the very ambiguities of the event, at least help to recapture the precise feel of *the ambiguity of the event* and its monumental disproportions. (AN, 53; my emphases)

As White argues in a different context, "no historical event is *intrinsically tragic*," and thus "the same set of events can serve as components of a story that is tragic *or* comic, as the case may be, depending on the historian's choice of the plot structure." Actually, for White, "all the historian needs to do to transform a tragic into a comic situation is to shift his point of view or change the scope of his perceptions."[9] However, Mailer's deliberate hesitation at the outset of these questions suggests that the ambiguity of the event itself requires different

7   See Linda Hutcheon, *Narcissistic Narrative: The Metafictional Paradox* (New York and London: Methuen, 1984), pp. 29, 94; *A Poetics of Postmodernism*, p. 117.
8   Compare T.V. Reed, *Fifteen Jugglers, Five Believers: Literary Politics and the Poetics of American Social Movements* (Berkeley et al.: University of California Press, 1992). Reed sees a deliberate hermeneutical and interpretive problematics at the core of *Armies*, so that the book "is constructed in such a way that the problem of reading the text and the problem of reading the event illuminate each other" (ibid., p. 90). 9. Hayden White: *Tropics of Discourse: Essays in Cultural Criticism* (Baltimore: The Johns Hopkins University Press, 1978), p. 84.
9   Ibid., p. 85.

approaches and perceptions, both tragic *and* comical – and still the complex reality itself eventually eludes any grasp of the historian.

What is especially idiosyncratic (or "Mailerian") here is that Mailer's own ego and character serves as a "tool" and "vehicle" in the approach to the "crazy" history, for "[o]nce *History inhabits a crazy house*, egotism may be the last tool left to History" (AN, 54; my emphasis). Therefore, reflecting on the very ambiguity of the event which requires an ambiguous protagonist, the author-narrator declares: "Let us then make our comic hero [Norman Mailer] the narrative vehicle for the March on the Pentagon" (AN, 54). Joseph Wenke accordingly connects the somewhat hybrid figure of the comic character Mailer with "the hybrid form of the nonfiction novel," while there is also an implication that approaching this "mysterious event" requires a new kind of literary form.[10] In this sense, Mailer uses "himself," the novelistic protagonist Norman Mailer, as a "mimetic," "thematic," and "synthetic" character component which would reflect the complex event itself.[11]

The Armies of the Night is Mailer's more or less conscious rewriting of Henry Adams's classic autobiography *The Education of Henry Adams* (1918) in which the author-narrator similarly tells about himself in the third person. In his essay about the method and ideology in intellectual history, focusing on *The Education of Henry Adams*, White contemplates how "the author seeks to characterize his own book, assign it to a genre and identify its specificity within the genre" and how the author "speaks of himself in the third person singular – as 'he,' 'Adams,' and so forth – splitting himself into both the speaker who is hidden behind the anonymity of the narrative form and the referent or the subject of the narrative, who occupies the center stage."[12] As White puts it, in connection with Adams's work, "the classic text reveals, indeed actively draws attention to, its own process of meaning-production and makes of these processes its own subject matter, its own 'content,'" and this content is primarily "the *ideological* content of the text as a whole."[13] As I see it, Mailer in his *Armies* also uses a specific kind of literary and narrative form (the "history/novel" or "the nonfiction novel," if you will) in order to present a certain "ideological" content. *The Armies of the Night* consequently serves as an example of such literary nonfiction which brings the form and the content into a complex, dialectic, and reciprocal relationship.

When reflecting on his narrative technique which aims "to study itself" and "to regard itself," Mailer notes that "such egotism" actually "finds itself therefore at home in a *house of mirrors*" (AN, 54; my emphasis). In a sense, the modernist situation requires a modernist narrative mode, or as Shlomith Rimmon-Kenan sees it, modernist and postmodernist novels "theorize" representation and subjectivity through strategies of narration, sometimes problematizing attempts to distinguish between "narrating subject and narrated object, container and contained, outside and inside, higher and lower narrative levels."[14] Here we are coming

---

[10]   See Joseph Wenke, *Mailer's America* (Hanover and London: University Press of New England, 1987), p. 139.

[11]   James Phelan discusses "the irreducibly synthetic component of character" in *The Armies of the Night* and analyzes characters "as artificial constructs playing particular roles in the larger construct that is the whole work." Phelan, *Reading People, Reading Plots: Character, Progression, and the Interpretation of Narrative.* Chicago: University of Chicago Press, 1989, pp. 2-3, 190-198.

[12]   Hayden White, *The Content of the Form: Narrative Discourse and Historical Representation* (Baltimore: The Johns Hopkins University Press, 1987), p. 207.

[13]   Ibid., pp. 211, 204.

[14]   Shlomith Rimmon-Kenan, *A Glance Beyond Doubt: Narration, Representation, Subjectivity* (Columbus: Ohio State University Press, 1996), p. 26.

close to paradoxical narrative structures and Möbius strip-like constructions. In his subsequent narrative about the 1972 Republican Convention, *St. George and the Godfather* (1972), Mailer consequently reflects that "moving around a ring made of a strip of paper, one finds oneself first on the outside, then on the inside," and thus "*history has moved from a narrative line to a topological warp*" (SGG, 35; my emphasis). Accordingly, when discussing the Watergate affair in his essay "A Harlot High and Low" (1976) Mailer contemplates "a vision of reality" which forces us to recognize that "Franz Kafka is the true if abstract historian of the modern age, and the Möbius strip is the nearest surface we can find to a plane" (PP, 203).

The narrative world of *The Armies of the Night* is both "mediated" and "warped" in various ways, and as a participant in the midst of the events, partly reflecting his role as the author-narrator, Mailer tries to find a clear vision of the happenings. Still he has to recognize that "the air was violent, yet full of amusement; *out of focus*" (AN, 81; my emphasis), and that "the fine line of earlier perception (and Vision!) got mucked in general confusion" (AN, 118). The confusing happenings of the demonstration are seen and perceived through different optical means and devices, so that the experience is both visual and "filtered" at the same time.[15] The March on the Pentagon is already a produced media spectacle, visually represented at the moment of its happening: "Newsreel, still, and television cameras were clicking and rounding and snapping and zooming" (AN, 105); Mailer and other participants are before "hundreds of Leicas and Nikons and Exactas in the hands of professional photographers" (AN, 106); they are walking "in this barrage of cameras, helicopters, TV cars, monitors, loudspeakers" (AN, 113); and as Mailer is obliged to feel in the middle of this media event, "if his head was busted this day, let it be before the eyes of America's TV viewers tonight" (AN, 107). According to Mas'ud Zavarzadeh's analysis: "The camera watches Mailer who also watches Mailer who participates in the March. The reality is filtered through so many reflectors a Chinese-box structure seems to surround the core of the alleged real."[16] As Morris Dickstein put it, Mailer has "made himself the protagonist of the story, *filtering the history* through the prism of his own ambivalence."[17] Thus the character Mailer reflects that "the participant was not only a witness and actor in these proceedings, but was being photographed as well!" (AN, 133); he also feels that he was "disembodied from himself, as if indeed he were watching himself in a film where this action was taking place" (AN, 129), and eventually focalizes that he "was seeing objects now with *[a] kind of filtered vision*" (AN, 139; my emphasis).[18]

---

[15] In the modernist period, new visual devices, techniques, and technologies have led to the emergence of new, modernist kinds of observers and visual relationships. See, for example, Karen Jacobs, *The Eye's Mind: Literary Modernism and Visual Culture* (Ithaca and London: Cornell University Press, 2001), p. 3. As I would argue, the "nonfiction novel" is a kind of natural (or should we say artificial) outgrowth from this cultural development.

[16] Maṣud Zavarzadeh, *The Mythopoeic Reality: The Postwar American Nonfiction Novel* (Urbana: University of Illinois Press, 1976), p. 167.

[17] Morris Dickstein, *Leopards in the Temple: The Transformation of American Fiction 1945-1970* (Cambridge: Harvard University Press, 2002), p. 159; my emphasis.

[18] Seymour Chatman proposes the term filter to mean a large field of mental activity experienced by the characters in the story world; the metaphor of filter thus corresponds to the idea of 'internal focalization' in which the narrative world is presented (or filtered) through the perspective, optical vision and cognition of one of its characters. See Chatman, *Coming to Terms: The Rhetoric of Narrative in Fiction and Film* (Ithaca and Lon-

Through various metaphorically optic devices, the events of the demonstration grow even more obscure and strange, as if Mailer were consciously using formalist techniques of estrangement and defamiliarization in his perception of objects and phenomena of the real world. Art's "estrangement" or "defamiliarization" techniques consequently foreground the artificial patterns and structures of a given literary work, directing the reader to pay attention to the textual construction itself. As the Russian Formalists, like Shklovsky, saw it, the special task of literature is to give us back our awareness of things which have become habitualized and automatized in our daily perception of them. The formalists accordingly foreground such art which, through its devices, leads people to see reality with "new" eyes. As White sees it, one way "we make sense of a set of events which appears strange, enigmatic, or mysterious in its immediate manifestations is to encode the set in terms of culturally provided categories, such as metaphysical concepts, religious beliefs, or story forms," and "the effect of such encodations is to familiarize the unfamiliar."[19] In *The Armies of the Night* Mailer employs various cultural frames which make the ambiguous and often chaotic event of the march and the demonstration more *meaningful* in a cognitive sense, at least to himself. For instance, when seeing and experiencing the random attack of the military police on the demonstrators, Mailer first contemplates this "odd" scene not knowing how to relate to it, until "this image" leads him to a further reflection and recognition: "[…] and *Mailer knew where he had seen this before*, this posture of men running in charge, yes it had been in *the photographs of Mathew Brady* of Union soldiers on the attack across the field, […]" (AN, 126; my emphases). As Barbara Lounsberry adds, seeing the charge repelled, Mailer imaginatively relives the Civil War experience of the protagonist of Stephen Crane's classic novel *The Red Badge of Courage*.[20] Here specific cultural frames, scripts, and schemas (in this case, well-known visual images and literary allusions) provide cognitive "naturalization" devices which familiarize the obscure and unfamiliar scene, making it meaningful and even understandable for the perceiving self.

In his study *The Mythopoeic Reality: The Postwar American Nonfiction Novel* Mas'ud Zavarzadeh argues (more or less persuasively) that the bipolar approach fictional/factual is no longer capable of dealing with current literary realities. On the whole his book is devoted to the discussion of "a zone of experience where the factual is not secure or unequivocal but seems preternaturally strange and eerie, and where the fictional seems not all that fictitious, remote and alien, but bears an uncanny resemblance to daily experience."[21] Instead of attaching "the nonfiction novel" either directly to the fictional or factual mode, Zavarzadeh proposes that works like Mailer's *The Armies of the Night* (one of his main examples) represent the *fictual* and *bi-referential* mode "becoming the concrete narrative

---

don: Cornell University Press, 1990), p. 143; compare also Dorrit Cohn, *The Distinction of Fiction* (Baltimore and London: The Johns Hopkins University Press, 1999), p. 177. Of course, the use of the filter also belongs to cinematographic technique in which various softening, obscuring, or colored filters in the lens of the camera render the narrative world in different ways, sometimes foregrounding a subjective perception of that world.

[19]   White, *Tropics of Discourse*, p. 86.

[20]   See Barbara Lounsberry, *The Art of Fact: Contemporary Artists of Nonfiction*. New York: Greenwood Press, 1990, p. 161.

[21]   Zavarzadeh, *The Mythopoeic Reality*, p. 56.

correlative for the fictuality of the present times."[22] Arguably, then, specific "unnatural" events of, especially, the twentieth century can only be approached with the help of techniques provided by literary modernism, as White also suggests. Consequently, White cites Primo Levi's way of laying bare his narrative devices in his subjective representations of the actuality of the Holocaust in *Il Sistema periodico*. In that book Levi reflects upon his own writing so that the reader realizes at a certain point that "this is not a chemical treatise," "nor is it an autobiography," "but it is in some fashion a history," and "it is – or would have liked to be – a microhistory."[23] In another context, Levi has discussed his attempts at producing "a filtered truth" through a "self-conscious book," thus anticipating Mailer's practices in his self-reflexive nonfiction.[24]

When compared to classic historiographical discourse or to realistic tradition in the novel, we may see how some modernist or postmodernist literary nonfictions do not aim at creating historical reality, or telling it "like it is," as seen through some transparent window to the real. As Reed suggests, Mailer's *Armies* "can be read through the lens of 'postmodernist realism'" which means "at once a mode of writing and a mode of reading, one that features self-reflexive, realism-disrupting techniques but places those techniques in tension with 'real' cognitive claims and with 'realistic,' radically pragmatic political needs."[25] Mailer occasionally stops his narrative in order to discuss what kind of work this is, thus foregrounding its self-consciously "historical" and "novelistic" devices:

> So the Novelist working in secret collaboration with the Historian has perhaps tried to build with his novel *a tower fully equipped with telescopes* to study – at the greatest advantage – our own horizon. Of course, the tower is crooked, and the telescopes are warped, but *the instruments of all sciences – history so much as physics – are always constructed in small or large error*; what supports the use of them now is that our intimacy with *the master builder of the tower, and the lens grinder of the telescopes (yes, even the machinist of the barrels)* has given some advantage for correcting the error of the instruments and the imbalance of his tower. [--] (For the novel – if we permit ourselves this parenthesis – is, when it is good, *the personification of a vision which will enable one to comprehend other visions better; a microscope* – if one is exploring the pond; a telescope upon a tower if you are scrutinizing the forest.) (AN, 219; my emphases)

After stating that "[t]he method [of this book] is then exposed" (AN, 219), Mailer argues that the "objective" approaches of conventional journalism and the mass media succeeded only in obscuring the history of the demonstration. What is therefore needed is a "subjec-

---

22 Ibid., 57. In the fhe following Zavarzadeh refers to Mailer's well-known "awareness of the complexity of reality and the impossibility of rendering it in a conventional, realistic manner" (ibid., p. 159). Zavarzadeh's study is one of the many which argue that new kinds of "postmodernist fiction," "transfiction" or "nonfiction novel" represent a reflection of, and are partly produced by, the "current realities" of contemporary America (e.g., experiences of entropy, absurdity, paranoia, and apocalypse).

23 See White, *Figural Realism*, p. 42.

24 See John Russell, *Reciprocities in the Nonfiction Novel*. Athens and London: The University of Georgia Press, 2000, p. 6. According to Russell, Levi's book is one of the masterpieces of "the nonfiction novel," a literary form which attaches itself to truthfulness but "slants" and "filters" actual experiences through the subjectivity and artistry of the author-narrator, producing a self-consciously "fashioned text" and "formal object" (see ibid., pp. 6-8, 107).

25 Reed, *Fifteen Jugglers, Five Believers*, pp. 18, 88. Compare also: "Postmodernist realism is a mode of writing that cuts across traditional genres and forms, since it has as one of its premises that narration (or narrativity) and other formal elements inform both fictive and factual, literary and nonliterary writing" (ibid., p. 21). As I see it, this contention comes close to White's position, and actually partly derives from it. Still, Reed's idea of postmodernist realism cannot be attached to simply postmodernist fiction.

tive" perception of the novel and its possibility to clarify the extreme complexity of reality: "The mass media which surrounded the March on the Pentagon created *a forest of inaccuracy which would then blind the efforts of an historian*; our novel has provided us with the possibility, no, even *the instrument to view our facts and conceivably study them in that field of light a labor of lens-grinding has produced*" (AN, 219; my emphases). As Mailers metaphors suggest, the world of reality ("the horizon") is contaminated and obscured by "a forest," and in order to see through the forest, to reach the horizon, one must "build the tower," that is, an appropriate textual construction. It is at this point of his novel/history that Mailer even feels like abandoning "history," for in crucial places and in crucial questions history and journalism must be replaced by "the novel."

Still, Mailers aim is not to replace "history" altogether with his "novel"; thus "the method" which is now "exposed," appears to be more complex, with a more complex function. As Reed sees it:

> Throughout the text the terms "novel" and "history" are fused and confused self-consciously until they seem to lose their autonomy as concepts, becoming some hybrid that questions the existence of novel and history as discrete writing forms, and that, in turn, questions the epistemological bases of these forms. The subtitle of the text, *History as a Novel, The Novel as History*, is emblematic of this questioning in that it does not resolve itself into some synthetic new term like nonfiction novel but is instead presented as an unstable chiasmus.[26]

It is only through the subsequent writing of the book that Mailer can make some sense of the "mysterious character" of the March on the Pentagon, in which he was a participant. The deepest aesthetic solution of *The Armies of the Night* is that Mailer's experiences as a character produce this book, and that the character's perception of the events is the "tool" through which the author filters his novel/history. As suggested above, then, "our *intimacy* with the master builder of the tower, and the lens grinder of the telescopes (yes, even the machinist of the barrels) has given some advantage for correcting the error of the instruments and the imbalance of his tower" (AN: 219; my emphasis). Mailer means here that any deep, complex, visionary, and finally trustworthy account of a real historical event can only be given through the subjective and intimate vision of a participant in that event. Even though this experience and vision is then moulded to a textual form, its power and accuracy potentially remains. Finally, the subjective and filtered vision may even "correct the errors" which are always produced by the so-called objective histories written by "objective" historians who detach themselves from the event.

The Absurdity of History: Oswald's Tale and the Assassination of Kennedy

As we have seen, in *The Armies of the Night* Mailer is himself a participant in the actual events, subsequently writing his novel/history on the basis of his own subjective experience of those events. However, in *Oswald's Tale* he must grapple with *texts*, various and conflicting documentary evidence of the mysterious case of Lee Harvey Oswald and the assassination of John F. Kennedy. As it appears in this context, Mailer would hardly agree with White and other supposed postmodernists in that the same set of historical events and factual documents can be plausibly represented and "figured" in different story patterns with

---

[26] Ibid., p. 98.

equal status, be they tragical or comical.[27] As White argues, "one narrative account may represent a set of events as having the form and meaning of an epic or tragic story, while another may represent the same set of events – *with equal plausibility and without doing any violence to the factual record* – as describing a farce."[28] As Lubomír Doležel sees it, in an article responding to the postmodernist, relativist, and constructivist understanding of historical narratives as represented by Barthes, White, and others, "[i]n the postmodernist perspective, historiography is a web of more or less interesting stories, governed by narrative patterns and tropological shifts, but with only an incidental connection to the human past and present."[29] The crucial example is provided by the so-called Holocaust test which suggests "that a mode of emplotment can be a distortion rather than an interpretation of history," insofar as we cannot reasonably argue that a comical representation of *this* historical event is as "plausible" as a tragic one.[30]

Apparently, a kind of "equal plausibility" and the question of making equally valid tragical and farcical representations of historical events is a sign of the "postmodern" stance that Mailer critically reflects upon in *Oswald's Tale*:

> We have come at least to the philosophical crux of our inquiry: It would state that the sudden death of a man as large in his possibilities as John Fitzgerald Kennedy is more tolerable if we can perceive his killer as tragic rather than absurd. This is because absurdity corrodes our species. The mounting ordure of a post-modern media fling (where everything is equal to everything else) is all the ground we need for such an assertion. (OT, 198)

The notion concerning the absurdity of events should be regarded in the context of Mailer's private philosophy and mythology, his "mystic existentialism." According to Mailer's scheme, which corresponds to Manicheanism and the Jewish kabbala, every act must be understood as meaningful in some sense, mirroring the larger battle between good and evil.[31] To draw a more or less persuasive analogy, in his book *The Prisoner of Sex* (1971) Mailer states that sex is "the mirror of how we approach God" (PS, 117), and thus every act (be it sex or murder) is always in some relation to God (or the Devil).[32] Therefore, as Mailer sees it, "the Lord, Master of Existential Reason, was not thus devoted to the *absurd* as to put orgasm in the midst of the act of creation without the cause of the profoundest sort" (PS, 87; my emphasis). As he suggests in *Oswald's Tale*, to admit that any act is absurd and

---

[27] Mailer concludes *Oswald's Tale* by noting that "one would like to have used [Dreiser's] 'An American Tragedy' as the title for this journey through Oswald's beleaguered life" (OT, 791).

[28] White, *Figural Realism*, p. 28; my emphasis.

[29] Lubomír Doležel, "Fictional and Historical Narrative: Meeting the Postmodernist Challenge."   David Herman (ed.), *Narratologies: New Perspectives on Narrative Analysis* (Columbus: Ohio State University Press, 1999), pp. 247-273 (p. 253).

[30] See ibid., p. 252. Actually, Doležel's conclusion is that White's theory of history fails the Holocaust test and that the failed test "reveals most tellingly [the] fundamental weaknesses of White's theory," its inability to take into account the truth-conditionality of historical representation, its "distortion" of the actual past by the emphasis on emplotment, and its adherence to "a formalist theory of historical writing [which] deprives historiography of any sociopolitical or ethical significance" (ibid., pp. 252-253).

[31] See, for example, Eberhard Alsen, "The Manichean Pessimism of Norman Mailer's An American Dream." Alsen, *Romantic Postmodernism in American Fiction*. Postmodern Studies 19. (Amsterdam and Atlanta: Rodopi, 1996), pp. 73-89.

[32] See also Jessica Gerson, "Sex, Creativity, and God." Harold Bloom (ed.), *Norman Mailer (*Modern Critical Views) (New York: Chelsea House, 1986), pp. 167-182.

meaningless is to suggest that there is no God and so "there was no logic to the event [the assassination of Kennedy] and no sense of balance in the universe" (OT, 606). On the other hand, if there is God (and the Devil), Lee Harvey Oswald's act – based upon the speculation that he was the actual assassin – is an individual act of "creation," mirroring either good or evil, and having the "cause of the profoundest sort." Mailer thus wants to *frame* Oswald on the basis of "the cabalistic sense" according to which God first conceives of the world and *then* makes it; thus to say that you have done something which you have not yet done becomes "the first and essential step in shaping the future," and "it is as if the future cannot exist without an *a priori* delineation of it" (OT, 569). At least this is Mailer's speculative interpretation of Oswald's personal aim and vision, which suggests his participation in the cosmic battle between good and evil powers, and without a clear knowledge of whether he is on the side of God or the Devil.

Mailer's mythology, firmly based on Jewish mysticism – which also explains, at least partially, the author's notorious ideas about sexuality – may sound like a world-model very different from White's adherence to modern Western thought (which, with figures like Hegel and Marx, still also lurks behind Mailer's mixed philosophy). If we reflect on the paragraph above about the absurdity of a historical event (the Kennedy assassination in this case), we may note that it implies *irony* as the master trope in our postmodernist sense of history. Joseph Tabbi sees that Mailer, being committed to a rhetoric of opposition in contemporary America, is concerned with the limitations that fashionable postmodernist irony presents, thus refusing "the easy acceptance of an irony that not only kills the sublime by reducing it to bathos but also too easily masks a bland acceptance of the consensus culture."[33] As White somewhat ironically puts it, the historian "can *misfire*" since the historian's audience would hardly accept "the emplotment of the life of President Kennedy as comedy, but whether it ought to be emplotted romantically, tragically, or satirically is an open question."[34] This notion may be right on target, since here (for once) White takes into account both the historian's constraints and the audience's expectations. Obviously, however, White is again more interested in the questions of emplotment and narrativization. Therefore, while historical situations are not inherently tragic, comic, or romantic, "they may be inherently ironic, but they need not be emplotted that way."[35] Because, for White, "a *serious theme* – such as mass murder or genocide – demands a *noble genre*, such as epic or tragedy, for its proper representation,"[36] he might share Mailer's belief that we should regard the Oswald/Kennedy case as a tragedy. In his *Metahistory*, White argues that "as the basis of a world view, *irony* tends to dissolve all belief in the possibility of positive political actions" and "its apprehension of the essential folly or *absurdity* of human condition, it tends to engender belief in the 'madness' of civilization itself."[37] There are, then, certain

---

[33] Joseph Tabbi, *Postmodern Sublime: Technology and American Writing from Mailer to Cyberpunk* (Ithaca and London: Cornell University Press, 1995), pp. 55, 73.
[34] White, *Tropics of Discourse*, p. 84; my emphasis.
[35] Ibid., p. 85.
[36] White, *Figural Realism*, p. 31; my emphases.
[37] Hayden White, *Metahistory: The Historical Imagination in Nineteenth-Century Europe* (Baltimore: The Johns Hopkins University Press, 1973), p. 38; my emphases.

affinities between Mailer's and White's notions as regards an antithesis between *ironic* and politically engaged world views.[38]

As it has been sometimes suggested, the age of American postmodernism starts on that fateful day in Dallas, 22 November, 1963. The assassination of Kennedy has been read as "the first postmodern historical event," and "as the inception of the American postmodern, the assassination is the terrible thing guiltily experienced long ago," being the ultimate event that "changed America, put an end to its innocent conviction of invincibility, gave birth to the culture of paranoia."[39] As Tabbi suggests when discussing the representations of the assassination, "if a total naturalistic or sociological representation of events is no longer possible, *if reality*, [--] *is no longer realistic*, that perception in itself is a basis for creating a recalcitrant, ambiguous, and self-consciously 'mysterious' fiction."[40] Tabbi still does not argue that the historical event itself is *fiction* or that it could be easily made such. When reading Don DeLillo's novel *Libra* (1988) he sees that the novel "seems purposely to sustain a sense of aimlessness and a schizophrenic flatness in which all items have an equal, and equally affectless, significance," but "the meaninglessness can be rescued only by the external reality of assassination."[41] As Daniel Lehman puts it, *Libra* presents the assassination "primarily through mediated images," but the reader's extratextual knowledge of the event (even though for most readers constructed by those same mediated images) brings some disturbing power to the reading experience.[42] In his emphasis on the materiality of (dead) bodies outside the narrative text, Lehman maintains that "a reader with specific experience of events off the page ([--] a reader with actual memories of the Kennedy assassination) will bring a thick and sometimes unmanageable response to the nonfiction text because she recognizes its ability to construe her experience off the page."[43] This ethically based notion should be juxtaposed with White's thesis that historical narratives, employing specific plots and story forms, create the experience of the event to those readers who have not experienced the event itself. White's notions become problematic at this very point when we recognize that people may also experience events (like the Holocaust, to take the crucial example) outside textual forms and literary plots.

However, as DeLillo's fictional representation of the assassination in *Libra* imaginatively envisions, the past event can perhaps only be grasped through well-known visual-cultural frames and images. The novel seems to be suggesting that everything is experienced as "a kind of simulation, as if even those present were seeing the event through one

---

[38] See also John Whalen-Bridge, *Political Fiction and the American Self* (Urbana and Chicago: Illinois University Press, 1998), p. 122. Whalen-Bridge is another critic who suggests certain similarities between Mailer and White, very briefly though.

[39] David Cowart, *Don DeLillo: The Physics of Language* (Athens and London: The University of Georgia Press, 2002), p. 95.

[40] Tabbi, *Postmodern Sublime*, pp. 176-77; my emphasis. In this context, Tabbi makes a reference to Mailer's early creed as presented through a fictional narrator in the short story "The Man Who Studied Yoga" (1952): "He does not want to write a realistic novel, because reality is no longer realistic" (AM, 163; my emphasis). Various critics have regarded this creed as representing, and anticipating, some of the central sensibilities in contemporary American writing; see, for example, Zavarzadeh, *The Mythopoeic Reality*, p.159.

[41] Tabbi, *Postmodern Sublime*, p. 191.

[42] Daniel W. Lehman, *Matters of Fact: Reading Nonfiction over the Edge* (Columbus: Ohio State University Press, 1997), p. 120.

[43] Ibid., p. 27.

or another of its many filmed versions."[44] In its strikingly executed climax, DeLillo's narrative represents the assassination scene as if in slow motion, imitating the frames of the famous 8-mm Zapruder film and successfully capturing those "seven seconds that broke the back of the American century."[45] In fact, when shooting the first two shots himself in the imaginary version of *Libra* – even though not the fatal bullet that kills the President – Oswald sees through the telescope of his rifle that "there was a white burst in the middle of *the frame,*"[46] as if Oswald were himself watching the film after "the fact." And indeed, after the third bullet coming from somewhere "Lee raised his head from the scope, looking right" and seeing "*a man on the wall with a camera.*"[47] That is Abraham Zapruder himself, of course; the historical event is already being represented. The assassination of Kennedy has become a paradigmatic example of such an historical event about which there exists much ambiguity and contradictoriness among "primary materials" or reliable documents, so that even a visual record of the event does not help to make the event "real" and "understandable."[48] As White also notes, the new electronic technologies of representation are able to produce manipulated images, even making a "seemingly unambiguously documented event virtually unintelligible as an event."[49] These visual and other devices have had a profound influence on literary modernism and postmodernism as well, as already noted in the case of *The Armies of the Night.*

The mysterious gap in the story of Lee Harvey Oswald is, apparently, the shooting of Kennedy: did Oswald do it? DeLillo's fiction actually represents Oswald with the rifle in the sixth-floor window of the Texas School Book Depository, whereas in Mailer's nonfiction there is a critical blank scene, a large epistemological-ontological gap at this ultimate point. As an eye-witness of the assassination (interviewed later by the Warren Comission) states it, "'I do not, of course, remember seeing any object or anything like that in the windows such as a rifle or anything pointing out of the windows... No activity, no one moving around that I saw at all'" (OT, 672). After this reproduced testimony Mailer constructs an imaginative speculation in his narrative: "Let us put ourselves in the mind of a rifleman who has set himself up in a nest of book cartoons on the sixth floor" (OT, 672). Still, this authorial reflection of the lone gunman's motives does not mean that we are really penetrating Oswald's mind; in effect, this is not a *representation* of Oswald's acts and thoughts in the same way as DeLillo's fictional construction is: "Lee was about to squeeze off the third round, he was in the act, he was actually pressing the trigger. [--] There was a white burst in the middle of the frame. A terrible splash, a burst. Something came blazing off the President's head. [--] *Oh he's dead he's dead.*"[50] Obviously, the assassination scene rendered in *Libra* is not so much DeLillo's personal creation as it is his *metarepresentation*, constructed from the basis of existing evidence and previous representations.[51]

---

[44]   Tabbi, *Postmodern Sublime*, p. 191.

[45]   Don DeLillo, *Libra* (London: Penguin Books, 1991 [1988]), p. 181.

[46]   Ibid., p. 400; my emphasis.

[47]   Ibid.; my emphasis.

[48]   See Cowart, *Don DeLillo*, pp. 97-98.

[49]   White, *Figural Realism*, p. 72.

[50]   DeLillo, *Libra*, p. 400; my emphasis.

[51]   See, for example, John F. Keener, *Biography and the Postmodern Historical Novel* (Lewinston et al.: The Edwin Mellen Press, 2001), p. 102. Apparently, even conflicting versions and representations of the Kennedy assassination (and there has been a lot of them) can be equally persuasive and plausible in a rhetorical sense.

The representation of a complex modernist event is the theme that is written inside De-Lillo's and Mailer's Oswald narratives, rendering both narratives as *metatextual* representa-tions. This kind of critical self-consciousness in representing events like the Holocaust or the Kennedy assassination is also reflected upon by White who notes that Art Spiegelman's famous "comic book" *Maus* "makes the difficulty of discovering and telling the whole truth about even a small part of it as much a part of the story as the events whose meaning it is seeking to discover," and accordingly "the story of the Holocaust which is told in the book is framed by a story how this story came to be told."[52] In its self-reflexive mode, *Libra* con-structs a fictional writer, a retired CIA analyst Nicholas Branch who is hired on contract to write the "secret history" of the assassination of John F. Kennedy and whose work with the various materials concerning the case reflect the actual working practice of DeLillo: "Nicholas Branch sits in the book-filled room, the room of documents, the room of theories and dreams."[53] Branch desperately feels that "there is enough mystery in the facts as we know them, enough of conspiracy, coincidence, loose ends, dead ends, multiple interpreta-tions," and DeLillo describes Branch as facing "the Warren report, with its twenty-six ac-companying volumes of testimony and exhibits, its millions of words."[54] Accordingly Mailer, in *Oswald's Tale*, reflects that "the twenty-six volumes [of the Warren Comission reports] will also be a Comstock Lode of *novelistic material*, [--] certainly to be honored for its short stories, historical vignettes, and vast cast of characters" (OT, 351; my emphasis).

   The metanarrative structure of *Libra* constructs Oswald as a kind of "always already" textualized character who cannot escape his fate as a created "patsy" in an all too complex conspiracy narrative. In his *Oswald's Tale*, Mailer is only able to represent Oswald's char-acter through texts and images, and his version of Oswald as a "tragic" figure, instead of an "absurd" one, is *his* vision, based on his own mythical story patterns. At some point it be-comes difficult, almost impossible, to decide what is "inside" and what is "outside"; where is the borderline between the historical event and its textual representation; where does a life end and where does its depiction begin? Again, as in Mailer's *St. George and the God-father*, history has moved from a narrative line to a topological warp. In any case, DeLillo's *Libra* is "conscious" of its own fictionality,[55] whereas Mailer's *Oswald's Tale* proceeds to this self-reflexive passage in the middle of its narrative:

As Eric Heyne suggests, referring to Libra, "it is not a matter of taking invention for fact, but rather of allow-ing a plausible blend of fact and invention to assume authoritative status in the absence of a superior compet-ing version, or of allowing the analogic truth of fiction to supply a gap in the record of verifiable truth." Heyne, "Where Fiction Meets Nonfiction: Mapping a Rough Terrain." *Narrative* 9:3 (2001), pp. 322-333 (p. 331). As White argues, rather obscurely though, "one can produce an imaginary discourse about real events that may be not less 'true' for being imaginary." White, *The Content of the Form*, p. 57.

52   White, *Figural Realism*, p. 31.
53   DeLillo, *Libra*, p. 14.
54   Ibid., pp. 58, 181.
55   DeLillo's "Author's Note" reads as follows: "This is a work of imagination. While drawing from the historical record, I've made no attempt to furnish factual answers to any questions raised by the assassination. Any novel about a major unresolved event would aspire to fill some of the blank spaces in the known record. To do this, I've altered and embellished reality, extended real people into imagined space and time, invented inci-dents, dialogues, and characters." There are "signposts" of fictionality in DeLillo's novel (as Dorrit Cohn would have it), such signs that should not be found in factual histories. In addition to the use of such fictive devices as the presentation of a character's consciousness, in Libra fictional characters and historical persons share the same space (thus blurring the levels of the world ontology). Most strikingly, we get an obscure vi-

Let me propose, then, that a mystery of the immerse dimensions of Oswald's case will, in the writing, create a form of its own somewhere between fiction and non-fiction. Technically, this book fits into the latter category – it is most certainly not fiction. The author did his best to make up no dialogue himself and attribute no private motives to his real characters unless he was careful enough to label all such as speculation. Still, it is a peculiar form of non-fiction, since not only interviews, documents, newspaper accounts, intelligence files, recorded dialogues, and letters are employed, but speculations as well. The author's musings become some of the operative instruments. Of course, speculation is often an invaluable resource of the novelist. The result can be seen, therefore, as a special species of non-fiction that can be put under the rubric of *mystery*. That is because all means of inquiry have to be available when one is steering one's way through a cloud – especially if there are arguments about the accuracy of the navigating instruments, which in this case are the facts. (OT, 353)

By emphasizing its "nonfictional" aims, Mailer's book also attaches itself to a truth-claiming function, and consequently it cannot feel free to use fictional imagination to fill in the gaps in the past history. Mailer, consequently, expresses his awareness of the distinct aims and conventions of specific textual types.

Conclusion: The Whitean Problem

In *Oswald's Tale*, subtitled *An American Mystery*, Mailer announces that "[e]vidence, by itself, will never provide the answer to a mystery" (OT, 775). Accordingly, in *The Armies of the Night* Mailer tries to make sense of an event with complex dimensions, trying, through his writing, "to elucidate the mysterious character of that quintessentially American event" (AN, 216). The "mysterious" case of Oswald and the Kennedy assassination, even more so than the "ambiguous" March on the Pentagon, provides a fruitful soil for Mailer's "peculiar" version of nonfiction as suggested in the authorial self-reflections of *Oswald's Tale*. Like Hayden White, Norman Mailer sees the form and the content as belonging together, also in nonfiction, so that a specific kind of "modernist" event seems to require a "modernist" literary treatment. However, while there may be certain interesting affinities between Mailer and White, as suggested above, Mailer's reflections upon the differences and similarities between fiction and nonfiction do not result in blurring and merging of the distinctions.

While some theorists maintain that the competing narratives about historical events can be distinguished from each other on the basis of their *correspondence* to the factual record, White argues that when it comes to historical narratives, their *coherence* (as a story form) is as equally crucial as their factual correspondence. Thus, for White, "the differences among competing narratives are differences among *the modes of emplotments* which predominate in them."[56] Therefore, "[h]ere the conflict between competing narratives has less to do with the facts of the matter in question than with the different *story-meanings* with which the

---

sion of Kennedy's real assassin shooting from the grassy knoll as imagined by DeLillo's narrator: "He [Raymo or Ramón Benítez] held on Kennedy's head. [--] He got off the shot. The man's hair stood up. It just rippled and flew." DeLillo, *Libra*, p. 402.

[56] White, *Figural Realism*, p. 30; compare *Tropics of Discourse*, p. 122. In fact, Monika Fludernik proposes that White's concept of 'narrativization' should more likely be understood as 'storification' since it "relies exclusively on the establishment of plot," Fludernik, *Towards a 'Natural' Narratology* (London and New York: Routledge), 1996, p. 34. As White puts it in one occasion, then, "there must be a story, since there is surely a plot." White, *The Content of the Form*, p. 9; my emphases.

facts can be endowed by emplotment."[57] According to White's well-known viewpoint, as verbal artifacts histories and novels are indistinguishable from each other. As I would define it, the main problem in White's theories about history as narrative/narrative as fiction may be located in his emphasis upon *formal* categories and definitions which exclude many pragmatic, referential, and contextual questions from his discussion. Dorrit Cohn is one of those critics who deliberately searches for formal and textual distinctions, certain "signposts of fictionality." These signposts would at least partly confirm the difference between fiction and nonfiction, including the presentation of a character's consciousness and the ontological story/discourse distinction.[58] It may be argued that these "signposts" are often signs of a specific literary genre or textual type as well, and in this way are able to direct our reading. We need to take into account multiple "framing" effects, including generic features, narrative devices, and many paratextual signs, which act "as a guide for reading the text in a sensible way, allowing the text to better realize its communicative function."[59] To put it briefly, then, White sees fiction (like the novel) and nonfiction (like history) indistinguishable as verbal artifacts because he only focuses on the formal level.

In our imaginative confrontation between Mailer and White, the latter would still stress that as a historical event the assassination of President Kennedy is "no longer observable, and hence it cannot serve as an object of a knowledge as certain as that about present events that can still be observed."[60] As White concludes, since the event is no longer observable, "it is perfectly respectable to fall back upon the time-honored tradition of representing such singular events as the assassination of the thirty-fifth president of the United States as a story and try to explain it by narrativizing (fabulating) it – as Oliver Stone did in *JFK*."[61] Actually, we may see White suggesting that Oliver Stone's controversial film *JFK* "is neither factual nor fictional but rather figurative."[62] This notion is connected with White's lar-

---

[57]   White, *Figural Realism*, p. 29; my emphasis. In White's general model, "narrativization" seems to both make and save history, but from an ethical viewpoint this notion sounds problematic: "That history employs narrative does not, however, turn history into fiction [--]; history's narratives of remembrance are 'a range of interpretations' of precious facts, to whose preservation the historian remains deeply committed: once lost, no narration will save them." Marianne Børch, "Introduction." Børch (ed.), *Narratives of Remembrance*. Odense: Odense University Press, 2001, pp. 7-12 (p. 10).

[58]   See Cohn, *The Distinction of Fiction*, p. 111.

[59]   Kalle Pihlainen, "The Moral of the Historical Story: Textual Differences in Fact and Fiction." *New Literary History* 33 (2002), pp. 39-60 (p. 48).

[60]   White, *Figural Realism*, p. 71.

[61]   Ibid., pp. 71-72.

[62]   Ibid., p. 187n. Some other critics would probably argue that *JFK* (which envisions the Kennedy assassination as a huge conspiracy involving almost every possible or, indeed, impossible agency) is an example of an impossible world model. This is because "impossible worlds are the branches that history failed to take in the past" and they "cluster at the periphery of the [world] system," based on illogical conclusions and destroying their "accessibility relation" to the actual world history. See Marie-Laure Ryan, *Narrative as Virtual Reality: Immersion and Interactivity in Literature and Electronic Media* (The Johns Hopkins University Press, 2001), p. 100. This notion would be based on a theory of possible worlds, according to which "the actual world is the realm of historical facts, possible worlds are the branches that history could take in the future" (ibid.; my emphasis). It is perhaps not a coincidence that DeLillo's fictitious writer inside *Libra* is called Nicholas Branch. As David Cowart puts it, DeLillo himself "insists on the distinction between embracing paranoia and representing it as historical reality," and consequently he "dismisses Oliver Stone's tendentious film JFK as 'Disneyland for paranoids.'" Cowart, *Don De Lillo*, p. 223n. Mailer's reflection on JFK in the middle of Oswald's Tale suggests that the film derives much rhetorical power from its paranoia hypothesis but that "it does not

ger discussion of such modernist events that seem to require "the new genres of postmodernist parahistorical representation," both verbal and visual texts that comprise of works like *Libra* and *JFK*, or Capote's *In Cold Blood* and Mailer's *The Executioner's Song*, for that matter.[63] What seems problematic here is White's subjective and rather non-reflective collection of texts which "[a]ll deal with historical phenomena, and all of them appear to fictionalize, to a greater or lesser degree, the historical events and characters that serve as their referents in history," and consequently his claim that "[w]hat happens in the postmodernist docudrama or historical metafiction is [...] the placing in abeyance of the distinction between the real and the imaginary."[64] On this basis, White even argues that "*everything* is presented as if it were of *the same ontological order, both real and imaginary.*"[65] As I see it, to consider distinct textual and literary modes as belonging to the same aesthetic, ontological, and epistemological level remains an unresolvable Whitean question.

---

come near to solving the immediate question: Did Lee Harvey Oswald kill JFK, and if he did, was he a lone gunman or a participant in a conspiracy?" (OT, 606).

[63] White, *Figural Realism*, p. 67.

[64] Ibid., pp. 67-68

[65] Ibid., p. 68. It is somewhat symptomatic, then, that for White these new genres of postmodernist parahistorical representation can be variously called 'docudrama,' 'faction,' 'infotainment,' 'the fiction of fact,' 'historical metafiction,' "and the like" (ibid., p. 67). Again, there seems to be no distinction between various textual types and literary genres.

CHAPTER 11

Olabode Ibironke

Monumental Time in Caribbean Literature

> No one has yet written a history from the point of view of the poets—from within their consciousness of the historical vocation of art[1]
>
> ---- Geoffrey H. Hartman.

The origins and vehicle of modern historiography reside in the rise to dominance of "the document" as the exclusive and irrefutable proof of human activity and achievement. The document from this standpoint is not the same thing as recorded history, but the very icon of modern civilization. In other words, the insistence by professional historians on the academic mode of documentation of evidence, and the status and totalizing authority invested in the archives, are perpetuated and valorized through their vital link to those processes powered by an auto-select mechanism of the trajectory of modernity. Consequently, the daunting task of our time is how to initiate an alternative discourse that is not overdetermined by the authority of the archives, in order to capture historical knowledges that were subjugated, thrown into disorder, turned awry by the rise to dominance of "the document." This task, I would argue in this paper, using Chamoiseau's *Texaco*[2] as an illustration, defines the project of writing history in the Caribbean through literature by invoking the question of space in constituting historical consciousness thereby challenging in a fundamental way, the dominance and objectivism of "the document."

An important understanding of the transformational stages of the historical discipline and the practices that could open the possibilities to a discursive shift is presented in Michel Foucault's *Archaeology of Knowledge:*

> To be brief, then, let us say that history, in its traditional form, undertook to 'memorize' the *monuments* of the past, transform them into *documents,* and lend speech to those traces which, in themselves, are often not verbal, or which say in silence something other than what they actually say; in our time, history is that which transforms *documents* into *monuments.* In that area where, in the past, history deciphered the traces left by men, it now deploys a mass of elements that have to be grouped, made relevant, placed in relation to one another to form totalities. There was a time when archaeology, as a discipline devoted to silent monuments, inert traces, objects without context, and things left by the past, aspired to the condition of history, and attained

---

[1]   Geoffrey H. Hartman, *Beyond Formalism* (Yale University Press, 1970), p. 356.
[2]   Patrick Chamoiseau, *Texaco* (New York: Pantheon Books, 1997).

meaning only through the restitution of a historical discourse; it might be said, to play on words a little, that in our time history aspires to the condition of archaeology, to the intrinsic description of the monument.[3]

Foucault here outlines at least three broad attempts in the writing of history: first, to transform monuments of the past into document; second, to transform *documents* into *monuments*; and third, to aspire to the condition of archaeology. Nowhere is the last tendency, that is, aspiration to make history into some form of landscaping more pronounced than in Caribbean literature. This aspiration is itself derivative of a revolutionary insight that the object of history is not singularly "the event" but the overall context of the formation of a subject. Thus, Michel-Rolph Trouillot raises a crucial point or stumbles over the confluence of literature and history when he exclaims, "subjectivity is an integral part of the event and of any satisfactory description of that event."[4] It is perhaps a similar insight that radicalizes Hayden White's notion of history as narrative – narrative defined as a basic literary phenomenon. In any case, conjoining the concept of history with narrative and space, as Chamoiseau does, in *Texaco*, must necessarily lead to a different understanding of history. The question is indeed: what are the justifications for such move?

The justifications for challenging the paradigms of modern historiography can be foregrounded in two broad imperatives, namely: the imperative of writing the history of the oppressed: those against whom the modern is defined, the ground upon which the wheels of modernity rolls; and the imperative of writing the history of the sublime. These two imperatives are one and the same, and could be illustrated by the following anecdotes. One is by the sagacious African writer, Chinua Achebe, the other by Immanuel Kant. In his novel *Anthills of the Savannah,*[5] Achebe tells the story of the irrepressible trickster, the tortoise, upon his historic encounter with the leopard, who had eternally been on a prowl for him. The leopard, king of the jungle, overjoyed that his age-long dream would now be accomplished, proclaimed triumphantly: "prepare to die!" The overawed and panic-stricken tortoise worshipfully pleads for a moment to prepare for his death. In what appears to be an inexplicable gesture, he digs up the earth and throws sand in all directions. Overcome by the intense and indescribable spell of perplexity and amusement, his executioner, the leopard asked what he was doing. His response, characteristically Olympian, is at the same time disarming, "… after I am dead I would want anyone passing by this spot to say, yes, a fellow and his match struggled here."[6] The story, like all riddles, ends at this point. The issue here is not so much about the past, but rather about what kinds of pasts are being produced as a necessary requirement for the functioning and legitimation of power and resistance. A story like this, if told under the moonlight in traditional Africa, would surely have ended in a series of questions: what do you think the leopard would do? Would he go ahead and kill the tortoise? If so, would the landmark of the struggle, staged by the tortoise, not ever stand beside his carcass and bones as a counter discourse? Or would the leopard, realizing that his victory would be diminished and neutralized, leave the tortoise and sustain a question mark on his omnipotence? Formulations like this qualify if not render fallacious, the assumption

[3] Michel Foucault, *The Archaeology of Knowledge* (London: Tavistock Publications, 1972), p. 7.
[4] Michel Rolph Trouillot, *Silencing the past and the Production of History* (Boston, Mass: Beacon Press, 1995), p. 24.
[5] Chinua Achebe, *Anthills of the Savannah*, (Ibadan: Heinemann, 1988).
[6] Ibid., p. 128.

that the subaltern cannot speak. The writing of the history of the oppressed introduces dilemmas into the grand narratives of modernity as much as it provides an opportunity for a reciprocal blackmail to beat back the intransigence of power. Wherever trust in archives is badly shaken, wherever documentary evidence is unavailable, veritable historical knowledge could still be gleaned.

The history of the sublime is related to the above because, for one to write the history of the oppressed, one must make an estimation of magnitude, which is not mathematical, but intuitive. The turn to landmarks, to monuments of suffering and of the enduring quality of the human spirit is a turn away from the mere empirical, quantitative and immanent. Immanuel Kant gives an idea of what it involves to attempt an intuitive estimation of magnitude in his *Critique of Judgment.*[7] In the first place, an intuitive estimation of magnitude is an aesthetic activity and precisely because historiography is conceived as solely dependent upon the faculty of logic – and since "all logical estimation of magnitude is mathematical,"[8] historiography necessarily falters in producing dimensions of history that are, according to Trouillot, subjective and subliminal. Kant's example, citing Savary, is that of an encounter with the pyramids of Egypt: "in order to get the full emotional effect from the magnitude of the pyramids, one must neither get too close to them nor stay too far away. For if one stays too far away, then the apprehended parts are presented only obscurely [...] and if one gets too close, then the eyes need some time to complete the apprehension from the base to the peak, but during that time some of the earlier parts are invariably extinguished in the imagination before it has apprehended the later ones, and hence the comprehension is never complete."[9] The speechlessness one feels before the spectacle and horror of events such as Slavery and the Slave Trade, the Holocaust, Hiroshima and Nagasaki, Colonialism, etc., is equivalent to the inadequacy of historiography to render these events in an estimation of "absolute magnitude." Indeed, the comprehension of history is ever incomplete without this estimation. The history of the oppressed requires, for moral and political as well as epistemological reasons, the intuitive estimation of magnitudes. It is these combined imperatives that compel experimentations such as we find in Caribbean literature and in particular, *Texaco*, which we shall momentarily discuss.

Texaco is a novel that self-consciously links the production of history literally to materiality and subjectivity. The quest of the author appears to be, how is the subject of a historical narrative constituted in relation to narrative spaces, both discursive and material? The assumption that undergirds the novel is similar to the conviction of the American experimental musician John Cage that "there is no such thing as an empty space or an empty time."[10] This allows one to understand *Texaco* along the lines of the position of there never being a "prehistory." Furthermore, because the novel demonstrates continuities of natural, psychological, social and narrative spaces, it calls into question the view that "nature appears as the vast territories of births. 'Things' are born, grow and ripen, then wither and die."[11] In essence, the whole philosophy of dialectics that opposes man and nature, fact and value, spirit and matter, time and space, and locates in the triumph of man over nature the

7 Immanuel Kant, *Critique of Judgment* (Indianapolis, Ind: Hackett Pub. Co, 1987).
8 Ibid., p. 107.
9 Ibid., p. 108.
10 John Cage, *Silence: Lectures and Writings* (Hanover, NH : Wesleyan University Press, 1973), p. 8.
11 Henri Lefebvre, *The Production of Space* (Oxford, OX, UK: Blackwell, 1991), p. 70.

origins of historical motion, is thrown on the trash heap. In its place, we find that a unique historical consciousness is constituted precisely through an account of space or "the tactics of the habitat." This preoccupation is amplified by the rationale for periodization employed in writing the history of Martinique around the material texture of Martinican hutches in such a way as to avoid the "pre-" and "post-" hierarchization inherent in modern historiography. Home, the space of human dwelling or "habitats," then becomes the focal point for writing the history of Martinique. The theory implicit in Chamoiseau's *Texaco* is significant for how it experiments with and opens up the possibility of constructing a history of a community, one that is based on the shared nature and transformations of landmarks, home, architectures and monuments.

The ambition of the novel as a revision and counterdiscourse of colonial history is foregrounded in the very structure and division of the novel into different ages. The task of the novel is not only to present to us the history of the Caribbean, but also to periodize it by transposing and condensing each period's unique spatialities into its historical metaphors. From the table of contents it is evident that Chamoiseau is preoccupied with making the determination of the rationality for laying out the chronology of the history of Martinique. It attempts to map out the situations that define each of its segmentations, setting the structural limits as well as the duration of their possibilities and transversalities. The novel is organized into two books: *Around Saint-Pierre* and *Around Fort-De-France.* The first book contains just one period, "The Age Of Straw (1823 [?]- 1920," the second book has three periods, "The Age Of Crate Wood (1903-1945)," "The Age Of Asbestos (1946-1960)," and "The Age Of Concrete (1961-1980)." However, there is another age "The Age Of Longhouses And Ajoupas," which does not appear in the table of contents of the book, but which appears in a chronology that Chamoiseau provides immediately after the content of the novel: "Milestones In Our Attempt To Conquer The City." The Age Of Longhouses And Ajoupas represents the "Genesis" because "at this point the site of the future Texaco is but thickets and mangrove."[12] One striking feature of the novel is that it is a story of this specific site projected as a history of the community itself. The novel could properly then be titled: The History Of Martinican Hutches And The Birth Of The Quarter! But, why would it appear to Chamoiseau that the history of Martinique could be told in this manner? It might be that if historicity were the story of the city, the city being the spectacle of modernity, then the counter-memory of modernity would be the story of the quarter, of the resistance to the expansion of the city, as setting the limits around the city. It is thus instructive that each book in the novel is titled "Around … [this or that city]."

Another reason Chamoiseau may have chosen this method of representing the past could be connected with the rhetorical question Marie-Sophie asks in the novel to which she simultaneously provides an answer, "Why this obsession about owning my own hutch? In City, to be is first and foremost to possess a roof."[13] In one word, the law of possession, of private property, of capitalism in the city could be seen as inducing the obsession with the hutch; since the city defines the condition of being, the standard of humanity to which Marie-Sophie is responding or is being, at some level, constituted by. Her statement reminds one of Bishop Berkeley's famous metaphysical proposition, "to be is to be per-

---

12 Chamoiseau, *Texaco,* p. 3.
13 Ibid., p. 275.

ceived." Clearly, Marie-Sophie makes a connection here between her hutch and her being-in-the-world as a worldly being. Elsewhere Marie-Sophie describes these hutches as "that jostling of epochs vibrant with the trace of my old Esternome, with straw, crate wood, tin sheets for the roof, and these new slabs brought here by the békés, which gave the illusion of a cement house. *Mmmmm dear Lordy...! asbestos...* to leave the straw and the crate wood and the white tin plate, for a home in cement!"[14] The architectonics in this case becomes an index of history and history, in turn, becomes the inscriptions of *presence*.

Marie-Sophie's obsession for a hutch mirrors the author's obsession about writing the history of Martinique as the history of the transformation of their homes, in the sense of architecture and material history. This move to inscribe the "tactics of the habitat" or what Chamoiseau calls "Texaco's logic"[15] is ingenious and can be seen as if responding to the challenge thrown down by Michel Foucault that "[a] whole history remains to be written of *spaces* – which would at the same time be the history of *powers* [...] – from the great strategies of geo-politics to the little tactics of the habitat, institutional architecture from the classroom to the design of hospitals, passing via economic and political installations. It is surprising how long the problem of space took to emerge as a historico-political problem."[16] The history of spaces is not limited to structures, but also includes nature itself, as motivated signs, living in the same way as language. The need to write the history of the quarter arises from its exclusion from the memory of City. The history of spaces that Chamoiseau writes enables him to capture what he calls monumental time and therefore redefine historicity to capture the competitiveness and simultaneity of histories: "All the stories are here, but there's no History. Only grand Time without beginning or end, without befores or afters. Monumental Time."[17] The idea of monumental time in the novel is further developed in the poem *Noutéka of the Hills*, Marie-Sophie's father, Esternome gives her the injunction: "you've got to read the landscape."[18] This emphasis on the textuality of space is held to be a definitive requirement of historicizing. This is probably why Chamoiseau will argue that he requires the form of the novel to write this kind of history, a history not just of spaces but also of the ways in which the individual and the collective shape and are shaped by the ecosystem of which they form a part. This is surely why further in Noutéka of the Hills Esternome is made to say: "The Creole Quarter exists with geography's permission. That's why places are called Valley-this, Mount-that, Ravine-this, Ravine-that... It's the land's shape which names the group of people"[19] just as the quarter, or "mangroves' chemistry"[20] defines Martiniquan subalterns. The emphasis on geography in constituting people's identity is not one of primacy but of the indissociableness of space from historical account. The materialist undertone of identity formation suggested here contrasts sharply with notions of *ethnoscape* in which the relationship between land and people is taken as spiritual and transcendental rather than as historical accidents best expressed in

---

[14] Ibid., p. 226.
[15] Ibid,, p. 220.
[16] Michel Foucault, *Power/Knowledge Selected Interviews and Other Writings, 1972-1977* (Hassocks, Eng.: Harvester Press, 1980), p. 149.
[17] Chamoiseau, *Texaco* p. 293.
[18] Ibid, p. 129.
[19] Ibid., p. 131.
[20] Ibid., p. 263.

the arbitrary, complex, yet necessary, metaphoric associations. Space, history, and people redefine each other as "exteriority of accidents."[21] However, in what ways should one then understand the animistic spirituality that so often surges in the novel in passages such as the following:

> In this abandonment, far away from everything, in the company of that old man, I never felt alone, I mean I never missed anything. There was no solitude: we had fallen into the water's rhythm, the barks' texture, the movement of birds landing on the ground. The grunting of four pigs, the hens' wing-flapping seemed to rise from us. No need to turn around to look at this mango tumbling down because we fell with it, nor mind the dry wood cracking: we were just as dry. I often heard voices hailing from far *Marie-Sophie Ola ou ye, Marisofi where are you...?* They seem to filter from another world without needing a reply. It was Carlo, it was Péloponêse, it was Pa Soltène, or others from Morne Abélard, left behind forever.[22]

This kind of portrayal integrating the rhythm of the ecosystem with that of social life through its pathetic fallacy of participation mystique is not limited to realities of the imagination alone; there are also claims that experiences of this sort recur in the very realities of perception. Maryse Condé, in what seems to be the parallel of this experience of immensity, narrates her dialogue with the island of Guadeloupe: "I went out and met with not so much of the people but the island itself. I learned how the island speaks to your mind; how it smells. It has a life of its own despite the meanness of individuals or their limitations. So, yes, I made peace with the island and having done so, I also made peace with myself in a way."[23] This argument about the Caribbean conception of the relation of man and his environment is not a detour but an integral part of the quarrel with modern historiography. The question then seems to be those of noumenousity and sublimity or what Gaston Bachelard characterizes as "how we experience intimate places;"[24] experiences that for all purposes and intent, like the subaltern past, are neither quantifiable nor translatable.[25] Spatial identity in the novel does not therefore correspond to *ethnoscape's* insistence on transcendental spirituality and connectivity of land and people.

The question of the role of space in the formation of identity and historical discourse brings us back to the Kantian notion of the intuitive estimation of magnitude and the interplay of subjective and objective realities. It is the contours of this interplay that Chamoiseau traces in the novel: questioning how a historian could possibly communicate or translate intuitive estimations of magnitude in the face of the pervasive "feeling that his imagination is inadequate for exhibiting the idea of a whole, a feeling in which imagination reaches its maximum, and as it strives to expand that maximum, it sinks back into itself."[26] These limits of the faculties confirm the position of poets as legislators of certain historical knowledges. Indeed, poetry emerges, on the one hand, precisely as a result of the failure of the

---

[21] Michel Foucault, *The Foucault Reader*, edited by Paul Rabinow 1st ed. (New York: Pantheon Books, 1984), p. 81.

[22] Chamoiseau, *Texaco*, p. 289.

[23] Maryse Condé, "'I Have Made Peace With My Island': An Interview with Maryse Condé," *Callaloo*, No. 38, Vol. 12, No. 1, (Winter 1989): p. 133.

[24] Gaston Bachelard, *The Poetics of Space*, translated by M. Jolas (Boston, Mass.: Beacon Press, 1994).

[25] Dipesh Chakrabarty poses the question: "Are there experiences of the past that cannot be captured by the methods of the discipline, or which at least show the limits of the discipline?" in *Provincializing Europe: Postcolonial Thought and Historical Difference* (Princeton, N.J.: Princeton University Press, 2000), p. 107.

[26] Kant, *Critique of Judgment* p. 109.

imagination and language and, on the other, as the resistance of human experience to translation beyond the "despairs of grasping and holding the genuine historical image as it flares
up briefly."[27] This could be because language is an arbitrary association naturalized by convention such that the expression of the depths of subjectivity and the sublime is deferred at
the moment of articulation to the nature of language as repression, just as much as the ho-
mogenizing power of conventionality continues to silence, absorb and imprison all speech.
It is here that one sees the necessity of history to embrace not only its narrative, but also its
poetic dimension as well.

It is within the interstices of the problem of the ever-retreating historical object and the
elasticity of language that poetic vision acquires its fascination as a supplementary mode,
one in which the extraordinary Caribbean experiences of "the irruption into modernity,"[28]
and participation mystique are brought together. Monumental Time is thus a view of the
universe as a space of the marvelous. The concept of marvelous realism has come to define
Caribbean literature precisely because of the conviction of the sublimity of the historical
experiences it captures, as it were; the writer in the Caribbean is before the inestimable
pyramid of nightmares. Marie-Sophie continually feels and relives the immensity of marvelous reality that essentially marks the eternal return of the momentary flashes of the past.
She says "my dear Esternome's spirit; more and more, he seemed to have come from a
faraway planet; which fact, along with distance, nostalgia, and maybe that familial impulse
that loneliness inspires, made him ever more appealing to me. As the years went by, he
grew in stature in my spirit."[29] Monumental Time, as Chamoiseau conceives it, can thus be
defined as the dynamics of how things and places in the past, present and future grow in
stature, how they transcend their immediate and ephemeral conditions of existence. It is not
the rationalization of space, but the enrichment of consciousness with the capacity to decipher *presences*. The most crucial aspect of this concept of time is enunciated when Marie-
Sophie says, "those words lived within me without my even knowing it, and without my
even understanding them.... A few got away from my memory, and from my words; I
barely brought back the idea of their presence."[30] Monumental Time is thus that which
gives us a new definition of history as *the idea of presence*. The category of presence as a
transcendental form is not the form of being but of the infinity and therefore, sublimity of
being. Marie-Sophie commissions the primary audience of the entire story: "can you,
Oiseau de Cham, write these futile nothings which make up the ground of our living
spirit."[31] The tautology of futility and nothingness is the coming together of time and narrative as double negation, which then renders monumental, the transcendence of the human
spirit.

---

[27] Walter Benjamin "Theses on the Philosophy of History," in *Illuminations*, ed. Hannah Arendt, trans. Harry
Zohn (New York: Schocken Books, 1969), p. 256.

[28] Édouard Glissant and J. Michael Dash, *Caribbean Discourse: Selected Essays* (Charlottesville: University
Press of Virginia, 1989), p. 146.

[29] Chamoiseau, *Texaco*, p. 222.

[30] Ibid. p. 291. In an article "The Truth of Fiction," in *Hopes and Impediments Selected Essays* (New York:
Doubleday, 1989). Chinua Achebe argues that the difference between literature and history is that between
good fiction and bad fiction respectively. Literature is benevolent fiction because it begins by setting out the
limitations of its truth. Whereas the historical discipline, even though shares such limitations, denies ordown-
plays them.

[31] Chamoiseau, *Texaco*, p. 310.

But monumental time is a metaphysical conceit that enables spatial imagery to take on poetic verve in transporting the passion and activities of humanity. In monumental time, space and psyche are engaged in a kaleidoscopic relationship, just as exteriority and interiority are mutually constitutive. The history of space therefore is always already the history of consciousness. It is in this sense that the history of the hutches can reflect and communicate an emergent historical consciousness. What we constantly observe in the novel is an attempt not only to define spaces: city and quarter, but also to read these spaces as inscriptions of human presence.

The attempt to give a definition of space in order to capture inner and outer realities as they interact to propel the motion of human activity and history is quite profuse in Caribbean literature. An example is Maryse Condé's *Segu* where she writes: "What is a town? It isn't a collection of mud or straw houses; market where people sell rice, millet, gourds, fish and manufactured goods; mosques where people prostrate themselves; temples where they spill the blood of victims. It is a collection of private memories, different for every individual, so that no town is like any other."[32] There is no better description of a monument than the transformation of a site into a collection of memories. City and quarter in *Texaco* are constantly imbued with the capacity to signify, and to endlessly generate narratives. Marie-Sophie's greatest regret concerning life in the city is that "everything had been built with no regard for memory,"[33] in contrast to which, Esternorme says about the hills, "in the torments of this cloudy earth, all had spread the *Trails*."[34] The words "legible" and "illegible" are used throughout *The Nouteka Of The Hills* to demonstrate the archaeological work that must be done in order for the task of writing history to succeed at translating subalterneity.

The question that perhaps appears most regularly and impetuously in the novel is: what is City? It is striking how, in all of the definitions offered, the association of interiority and exteriority, and of geography and history is constant. These definitions press the case for a history that is more and more archaeological: an archaeology of sites and minds that brings trails and memories, tangible and intangible evidence together. "A City is the ages all gathered in one place, not just in the names, houses, statues, but in the not-visible,"[35] "[the city] throws you off by showing you her streets while in reality she's well beyond streets, houses, people, she's all of it and takes on a meaning only beyond all of that."[36] Another answer to the question what is city appears in the longest sentence in the novel:

> They say City, he said, City, but that's what City is before anything else, it's like flowing daydreams, misfortune pulled apart, love withered with old bouquets, there, look at the slips of old women who never figured out what the flesh was for, there, look at the fifty thousand longings of old blackmen whose bones look like tools, and over there, moths burnt by electric bulbs, and there twelve syrian nightmares where bullets still fart, and there the pierced heart of a small Syrian girl they wanted to marry off to a faraway syrian, and there Carib sea-tongues which surface from the ocean without saying why and which howl ugly screams into the conches' pink depth, and there the clotted blood of oxen escaped from Portorico which no one was able to turn into pudding, and there, fishermen's gum-tree canoes which rot away since City calls on liners, and there . . . the misery, I tell you, of the coolie souls who have not found the boat home, and there... the chinese sweat speedily departed, leaving us their fear, City they say, everyone wants City and starts running to it like flies to

---

32 Maryse Condé, *Segu, a Novel* (New York: Viking, 1987), p. 157.
33 Chamoiseau, *Texaco*, p. 167.
34 Ibid p.126. His emphasis.
35 Ibid., p. 173.
36 Ibid., p. 287.

syrup, but I posted here, I see the other side of the light, I know the wanderings which peel memories, I see the scales of the seven-headed beast, I feel its blood, its chiggers, its filth, its slops; they say City, they want City but what to do with all of this, where to throw it, City mingles its feet in City and no longer knows what to do with its own body, they say City I say the *béké's kitchen.*[37]

It is very interesting that in answering the question of what City is that a whole history emerges. The repetition of "there" is an insistence on telling history not from the point of view of human agents but from the metaphorical conjunction and actuality of site and experience;[38] the aura of City as a monument of depravity is thus prevalent in the novel. The application of the notion of aura to the story of City is an attempt to restore to history the very essence of the relations of forces that have been expended in a particular place. Aura is what the Urban Planner refers to as radiation. "Texaco […] this irreplaceable wealth which is memory. Possessing so few monuments, the Creole city becomes a monument through the care given its places of memory. The monument, there as in all the Americas, does not erect itself as monumental: it radiates."[39] Historical events according to this theory have a radiational dimension; the effervescence effects that alter and regulate the chemistry of human personality. This radiation is the evanescence and poeticality of memory that events leave in their wake. The novel also attempts to define this poeticality of memory thus:

> "So Idoménée would say: But what is memory? It's the glue, it's the spirit, it's the sap and it stays. Without memories, no city, no Quarters, no Big Hutch. How many memories? she would ask. All the memories, he would answer. Even those the wind and the silences carry at night."[40]

Memory serves as the connecting rod between events of the past and the places that have witnessed these events. This poeticity is possible because of the comparative nature of metaphor, which allows the condensation, and superimposition of signifiers, one hidden, and another foregrounded; such that, the archeology of hutches is the *rendered* but the people's history is the *embodied.*

However, Caribbean writers are not writing microhistory or history from below. This is why the move in *Texaco* to distinguish between shantytown and quarter. The urban planner writes, "I understood suddenly that Texaco was not what Westerners call a shantytown, but a mangrove swamp, *an urban mangrove swamp.* The swamp seems initially hostile to life. It is difficult to admit that this anxiety of roots, of mossy shades, of veiled waters, could be such a cradle of life for crabs, fish, crayfish, the marine ecosystem. It seems to belong to neither land nor sea, somewhat like Texaco is neither City nor country."[41] The history of the shantytown will produce a microhistory, however, the history of the quarter calls forth a

---

[37] Ibid., p. 281.

[38] Bachelard has explained that not only by visiting monuments or sacred sites do we experience the aura and transformation of space, even "by changing space, by leaving the space of one's usual sensibilities, one enters into communication with a space that is psychically innovating. This change of concrete space can no longer be a mere mental operation that could be compared with consciousness of geometrical relativity. For we do not change place, we change our nature... But, since these problems of the fusion of being in highly qualitative, concrete space are interesting for a phenomenology of the imagination – for one has to imagine very actively to experience new space," *Poetics of Space,* p. 206. Therefore in order to write the history of spaces, and man's experience of space, poetic imagination must be a part of our instrument.

[39] Chamoiseau, *Texaco,* p. 336.

[40] Ibid., p.178.

[41] Ibid., p. 263.

subaltern past. The difference according to Chakrabarty is that whereas the subaltern past questions the possibility of the historical discipline to capture its reality, microhistory does not.[42] This is precisely because a subaltern past appears as if it were lost. An urban planner is writing the history of Martinique in this novel because "Out of the urban planner, the lady [Marie-Sophie] made a poet. Or rather: she *called forth* the poet in the urban planner. Forever."[43] "The Creole urban planner must from now on restart new. That's why the architect must become a musician, sculptor, painter… – and the urban planner a poet."[44] The task of writing history has always implied "calling forth" the past but only now does it encompass both the evocative and invocative aspects of that act.

Texaco is the oral transmission of the genealogy of Marie-Sophie's family. It has a radically different approach to the question of history, an approach that is simultaneously historical by pointing to the realities of some time past and theoretical, by engaging on the level of the anecdotal and metanarrative, the construction of historical conditions, documents, archives and monuments. This simultaneous engagement with history and theory is continuous with "the deployment of the conceptional weaponry of semiotics and the semiological notion of the text, [through which] daily life itself soon became a 'legible,' if not ultimately a 'traceable,' phenomenon."[45] The history, from the point of view of the poet, fascinating as it may be, leaves us with a paradox, namely: every monument becomes a document. Thus, in monumental time we are not providing an alternative to "the document" but an appropriation of oral and spatial histories into the dominant modes of textuality. Though such appropriations are ineluctable, the writing of history must be informed by Trouillot's remarkable insight in his important book: *Silencing the Past* that "theories of history have a rather limited view of the field of historical production. They grossly underestimate the size, the relevance, and the complexity of the overlapping sites where history is produced, notably outside of academia."[46]

[42] Chakrabarty, *Provincializing Europe.* This argument was made in the chapter entitled "Minority Histories, Subaltern Pasts."
[43] Chamoiseau, *Texaco*, p. 341
[44] Ibid., p. 361.
[45] John Mowitt, *Text the Genealogy of an Antidisciplinary Object* (Durham, N.C.: Duke University Press, 1992), p. 47.
[46] Trouillot, *Silencing the past*, p. 19.

CHAPTER 12

Lara Okihiro

Divergence and Confluence, Mapping the Streams of Hiroshima

Although he completed a documentary on the Holocaust entitled *Nuit et brouillard*, when the producers of the film asked Alain Resnais to make a second film on the atomic bomb he chose to use a melodramatic narrative to tell the story. Resnais explains that he had seen several films on Hiroshima and it seemed impossible and useless to remake what had already been done. Instead he proposed making a love story that would take place in Hiroshima: a context infused with "the knowledge of the misfortune of others."[1] No longer about the city of Hiroshima but about a love affair that takes place in Hiroshima, the film's focus sustained a connection to the city's traumatic history through the fictional characters and the memories they could not escape. The lovers were "two characters for whom the memory [of the past] is always present in the action"[2] of the film. Thirty-five years later, director/actor Robert Lepage and members of the Ex Machina production company similarly set their sights on Hiroshima. The theatre production, *The Seven Streams of the River Ota*,[3] also establishes love affairs at the site of the atomic bomb. Rather than portraying any single story or affair set in Hiroshima, however, Ex Machina uses seven storylines spanning decades and taking place across different continents to tell a story inspired by the city's history. Lepage and his collaborators also use the Ota River on which Hiroshima was built to metaphorically link the storylines of the play. Though not directly dealing with Hi-

---

[1] Yvonne Baby, "Alain Resnais: 'J'ai essayé de trouver l'équivalent d'une lecture au cinema,'" *Le Monde*, my translation (10 and 11 May 1959), p. 11. All subsequent translations from French to English within the text are my own. In the newspaper interview Resnais describes meeting with the writer Marguerite Duras and explaining his vision for *Hiroshima mon amour* as a fictional love story that remains inevitably tied to the past (World War II and the bombing of Hiroshima): "J'ai rencontré la romancière, je lui ai dit: «Il serait curieux d'«engluer» une histoire d'amour dans un contexte qui tienne compte de la connaissance du malheur des autres et de construire deux personnages pour qui le souvenir est toujours présent dans l'action.» À ma surprise elle s'est intéressée à ce sujet et elle a écrit un scénario auquel nous avons travaillé ensemble."

[2] Ibid.

[3] *The Seven Streams of the River Ota* was created by 13 artists (Éric Bernier, Normand Bissonnette, Rebecca Blankenship, Marie Brassard, Anne-Marie Cadieux, Normand Daneau, Richard Fréchette, Marie Gignac, Patrick Goyette, Ghislaine Vincent, Macha Limonchik, Gérard Bibeau, and Robert Lepage) working in collaboration under the directorship of Robert Lepage. The creative process that gave way to the play began in January 1994 and there have been at least four versions of the play as it developed over time. The first full length (8 hour) version of the play was performed at the Carrefour International de Théâtre de Québec in Quebec City on 17 May 1996. Also in 1996 a version of the play was published based on the Vienna performance in June of the same year: Robert Lepage and Ex Machina, *The Seven Streams of the River Ota*, introduction and commentary by Karen Fricker (London: Methuen Drama, 1996).

The play has continued to developed and for this paper, unless otherwise noted, all references pertain to the version of the play that was last updated in 2002: Robert Lepage et al., *Les sept branches de la rivière Ota / The Seven Streams of the River Ota*, updated by Marie Gignac (Manuscript received directly from Ex Machina, Quebec City. 2002).

roshima and its survivors, the metaphor of the river implies that the stories being told within the play are like streams or lines, and by following these lines we can (re)map Hiroshima.

For both Resnais and Lepage, the weight of the historical event of the bombing of Hiroshima informs and inspires the creative process of constructing a narrative text. Both artists deliberately and thoughtfully use a fictional narrative form in relation to an incredibly destructive historical event. Merging an event of historical atrocity with the making of a film or a play, however, begs a number of questions regarding the relationship of artistic representation to the traumatic history; in this case a relationship involving a level of respect and ethical negotiation. The problem is outlined well by Hayden White in "Literary Theory and Historical Writing"[4] when he considers how literary techniques can influence our understanding of history. The facts of an event are one thing, and indeed, only a part of what constitutes our understanding of an historical event. The way we cast facts in the process of communicating or explaining an event also affects the meaning of the facts. White writes,

> A mode of representation such as irony is a content of the discourse in which it is used, not merely a form . . . .
> When I speak to or about someone or something in an ironic mode, I am doing more than clothing my observations in a witty style. I am saying about them something more and other than I seem to be asserting on the literal level of my speech. So it is with historical discourse cast in a predominantly ironic mode, and so it is with the other modes of utterance I may employ to speak about anything whatsoever.[5]

As White indicates, when we work with facts we are implicated in an undetermined process of shaping the meaning of these facts. Indeed, facts themselves can be considered indecisive claims. Of course, there are facts that cannot be denied and events in the past that have most certainly taken place, but as soon as we begin to qualify these events we find we run into some difficulties. Reflecting on the atomic bombings of Hiroshima and Nagasaki, for example, we cannot determine how many people were killed, the exact effects of the bombs, what it was like in the centre of the fireball, nor how exactly the bombs affected peoples' health many years after 6 and 9 August 1945. In his introduction to *Figural Realism*, White asserts that there is no pure empirical or factual point of understanding outside of using thought and theory to try and make sense of a thing or an event. However, he does admit, "there is good theory and bad theory,"[6] by which he means, "theory that conduces to morally responsible thought and that which leads us away from it."[7] Similarly for artists explicitly interested in creating works in relation to an historical event we can consider there is good representation and there is bad representation, where good representation challenges audiences to think beyond any singular or established interpretation and bad representation encourages audience members to forget an event, or at least to remember it in a particular and limited way.

In the following inquiry I will explore the question of factual knowledge and how artistic representational and narrative form lend themselves to this question; namely, how artistic representation can account for history and the problem of an ethical or 'good' representation. My aim is to consider what is at stake in constructing a narrative around the event of

4   Hayden White, *Figural Realism* (Baltimore, Maryland: Johns Hopkins University Press, 1999), p. 1-26.
5   White, *Figural Realism*, p. 12.
6   White, *Figural Realism*, p. viii.
7   Ibid.

the bombing of Hiroshima, most particularly with reference to *The Seven Streams of the River Ota* by Lepage and Ex Machina. To begin, I will outline how narratives and representations fail as testaments to history. That is, how historical referents, opened up to the present and the process of representation, are emptied of their particular significance causing them to appear as distilled or empty icons. Secondly, in providing some considerations on how the play meets with and recedes from the challenge of representing Hiroshima, I will explore how reductive narratives may actually lend themselves to the challenge of representation. Narratives focusing on themes such as 'nation' or 'peace', or moral claims too simple or singular to contain and convey Hiroshima and its history, are still able to convey something about the traumatic history and our relationship to it. To conclude, I will touch on the use of the Ota River metaphor, which combines story telling and mapping as a model of remembering and representation that encourages viewers to think about an event in a more critical and complex light.

First, how faithful should an artist invested in historical events aim to be to the event she is attempting to represent? Where there exists the desire to remain loyal to the historical facts and the memory of the event, insofar as the creative process entails creating something that will engage audiences one is also required to pull the story elements together: to select them, to arrange them, and to shape them. Part of the process includes framing the historical elements and the facts so that they come across to the audience in a particular way that will help form the cohesive text. Another part of the process is filling in or sidestepping gaps in our knowledge of an event in order to construct a comprehensible narrative or a story. The danger in trying to transmit meaningful events arises when that which is conveyed in the process of framing and selection does not indicate the weight and magnitude of the traumatic event, and rather distances or distils the event into emblematic narratives or images, such as a moral story of peace or the image of the mushroom cloud. Art critic Kyo Maclear describes the effect of iconic remembering not as a means of recalling the traumatic event but rather as a means of forgetting it,

> With each passing year, the image memory relating to Hiroshima and Nagasaki seems to grow feebler; these events begin to merge into a background mutter of forgetfulness, a screen of clichés. Across the Pacific, an increasing number of North Americans have seen very little visual documentation of the bombings. When asked, many identify the mushroom cloud as the only image they can recall.[8]

The emblematic image of the mushroom cloud is not able to evoke the immensity of the historical traumatic event because the historical specificity of the event is elided as the image comes to stand as a phenomenon in its own right. The iconic image or narrative, as something singular and complete, distils the destruction and horror it is meant to represent and diffuses any sense that gestures toward a more complex understanding of the bombings of Hiroshima and Nagasaki. In effect, the iconic image or narrative and our reliance on it wholly replace the traumatic histories as traumatic in our understanding of them. What we have instead is something that appears to us as fully recognizable, and in a metonymic turn, it even seems that the event can be fully identified by the image we see or the story we are told.

---

[8] Kyo Maclear, *Beclouded Visions: Hiroshima-Nagasaki and the Art of Witness* (Albany, NY: State University of New York Press, 1999), p. 52.

Given that Resnais and the Ex Machina company are tied by their film and theatre projects to the problem of constructing a narrative of the bombing of Hiroshima, how do they, and most particularly Lepage and his collaborators, negotiate the problem of potentially distancing and freezing the event in the process of trying to represent it? It is interesting to consider here that the experiences that help inspire the artists in their projects are very much in line with the cliché sentiments that appear to erase the specificity of Hiroshima. Describing his experience in Hiroshima Resnais admits, "I did not leave to discover Hiroshima but to see if the city resembled that which we had imagined. We were not surprised, but were struck by the presence of death at once denied and constant. Hiroshima is the city of forgetting."[9] Almost a reverse mirroring of Resnais' sentiment Lepage's visit to Hiroshima is summarized in the introduction to the published version of *The Seven Streams of the River Ota*: "on his first trip to Hiroshima, expecting to find devastation, Lepage instead discovered a place full of vitality and sensuality. He was so struck by Hiroshima that he decided to create a production that took the city's unexpected liveliness as its jumping-off point."[10] Both artists were struck by the way in which Hiroshima did not fit their expectations. And both artists found in Hiroshima a totalizing experience. For Resnais, Hiroshima was infused with death even where it was denied. For Lepage, Hiroshima was the symbol of life and regeneration.[11] The emblematic narratives on which Resnais and Lepage have picked up deny, as much as they indicate, the recognition of the specificity of the historical traumatic experience. There is something in the unexpected, in the presence of death, and in the vitality and sensuality that suggests more of their enchantment with Hiroshima, something that cannot be fully indicated. Yet, their descriptions also resonate with guidebooks prepared for visitors to the cities, which "have generally emphasized [Hiroshima and Nagasaki's] tragic position [(death)] as testaments to the need for world peace and nuclear disarmament [(life)]."[12] These tourist approaches to the cities and their histories frame the magnitude of the bombings in a symbolic, moral, or pedagogical way, solidifying the memory of the destruction laid on the cities into simple, unequivocal lessons on peace and humanity for those who come to visit.

The use of simplified narratives – such as death and life, wrong and right, or war and peace – to convey historical traumatic experiences is a provision that is reproduced even within the creative works of Resnais and Lepage. For example, in *Hiroshima mon amour* the significance of the city as the location of the first atomic bomb dropped on a civilian population,[13] a city whose population was decimated during the Second World War, is

---

9   «Je ne suis pas parti pour découvrir Hiroshima, mais pour voir si la ville ressemblait à ce que nous avions imaginé. Nous n'avons pas été surpris, mais frappés par la présence de la mort à la fois niée et constante. Hiroshima, c'est la ville-type de l'oubli.» Baby, "Alain Resnais," p.11.

10   Lepage and Ex Machina, *The Seven Streams*, 1996, p. v. From the introduction by Karen Fricker.

11   There is about a thirty year difference between Resnais and Lepage's trips to Hiroshima, which may account for their differing views on the city. However, my concern here is less with the quality of their opinions than it is with the effect of their opinions, both of which indicate the event and cannot help but lay claims on it.

12   Peter Siegenthaler, "Hiroshima and Nagasaki in Japanese Guidebooks," *Annals of Tourism Research* 29 (2002): p. 1115.

13   In thinking about how history is framed, it is appropriate to note that most organizations invested in memorializing the bombing of Hiroshima and Nagasaki refer to the "Little Boy," the code name for the atomic bomb dropped on Hiroshima, as the first atomic bomb used on civilian populations. On the other hand, organizations invested in the atomic bomb more as a celebration of human intelligence tend to describe the bombing of Hi-

eclipsed by the story of peace. Hiroshima becomes the location for inquisitive tourists on bus tours and for films and parades about peace. Even in the interchange between the characters, a French woman and a Japanese man, the horror that is central to the event is erased, for the man never explicitly talks about the bombing, and in the woman's experience the news of the bombing is associated with the end of the war:

> He: What did Hiroshima mean for you, in France?
> She: The end of the war, I mean, really the end . . .
> He: The whole world was happy. You were happy with the whole world.[14]

The particular history of Hiroshima does not come into the sight and understanding of the woman. Rather, the bombing ends up affirming and reflecting the woman's experience as a French citizen living in France during the war. As Cathy Caruth explains in her examination of the film,

> For the French, Hiroshima did not signify the beginning of the suffering of the Japanese, but rather precisely the end of their own suffering. The knowledge of Hiroshima, for the French, understood not as the incomprehensible occurrence of the nuclear bombing of the Japanese but as the knowledge they call "the end," effaces the event of a Japanese past and inscribes it, as a referent, into the narrative of French history.[15]

The bombing is not recognized for its horror and destruction, but is known in all truthfulness as the end of the war and the beginning of peace, or as the moment that commences the reconstruction of France and Europe. That the destruction of Hiroshima becomes synonymous with a new beginning is emphasized in the film through the account of the woman's personal history. Previously shunned as a traitor for loving a German soldier, the French woman begins a new start in Paris at the end of the war. As Caruth points out,

> Telling the 'when' of her arrival in Paris as the moment that she learned of Hiroshima, the woman connects her own arrival, her insertion into collective French time, with a factual knowledge of Japan's catastrophe, which . . . has meant for her only 'the end of the war.' The arrival into national history thus erases not only her past but that of other nations as well.[16]

Further to erasing the history of the other, the French woman ends up erasing the specificity and individuality of her lover. He becomes for her a conduit for remembering the tragedy of the war as she experienced it, and as a result he comes to represent for her both the loss of her first love, by doubling as her German lover, and the tragedy of the inhabitants of Hiroshima, as a survivor and her Japanese lover. As a tragic figure the man is also the figure upon which the woman is able to project and see (or sense) the tragic history of the city and its destruction, and in the final lines of the film the woman addresses the man:

---

roshima as the "first wartime use of an atomic bomb" erasing the human element from the destruction and adding an element of justification, i.e. the destruction was laid in the name of war. The Bureau of Atomic Tourism [online]. 2001 [cited 17 February 2004]. Available from World Wide Web: (http://www.atomictourist.com/).

[14] Marguerite Duras, *Hiroshima mon amour*, trans. Richard Seaver (New York: Grove Press, 1961), p. 33-34.

[15] Cathy Caruth, "Literature and the Enactment of Memory (Duras, Resnais, *Hiroshima mon amour*)," *Unclaimed Experience: Trauma, Narrative, and History* (Baltimore, Maryland: Johns Hopkins University Press, 1996), p. 29.

[16] Caruth, "Literature and the Enactment of Memory," p. 33.

She: Hi-ro-shi-ma. That's your name.
(They look at each other without seeing each other. Forever.)
He: That's my name. Yes. Your name is Nevers. Ne-vers-in France.[17]

The man's experience has become the measure of the destruction of a whole city, and the destruction of Hiroshima has become as intimate as her lover and his story, yet they miss seeing or knowing each other completely. Through their interaction the characters gain a level, even a deep level, of insight into each other's lives. Besides the facts of their lives (the woman's first lover, her imprisonment, and her madness; the man surviving the bombing of Hiroshima by his absence), they gain a sense of the inaccessible parts of each other, and with that, a fear of losing or betraying those precious, identifying parts to the other. What is significant about the relationship that develops between the characters is that their encounter begins, and arguably remains, though more self-consciously so, with the knowledge of each other in reduced and simple terms, as Nevers and Hiroshima. That is, where they have fit the experience of the other into something that appears graspable and reconcilable to their own terms, and where their experiences have been reconciled to the terms of the other.

Inscribing the bombing into an understanding that allows the event to lose its specificity and for others to lose a sense of the magnitude of the event is something that can similarly be found in *The Seven Streams of the River Ota*, predominantly because the play deals with so many different issues making it hard to lend focus or privilege to any one. One critic, quoting Lepage, deems that *The Seven Streams of the River Ota* "concerns itself with 'the Nazi persecution of the Jews, the nuclear bomb and AIDS' [...] Admittedly, these are often explored [in the play] through personal and again domestic examples, but their accumulation and mutual contextualization tends to make them seem somewhat iconic, even generic."[18] Criticizing the play as presenting "Japan as a vehicle for Western nostalgia"[19] Jennifer Harvie shows how far from its aim, representing and paying tribute to Hiroshima, the play can appear. If Lepage's play is inspired by visiting Hiroshima, then it may seem odd that some of the storylines that comprise the play not only do not take place in Hiroshima but do not include any significant roles for characters that are linked to Hiroshima. Though there are seven different stories in the eight hour long play, Hanako, who is the only character who survives and is a direct witness of the event (a hibakusha[20]), is not given the oppor-

---

[17] Duras, *Hiroshima mon amour*, p. 83. In the entire film this is the closest the characters come to addressing each other by name.

[18] Jennifer Harvie, "Transnationalism, Orientalism, and Cultural Tourism: La Trilogie des dragons and The Seven Streams of the River Ota," *Theatre Sans Frontières: Essays on the Dramatic Universe of Robert Lepage*, ed. Joseph I. Donohoe Jr. and Jane M. Koustas (East Lansing, Michigan: Michigan State University Press, 2000) p. 119.

[19] Harvie, "Transnationalism, Orientalism, and Cultural Tourism," p. 123.

[20] Hibakusha is the Japanese (transliterated) term used for the survivors of the bomb or for those who experienced it. From a description by Robert Jay Lifton, "*Hibakusha* is a coined word whose literal meaning, 'explosion-affected person(s),' suggests a little more than merely having encountered the bomb and a little less than having experienced definite injury from it." Lifton goes on to discuss the four categories of exposure that fit under the term Hibakusha. These range from people who were in the city when the bomb exploded, those who came into the city within fourteen days after the bomb, those who came into physical contact with bomb victims, and those who were in utero at the time of the bomb. Robert Jay Lifton, *Death in Life: Survivors of Hiroshima* (Toronto, Ontario: Random House, 1967) p. 6-7.

tunity to tell her story, the story of Hiroshima, except in a short monologue. The monologue opens the production (2002 version) and is repeated at more length in the last act of the play. The monologue begins, "I really saw the end of the world. When I was five years old, during the last year of the war, I saw a final flame that burned my eyes."[21] The monologue is cited as an extract from Yukio Mishima's *Five Modern No Plays* suggesting, however, that Hanako's experience of Hiroshima does not in fact refer back to Hiroshima, or at least the degrees of separation are more tenuous. And when repeated in the final act of the play we find that it is not Hanako telling the story, but her friend Sophie who is acting in a production of Mishima's plays, causing the account to appear even further removed from Hiroshima, its inhabitants, and its horrific history. The monologue account of her blindness is not, as we may expect it to be, the story that contains and relates an individual experience of the bombing. Indeed, in considering Hanako simultaneously as a figure of Hiroshima and as being without a story of her own, a sense of distance and forgetting appears reminding us how far away from Hiroshima and Hanako's history our thoughts are.

As a translator by profession, Hanako effectively never tells us the story of her experience of the bomb but is constantly in the process of translating and telling someone else's story. In the middle of *The Seven Streams of the River Ota*, and in the absence of a story that is specifically her own, Hanako even translates a French farce by Georges Feydeau for an audience attending the World Fair in Osaka, Japan. Like the history of the Man in *Hiroshima mon amour*, here Hanako's history appears to be replaced by the history of France – only this time by its dramatic, literary history – and Hanako is left translating the nation affirming words, "Vive la France."   Yet, Hanako also reminds us of the problem with trying to make sense of something and with the very process of translating or of putting an experience, sentiment, or event into our own terms. In the third act of the play entitled "Les Mots / Words"[22] Sophie and Hanako have a telephone conversation that is theatrically and thematically accented by the use of translators who translate their French conversation into English. At one point, however, the translation comes apart:

> Hanako/Translator: Mishima dit que les mots sont comme des masques et qu'à cause des mots, la pensée est travestie. / You know Mishima says that words are like masks and because of the words, he thinks of transvestites.
> Hanako: C'est pas ce que j'ai voulu dire.
> Translator: I'm sorry?
> Hanako: This is not what I wanted to say. J'ai pas dit 'il pense aux travestis', j'ai dit 'la pensée est travestie'.
> Translator: Because of words thought is betrayed.
> Hanako/Translator: Traduttore, traditore . . . . / Translator, traitor . . . .[23]

---

[21] «J'ai vraiment vu la fin de ce monde. Quand j'avais cinq ans, pendant la dernière année de la guerre, j'ai vu cette flamme finale qui m'a brûlé les yeux» (Lepage et al., *Les sept branches*, 2002, Prologue, p. 1). The monologue is quite beautiful and I have decided to include a further portion of it here: «Et depuis, cette flamme, cette flamme de la fin de ce monde continue les brûler. Comme vous, j'ai essayé bien des fois de me dire que ce que je voyais n'était qu'un calme soleil couchant, mais en vain, car ce que je vois est bien un monde en proie aux flammes."   It is interesting to notice the way in which the audience is indicated in a communal denial ("like you I tried to tell myself that what I saw was a beautiful sunset") suggesting that we have tried hard to not recognize the reality and horror of the bombings and to be, like Hanako, blind. By addressing us the audience is implied as participants in the task of remembering. I will return to this idea.

[22] This act was later developed into the film *Nō*. Robert Lepage: *Nō*, prod. Bruno Jobin, dir. Robert Lepage, 85 min., Alliance, 1998, videocassette.

[23] Lepage et al., *Les sept branches*, 2002, Act 3.8, p. 28.

Hanako reminds us that in the act of translating, of taking something and making it mean-ingful in another system, the translator also betrays it. The translator, like anyone who is involved in making foreign things (other languages or other experiences) clear and evident to her audience, assigns a thing with traits and characteristics that make sense to their audi-ence but fail to reveal or contain the reality of an event in its entirety.

No matter how we approach the bombing of Hiroshima with the intention of seeing it and relating it to others, the task of mediation – translation and representation – implies a distance between our comprehension and an event. Furthermore, as it is suggested by the characters in both *Hiroshima mon amour* and in *The Seven Streams of the River Ota*, at-tempting to capture an event or experience returns to us an image of our own experience rather than bringing us closer to the experience of the other. Turning on the notion of me-diation as a means of distancing us from an event and rendering us blind to an experience, let us consider Hanako and her blindness as a figure for the audience. Where Hiroshima is the starting point and the love stories and chains of events in the play move out and away from the first affair in Hiroshima, it is not surprising that the audience should quickly lose sight of Hiroshima and its traumatic past. However, having reached this point we must also ask if we ever did have sight of Hiroshima or if indeed we can have sight of Hiroshima. Like Hiroshima, Hanako is never the central figure or focus of the play but she remains throughout the story like a consistent thread holding the stories together. As a witness and a survivor, Hanako is also our most direct connection to the bombing. However, if Hanako is the one who could tell us what it was like she is also the one who did not see the event, for in the process of her seeing she became blind and lost all means of visual reference. How then does one aim to tell or represent a traumatic past when arguably there are no first-hand witnesses to the horror? As Maclear explains the problem,

> *It is profoundly difficult to fully imagine what happened in Hiroshima and Nagasaki.* From survivor accounts, we can gather only a sparse chronology. We know, for example, that the bomb fell upon residents of Hi-roshima and Nagasaki from a serene sky – just after an all-clear siren had sounded in the case of Hiroshima. We know, too, that civilians who survived the three-second blasts were left to wander the ruins in states of ex-treme shock and disfigurement, many literally blinded by the event. Beyond this accounts are muddy and dis-persed . . . .
> *It is profoundly difficult to fully imagine what happened in Hiroshima and Nagasaki,* for the terror in both in-stances was compressed into a single instant, which left strange – even illegible – visual traces. The physical force of these disasters overwhelmed comprehension by virtue of their sheer and sudden magnitude."[24]

Maclear's account indicates two different ways that make the representation of the bomb-ings of Hiroshima and Nagasaki problematic. In one way, there is a lack of physical docu-ments and facts, from survivor accounts for example, which would be helpful in piecing together the traumatic events either in order to represent the event or to verify and measure a representation for its accuracy. In another way, representing what happened in Hiroshima and Nagasaki is difficult because the experience and the destruction that resulted from the

---

[24]   Maclear, *Beclouded Visions*, p. 4. Writing about the Holocaust Primo Levi makes a similar suggestion about there being ultimately no witnesses to a horrific event, "we, the survivors, are not the true witnesses. [. . .] we are those who by their prevarications or abilities or good luck did not touch bottom. Those who did so, those who saw the Gorgon, have not returned to tell about it or have returned mute."   Primo Levi, *The Drowned and the Saved*, trans. Raymond Rosenthal (New York: Vintage International, 1989) p. 83-84.

bombs defied comprehension. Speaking in more psychological or experiential terms, the event was so much beyond habitual ways of understanding the world and one's experiences that it eluded the means of reception and comprehension available to survivors.[25] Those who witnessed the event were at a loss to grasp what had happened to them. There were no means for them, as there appears few means for us in our experience now, to gain the perspective of the bombings that the traumatic events in their magnitude demand. The loss of perception located precisely at the point of Hanako's blindness mirrors the audiences' own inadequacy toward understanding the traumatic history of Hiroshima. Like Hanako we can look at the horizon of the traumatic event but we cannot see and grasp the bombing in full comprehension. What we find here instead is a gap or a point of blindness that is not easy to fill in, but remains outside of comprehension no matter how hard or how often we attempt to inscribe it in our understanding. Returning to Resnais and Lepage's opposing opinions on Hiroshima, viewing Hiroshima as being at once emblematic of death and life reveals the instability at the centre of the attempt to label and contain Hiroshima. Regardless of the directors' intentions Hiroshima slips past and between the terms they use to ascribe to the sentiment that visiting Hiroshima inspires in them.

Unable to see Hiroshima, know Hiroshima, nor convey the magnitude of the bombing of Hiroshima, *The Seven Streams of the River Ota* can be seen as presenting us with our own seeing. A seeing that works around, covers up, and inevitably inscribes the destruction and reconstruction of the city in and through the other histories and issues that are taken up in the play. However, the story of the city and its violent history cannot be fully inscribed, for the very question of representation calls us back to our relationship (even Lepage and Resnais' relationships) to the event. For those of us who are engaged in representing or in somehow coming closer to and even capturing Hiroshima, what concerns us so much in finding an appropriate representation is that we recognize something of the magnitude of the event and that we are inspired through our encounter with the city and its history to make some gesture of acknowledgement. The gesture toward Hiroshima, the history and event existing for us as an incomprehensible blind spot, acknowledges not the bombing of the city but more specifically our desire to reach out and grasp Hiroshima. The play is a consequence and representation of the desire to do something or to say something about Hiroshima, and conversely, the strength and uniqueness of this appeal stands as a testament to the uniqueness of the city, its history, and its destruction. The attempt of Lepage and his

---

[25] For Sigmund Freud, traumatic experience is directly linked to a person's inability to register the event. Freud imagines that we build a psychological protection based on the gradual accumulation of experiences and habitual occurrences. As we accumulate experiences we are able to bind the disruption they would cause in the psyche and diffuse the excess energy in what he calls the pleasure principle. In trauma, however, the experience cannot be bound. Instead, it breeches the protection afforded to the psyche. Freud writes, "trauma is bound to provoke a disturbance on a large scale in the functioning of the organism's energy and to set in motion every possible defensive measure. At the same time, the pleasure principle is for the moment put out of action. There is no longer any possibility of preventing the mental apparatus from being flooded with large amounts of stimulus, and another problem arises instead – the problem of mastering the amounts of stimulus that have broken in and of binding them . . . so that they can then be disposed of." Those who survive trauma are both witnesses to and have missed the event, for they were unable, in any psychological way, to mark the event and make sense of it. The effect is a moment of lost reception, a moment where experiences and events are not registered. Sigmund Freud "Beyond the Pleasure Principle," *On Metapsychology: the Theory of Psychoanalysis*, trans. James Strachey, comp. and ed. Angela Richards (New York: Penguin Books, 1991) p. 301.

collaborators to mark their desire to grasp Hiroshima begins almost in the only way it can. It begins from their perspectives and experience and it maintains a balance that reminds us that the play is not making claims on the nature and the experience of the bombing of Hiroshima, but is reaching out to meet and sometimes receding from the experience. The balancing factors, which work to counter the reductive claims that the play must make to convey a coherent story, arise through the moments where the play helps to remind us of the danger of asserting a version of the story onto the incomprehensible traumatic history. For example, there are instances in the play that intentionally lead the audience/reader to question how events are framed and transmitted, and in a sense, Lepage and his company have brought to the foreground the predicament of wanting to formulate a response to the traumatic history and being unable to ascertain how. The problem of how to conceive of the history of Hiroshima surfaces, for example, when a Dutch character named Ada looks for a book for her friend Jeffery 2 (the second born):

> Ada: Excuse me sir. Do you speak English?
> Librarian: Yes, a little bit . . . . Can I help you?
> Ada: I'm looking for a book by an American soldier called Mike Osborne. It's on the Second World War.
> Librarian: This whole department is about World War II . . . . On what front? (Ada looks at him quizzically.) The Russian front . . . The African Corps . . . The Battle of Normandy . . . The London blitz . . . The Battle of the Pacific . . .
> Ada: Pacific
> Librarian: What event? Pearl Harbor, Philippines, Guadalcanal?
> Ada: Japan.
> Librarian: Japan is a country, Mam, not an event. Before the bomb or after the bomb?
> Ada: After the bomb.
> Librarian: So, you mean the occupation of Japan by the U.S. Army . . .
> Ada: Yes
> [The Librarian looks for the book]
> Librarian: I'm sorry, it doesn't exist.
> Ada: What do you mean it doesn't exist?
> Librarian: Sorry, Mam, if we don't have it, it doesn't exist.
> Ada: Listen, I know it exists. It's a book with articles and photos taken right after the war.
> Librarian: Ah! ah! ah! Photography! That would be in the World War II iconography section.[26]

In the way that it lists numerous other events that took place during World War II, the conversation between Ada and the Librarian does two things. On one hand, it reminds us that besides the bombing of Hiroshima a number of other atrocities took place during the war, some of which place the Japanese as the aggressors. On the other hand, in recalling these other events, the scene also warns of how easy it is to lose sight of the specificity of the different events either as they are eclipsed by each other or by the abstract notion of war. In an attempt to place the traumatic historical event, the ungraspable, incomprehensible aspect of the history is replaced with something seemingly more tenable, or at least misplaced. The bombing of Hiroshima becomes synonymous with the entire country and its history causing Japan to become reduced to the terms of Hiroshima's destruction, and the bombing of Hiroshima to lose its specificity in a continuum of Japanese history and the history of World War II. Ironically the scene suggests that the bombing of Hiroshima has become so ab-

---

[26] Lepage et al., *Les sept branches*, 2002, Act 4.2, p. 1-2.

stracted that there are no documents or records to testify to the traumatic historical event but only emblematic labels and iconic pictures to take their place.

In examining how *The Seven Streams of the River Ota* meets the challenge of representing an historical traumatic event it is interesting to return to the image of the river delta invoked by the play's title. The concept of seven stories that are connected to the geography of a site, like the streams that run through Hiroshima, suggests that story narratives are a means of coming back to a place, not simply as a tourist who cannot turn away from the moral lessons on peace or the iconic images of the mushroom cloud, but perhaps as one who also sees deeper to the many other textures and layers. Like the branches of the river that diverge and cross the landscape, the stories that are told through and around the city and its history, rather than directly of the bombing, lap against and uncover connections that cause the audience to feel and to think more deeply about the event that remains in the periphery. These moments foreground the limits of representation and of our understanding of the event, for, they remind us of how much we fail to see and know about what took place at Hiroshima. By turning the inquiry into a self reflection and revealing the challenge to simultaneously sustain a fidelity to an event while using representation and narrative to describe it, the play provides viewers with the tools or reminders they need to think beyond any limited formulation that even the play cannot help to escape. What we gain from the play is not confirmation of what we think we understand or lessons on the significance of what happened at Hiroshima, but an understanding of how limited our conception of the event is and continues to be. Where our aim may be to distinguish Hiroshima, we are always delayed from grasping its meaning fully and completely.[27] Making claims in order to distinguish and make sense of experiences and events, however, is not a bad or false thing it is a necessity. And the very fact or literalness of our desire for narrative and representation to bring us into an unmediated relationship with the past or with the event is itself the ges-

---

[27] In "Differance" – Jacques Derrida, "Differance," *Margins of Philosophy*, trans. Alan Bass (Chicago, Chicago University Press, 1982. p, 129-160) – Derrida unfolds the meaning of the verb 'to differ' as, in one sense, "the action of postponing until later, . . . a delay, . . . a representation, . . . a detour that suspends the accomplishment or fulfilment of 'desire' or 'will' . . . . The other sense of 'to differ' is . . . the sense of not being identical, of being other, of being discernible" (Derrida, "Differance," 136). In the concept of "Differance" there is always a distance or delay that prevents us from grasping an object in full knowledge. Subject to this inevitable delay from arriving at an otherness (object) that is unmediated we instead make use language and representation to differentiate things. Of course, through language we can never capture the thing in itself. Hayden White discusses "Differance," along with 'intransitive writing', in "The Problem of Truth in Historical Representation" (White, *Figural Realism*, p. 27-42). For both Derrida (staying with the difficulty of a passage and repeating it, Derrida 154) and White (speaking of something as though you have passed through it, White 37) it is important, in an ethical approach to knowledge and history, to work through something giving it the time and attention it deserves in order to do it a sort of justice. White explains that this complex way of treating an object develops through a middle voice or by a "posture that is neither subjective not objective, neither that of social scientist with a methodology and a theory nor that of the poet intent upon expressing a personal reaction" (White *Figural Realism*, p. 37). What I think is most important about working in this middle area is that doing so gives rise to the realization of our own limits and the suggestion of something more beyond them. I would suggest that the middle ground that we need to work through is actually here, between the limits of our world (considered either as subjective or objective) and the impression of a trace or of the possibility of otherness. In this way we are always already in the middle space, or between the limits of our understanding and the prospect of understanding the world in another way. By recognizing the limits of our comprehension, we arrive at the opportunity of taking responsibility for how we lack knowledge of another experience (history) or how we try to reduce it to our own.

ture that begins to touch the core of Hiroshima. Where the magnitude of the event is ulti-mately unknowable, the desire to bridge the gap between the present and the past event, our desire to know it, stands as a testament to the significance of the event. However, the meta-phor of the river also suggests that there is go guarantee that the significance of the gesture, as a mark of the desire to want to grasp the immensity of the event, will reach the audience. Likewise, there is no guarantee that we will take up the traces and challenges that are pre-sented by the text to help us think beyond our limits, nor that we will be self-reflective about our process of theorizing and making meaning. Ultimately the theme of the river delta simply refers to the streams passing through a landscape, lines on a map, a pattern from which significance may be discovered or left forgotten, settled, or simplified. Narratives, like the streams of the Ota River, lay open, a pattern of courses in which we as good, re-sponsible theorists are left to find meaning.

NOTES ON CONTRIBUTORS

The editor of the book

Kuisma Korhonen is the author of *Textual Friendships: The Essay as Impossible Encounter* (Amherst, NY: Humanity Books, 2005). He has published numerous essays and articles in Finnish, English, and French, and taught comparative literature at the University of Helsinki. Currently he is a docent (adjunct professor) of comparative literature and a Fellow at the Helsinki Collegium for Advanced Studies, University of Helsinki, Finland.

Contributors

Hayden White is Professor Emeritus of the history of consciousness at the University of California, Santa Cruz, and the professor of comparative literature at Stanford University. He is the author of numerous widely influential books, including *Metahistory*, *Tropics of Discourse*, *The Content of the Form*, and *Figural Realism*, most of them translated in numerous languages. His work has had a profound influence on conceptualization and practice in all humanities disciplines.

Herman Paul is currently writing a Ph.D. thesis on Hayden White's philosophy of history at the University of Groningen, the Netherlands. He has published an essay on the use and abuse of victim's perspectives in historical writing: *Slachtofferperspectieven in de geschiedschrijving. Een geschiedfilosofische analyse* (Groningen 2001). He has also co-edited a volume on religious *lieux de mémoire* in the Netherlands (2004).

Stanley Corkin is Professor and Director of graduate studies in the English Department at the University of Cincinnati. His books include *Realism and the Birth of the Modern US: Cinema, Literature and Culture* (1996) and *Cowboys as Cold Warriors: Hollywood Westerns and Post War U.S. History* (Temple University Press, 2004). His essays on US cinema, literature and culture have appeared in a number of journals, including *Cinema Journal*, *Journal of American History*, and *Modern Fiction Studies*. He and Professor Frus (see below) have collaborated on a number of projects.

Phyllis Frus is Associate Professor of English at Hawaii Pacific University, where she chairs the writing program and teaches in the film studies program. She is the author of *The Politics and Poetics of Journalistic Fiction: The Timely and the Timeless* (Cambridge, 1994), "Documenting Domestic Violence in American Films," in *Violence and American Cinema*, ed. David Slocum (AFI/Routledge, 2001), and many articles on the relation between fiction and nonfictional texts. She and Professor Corkin (see above) have been collaborating since 1993, focusing on historical readings of literary works. They have published essays on Willa Cather and Zora Neale Hurston, two review essays on educational reform and the culture wars, and an edition of Stephen Crane that includes texts by writers of his time. They are working on a book about U.S. history-based films, including documentaries.

Kalle Pihlainen is a Research Fellow at the department of Cultural History at the University of Turku, Finland. He has published numerous articles in anthologies and journals like *Rethinking History* and *New Literary History* on narrative theory and the significance of literary knowledge in historical research. His doctoral dissertation, entitled *Resisting History* (1999), dealt with the ethics of narrative representation with a focus on the thinking of Hayden White, Michael Riffaterre and Jean-Paul Sartre. Currently he is working on a manuscript dealing with strategies of representation in historiography and biography, with a focus on Sartre's *L'Idiot de la Famille*.

Karlheinz Stierle has been Professor of Romance literatures at the University of Konstanz. He is one of the leading literary scholars in Germany, and has published numerous books on literature, theory, and arts, including *Text als Handlung, Der Mythos von Paris* (translated in French), *Dimensionen des Verstehens and Ästhetische Rationalität*.

Matti Hyvärinen is currently a Fellow at the Helsinki Collegium for Advanced Studies, University of Helsinki, Finland. He has just finished a study on the conceptual history of Finnish 'power' (*valta*) and has led a research project on the conceptual history of Finnish political culture. By education, he is a political scientist and sociologists, and he has completed his Ph.D. in 1994. His current interests include the political theory of narrative, and he is beginning a new project on the conceptual history of narrative. He is the coordinator of the Finnish Network of Narrative Studies.

Claire Norton is at present a History Lecturer at St Mary's College (University of Surrey). Her doctoral thesis was entitled *Plural Pasts: The Role of Function and Audience in the Creation of Meaning in Ottoman and Modern Turkish Accounts of the Sieges of Nagykanizsa* (University of Birmingham, 2003).

Fiona McIntosh-Varjabédian is *maître de conférences* of comparative literature at the university of Lille III. She studied at the Ecole Normale Supérieure in Paris. She has published *La Vraisemblance narrative en question* (PSN, 2002), and edited a collection of articles on the representation of the primitive man (*Discours sur le Primitif*, Lille, 2002). Her researches are centered on the writing of history in 18th and 19th century France and Great Britain and the boundaries between fact and fiction.

Andrew Burrell is a Sydney-based interdisciplinary writer, sculptor and audio artist. His work has been shown both across Australia and internationally. He has been involved in several projects in Finnish Lapland, which have culminated in a body of work entitled *Notes From a Fish out of Water*, which has been exhibited in several incarnations in both Australia and Finland. His doctoral dissertation, *Notes Towards the End of Time* (University of Sydney, 2005) explores notions of personal narratives and the collected object. For his artistic work, see www.miscellanea.com

Markku Lehtimäki has been a Researcher and Assistant Professor of comparative literature at the University of Tampere, Finland. He has published numerous essays in Finnish and English on narrative theory, American literature, fiction / nonfiction, Norman Mailer, and film history, the most recent being "'That was how she read him': Free indirect discourse and reflexive reading in nonfictional narratives" (*FID Working Papers 1*, 2003). His forthcoming publications include his doctoral dissertation *The Poetics of Norman Mailer's Nonfiction: Self-Reflexivity, Narrative Rhetoric, and Literary Form* (2004).

Olabode Ibironke has been an instructor at Obafemi Awolowo University Ile-Ife, Nigeria, and has published several essays on African and Caribbean history and literature. He is currently a Ph.D. candidate in Comparative literature/English at Michigan State University. His interests include historical fiction, theories of literary production, and archaeology of knowledge.

Lara Okihiro has studied literature and psychoanalysis specializing in English Romantic poetry and the problem of representing trauma. Extending her interest in the representation of historical traumatic events Lara has researched the internment of Japanese descendents in Canada during the Second World War. Currently, she is working on a film project that aims to consider the history of Japanese Canadians alongside the history of Hiroshima and the current western policies of dealing with 'enemy' populations.